Find out more about the author and upcoming books online on;
https://linktr.ee/Carrie_Weston

Other books by Carrie Weston;

The Xander Chase Series (YA crime fiction/ fantasy)

1. Xander Chase and the Unicorn Code

2. Xander Chase and the Lost Wing

3. Xander Chase and the Battle for Deaths Throne

A Dark Fairy Tale (Fantasy fiction 12+ novella)

0.5 - P.E.T empathiser's PREQUEL (Short Story)

1- Pet Empathiser Team

2- Fractured

3. Fabric Of Magic

4. The Fabric Of Magic

Ghost Possessor (YA Paranormal/ fantasy mash)

Ascender

Standalones

An Ampoule of Terror (Horror 18+)

Anthologies

Suddenly, the scene hit fast-forward with a jarring blur as the aroma of sweet-scented roses were replaced with a repugnant meaty layer beneath the foul stench of iron. Her breath caught on a heave and immediately her hands were there to shield her nasal passages from the abominable stench.

She knew what was coming next. Knew if she looked up now that she would be staring into the blotchy, red face of her brother as heart-wrenching tears dragged glittering trails beneath his eyes.

She couldn't help but screw her eyes shut, praying the nightmare would end without its horrific conclusion. But all too fast, she heard her dream self screaming,

'Just go! Get out of here, Donnal. I mean it, scat!'

Before she knew it, she was sucked into the dream completely, melding with her dream self as her lungs seared with the chastising words hurled at her snivelling brother before her.

"I - I'm telling mum!" he wailed, running so fast he stumbled up the crest of the little hill, sprinting from view.

Tia gently swiped at her own cheeks, turning back to the darkened mass she knew lay beneath the shade of the large oak tree. Her heart beating a rhythm so hard it vibrated through her footsteps; she tiptoed closer.

Chapter 1

Tia

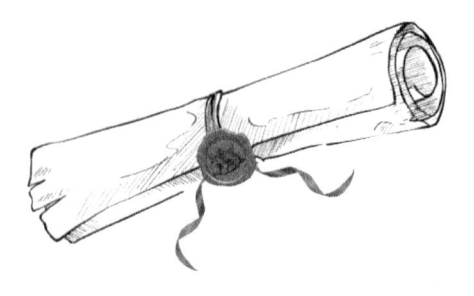

Not here. Not now. Please!

It started with a rare wave of peacefulness. Roses, the kind tended to regularly and groomed to perfection, lined a small, almost pointlessly low, wall separating the garden from a row of apartment blocks. Tia knew where she was now and dread crept up on her like a demon shadow devouring her soul.

Donnal, her overbearingly enthusiastic brother, ran into the communal garden, followed closely by their mother - until she saw an elderly neighbour and stopped to chat. Meanwhile, Donnal ran ahead to where Tia glimpsed a shadow of her dream self in the nightmare beneath *the* tree.

About the Author; Hello everyone thanks for your continued support and I hope you enjoy reading this book. G-poss is one of the very first books I wrote it's just taken a long time to get it out there. Thanks for staying tuned

Hearts & Kisses

Carrie

1- Natural Beauty in The Book of Love
2- Cutlemans Rise in The Gift and Other Stories
3- Fallen Elf in Snowflakes & Sleighbells

Copyright © Carrie Weston 2024

This novel is a work of fiction. Names, characters, businesses, places, events and incidents are either the products of the author's imagination or used in a fictitious manner. Any resemblance to actual persons, living or dead, or actual events is purely coincidental. All rights reserved in all media. No part of this publication may be reproduced, stored in retrieval system, copied in any form or by any means, electronic, mechanical, photocopying, recording or otherwise transmitted without written permission from the author and/or publisher. You must not circulate this book in any format. Any person who does any unauthorised act in relation to this publication may be liable to criminal prosecution and civil claims for damages. For permission requests, please contact: authorcarrieweston@gmail.com Produced in the United Kingdom.

The shading canopy of intertwining leaves cascaded a dull light down on its roots, as if the tree itself was in mourning. Tia bowed her head in acknowledgement, her chest suddenly cramping, her hand settled firmly at her throat as she wheezed out a shred of icy spiked air.

Heart pummelling her constricting ribs, she shivered, wrapping her arms around herself and puffing out a huge, steamy breath nipped at by her chattering teeth. Ice spurted from the hanging branches around her like coiled ropes of barbed wire. Tiny prickles stabbed at her skin as hair follicles stood erect, a huge shiver raked her spine and then she heard it –

Drip.

Drip.

Drip.

The peaking crescendo of droplets slowly drowned the sanity in her mind. She wrapped trembling hands around her skinny frame, swallowing hard as she faced the plague of her nightmare.

Sheathed in a frozen mist, a partially formed Spector desperately reached out towards her. Its nailless fingers were smothered in crimson droplets that streaked towards the earth like scarlet ribbons.

A lung burning scream punctured though her terror, her slight body shook with bone rattling churns as the blood in her veins prickled with ice to the very depths of her demon haunted soul. Her breath hitched, stopped, then she smashed into the cold biting grip of the classroom's stone floor.

Jolting awake, maths paper confetti rained around her and her upturned stool. Sweat burst from her pores, her heart hammered the beat of a victim who no longer had a place to hide. Slowly, her vision began to clear, blinking back into A1.

Tia shrunk amidst the onslaught of laughter from her peers, gritting her teeth until they ground enough to make her jaw ache.

"Nice trip?" Reece, a tall, gangly boy with a mop of dark brown hair, asked in his Welsh twang, a smile quirking at the edge of his lips as he stopped to help her retrieve her fallen papers.

"Piss off!" Tia yelled, grabbing the eraser from the neighbouring desk and lobbing it at him. He shrunk back playfully, a glaring wide smile on his tanned face.

Jerk, thought Tia as she righted her stool and slumped unceremoniously back onto it.

"Tia Morgan!" roared the mentor.

Tia sighed, trying to recall the woman's name - Rachel, Rafael, something like that. There was really no point in cramming such pointless information into the files of her already stuffed to bursting mind.

Tia eyeballed the woman as she swayed her way through the desks to stand before her. "Your audacity is astounding, Tia. This is the very last class you have to attend before your ascension and still you cannot be bothered to pay attention. You swear in my class, you fall asleep! I wash my hands of you, Tia, I really do."

Boo-hoo, snipped Tia in her mind.

"One hour. That's all my class is, just one hour. The information I give you could save your life one day. But no, you just don't listen. Tia, you have taken this rebellious attitude too far, I…"

Tia sucked in a deep lungful of air and yawned loudly, watching the woman's eyes bulge with fury, her cheeks a raging peruse. "Get out of my class!" she screamed.

Thank God! Thought Tia.

It's about bloody time! Tia swaggered her way past the desks with Li's - only the most handsome guy at the academy - disapproving glare incinerating her back. She stuck up her chin defiantly at his silent scolding and barged through the old wooden door. Her heart gave a little squeeze at his blatant disapproval.

What? she thought - *bloody bitch started it! Why does he have to look at me like that? Mentor started it. It wasn't her fault that she fell off her stool because the lesson was so boring. It's not like she hadn't tried her utmost to stay awake.* She slumped against the corridor wall facing the classroom where she watched Li's head turned to stare at Anka. The girl was, in short, beautiful. She had long, corn-coloured hair, bright blue eyes, an irritatingly perfect voice and the body of a supermodel. *Bitch! Why can't Li stare at me like that?* thought Tia, her heart giving a flip-flop in agreement.

Pushing herself away from the wall, Tia stalked down the long flagstone corridor. Landscape pictures adjourned the magnolia walls.

What was it with pictures anyway? Why did people like them so much that they would stay inside buildings to gaze at them instead of being free to experience the beauty outside? She pondered, staring at one after another, trying to decipher something, anything that would content her soul.

Until she caught her reflection staring back at her from a shimmering silver pond with scrolled renaissance filigree.

Stepping up to it, she felt her breath hitch at the reflection staring back. She didn't have a round face, not like her brothers and her eyes weren't slate like her mother's, but the startling cobalt blue of her father's. *A dreamer's eyes*, he used to say.

Heart clenching at her own resemblance, she squeezed her eyes shut, swiping angrily at an errant tear as it escaped its confines with the bending will of her mascara as it streaked down her pale face.

I will be with you again. I swear it! I've got a plan, she confided to the eyes which stared back at her with her father's intelligence – *I promise. I'll be free of them soon.*

She watched her thick bottom lip wobble. *That's one thing we all have in common,* she thought, cheering her soul a little. She remembered her mother used to joke that Tia spent a lot of time kissing windows to achieve such a look - but her mother had it too.

Suddenly, a palm smoothed down the raven hair that had escaped from her French plait before it settled on her shoulder. She didn't jump. Instead, anger rolled through her system, stealing the vulnerable rawness she seconds ago admitted as she recognised the ring on Paul's hand. Recoiling, she glared daggers at him.

Oh God, this isn't my day. I seriously don't need a 'I'm here for you' lecture from Paul, the creep. She rolled her eyes, the effect heightened by the gothic smear underlining them.

As always, he wore the most expensive 'acceptable' version of the academy's uniform. Complete with labels no other student would get past the mentors - but lucky for him his uncle was in charge. The most unfortunate part of this was the fact that he made the clothing look ridiculously good.

How anyone could make a black polo shirt and slacks look fashionable was beyond her. His wrist bore the latest G-shock watch which rounded off the ensemble. How he managed to get away with having Bluetooth on his watch was a miracle considering the mentors' daily search for 'banned' items, mobiles being their top priority.

"You okay there?" Paul asked, his brow furrowing. He tucked his hands into the pockets of his tight slacks as a slight glow pinkened his cheeks.

"Yeah, fine!" she roared, storming down the corridor and away from the pressure of Paul's soul-searching eyes.

Tia slammed through the cafeteria door and stormed into the 'pigpen', her feet smacking the cobbled floor in warning to the students who might dare intercept her. She plonked down into her booth at the back of the room, wrenched a pen from the pocket of her trousers, and rhythmically stabbed it into the graffiti covered table.

"What-cha-doing?"

Tia's gaze flicked up to Ella, her soul sister by circumstance. The thirteen-year-old slid into the seat opposite Tia, one hand twirling her blonde-dyed-black pigtail while the other clenched a bright orange cup.

"Stabbing the table. What does it look like?" Tia snapped, glaring as the young girl shook her head back and forth like a confused puppy, her blue eyes widening. Tia shivered at the mere thought of a puppy. She hated them. Hated the G-Poss. Hated the mentors – the bloody Jailers. Hated her life!

"What's up, Ti?" Ella's question had her thoughts jarring back to the scar that was her reality.

"Ghost Possessors," snorted Tia. "They run around thinking they do the world a favour!"

"Well, they kinda do. Menta Tom says—"

"You mean *Jailer*," Tia interrupted. "And since when did you care what they say?"

"I meant Jailer. Jailer Tom," Ella sniggered. "He says the G-Poss stops the ghosts' ectoplasm from overcrowding our world.

Did ya even know they could do that - over crowd the world I mean?"

"Classic G-Poss textbook," grunted Tia. "Just because they possess ghosts and help them fulfil their unfinished business doesn't make them superior. They can't do whatever they like. They don't even care that they ruin people's lives!" Tia slammed her hands down on the table, snapping the pen in half as a fiery light sparked in her eyes.

"I know, I hate 'em, too. If they didn't exist, then my mum and dad would still be alive." Ella hiccupped, tears twinkling in her eyes.

Tia ran a hand down her braid, biting her thick bottom lip as her fingers walked across the table to take her friend's hand. She watched Ella slurp up enough icy juice to freeze her brain forever, and waited for her to talk.

"They didn't even get buried," Ella sniffed. "They died in the past, Ti, when they were transporting their assigned ghosts back to sort out their unfinished stuff. I didn't even get to say goodbye," Ella sobbed as Tia patted her hand gently.

"Come on, let's get some cookies. They're your favourite, white chocolate and raspberry." The promise of sugary junk food had Ella half smiling through her morbid thoughts as they slid from the booth, gathering up more cookies than they both could eat, and sneaking them into the pockets of their slacks to avoid detection. They raced from the canteen and up the main stairs, laughing, pulling cookies out to munch as they walked the corridors to Ella's room.

Quietly entering the room, Tia and Ella opened her desk drawer, stashing the cookies for whenever the morbid thoughts of Ella's parents' death might cross her mind. "I suppose I had better get going," Ella sighed, kicking at a large crumb on the floor by her messy bed.

"What class do you have?" Tia asked.

"Ghost Types and Traits," Ella murmured before scoffing down another cookie.

"Isn't that with Jailor Sady?" Tia asked, curling her lip in disgust. She had never gotten on with the bossy, overbearing mentor. Ella laughed, erupting in a spray of cookie crumbs and spittle. "It's Sandy. You always get it wrong."

Tia shrugged. "Whatever. It's not like I care." She walked from the room, deciding Ella's deceased parents wouldn't want Ella to miss lessons - no matter what a waste of time Tia thought they were.

The hallways were large and imposing, as much of the academy was, and one could find themselves lost very easily amid the magnolia maze. The only real clue to tell them apart were the irritating paintings and occasional spidery crack that splayed from areas of the building that predated even Jailor Georges. The head mentor wasn't particularly old but his idealistic views concerning the 'running' of the academy were definitely prehistoric.

The staircases were something of an anomaly to the magnolia rule as they were huge carved monstrosities embellished with gargoyles most would find disturbing. But Tia loved them. Their raw ugliness was one thing the academy couldn't hide.

As they walked down the last few steps, the sound of slamming doors echoed ominously throughout the building. Class was in session, and Ella was late. The two of them doubled their pace, rounding a corner before halting at a large wood door inscribed *Phantasm Room 1*. Giving half a smile, Ella pushed open the heavy door, sliding inside, as a string of conversation drifted from the room.

"No, Spencer. Ghosts can't write. No matter how active they are, they cannot manipulate an object long enough to establish co-ordinated writing."

"Poltergeists can!" butted in a shrill voice.

Tia smirked, imagining the agitation Jailor Sandy must have felt.

"No. They cannot," the first voice snapped. "Next time, Lizzy, raise your…"

Slam!

The door shut and Tia was left alone in the corridor stripped of artistry. She shivered, its sterile appearance reminding her of the hospital where the G-Poss had 'acquired' her as a child.

She could still hear the echoes of her mother's frantic screams when she realised her only daughter was missing. She shook herself hard - that's why she didn't dare sink too far into the memories of her past.

They haunted her.

Shaking herself loose of the trauma of her past, Tia walked out of the trigger zone, around a corner and straight into the broad chest of… Paul?

For Christ's sake, can't you cut me some slack?

"You all right, Tia?" he asked, swiping his shaggy brown fringe from his ebony eyes.

"Yeah, obviously!" Tia roared, ascending the main staircase, taking the steps two at a time.

"We all have a ghost in our closet, Tia," he called, his chuckling quieting as the distance between them grew and her raging heart calmed its erratic staccato. She didn't have to look back to know a goofy smile was plastered all over his sly face.

Finally, she stumbled onto the second floor, panting as she reached her door. Pushing it open, she sighed with relief as her eyes scanned the area for her roomie.

Tia slumped down onto the bottom bunk, pulling her quilt over her head. Three deep breaths and she had calmed her shaking body. Her shoulders sagged as exhaustion caught up with her. She was not a natural insomniac, but the fear of those nightly terrors pushed her body to keep going. Still, on occasion, her system would disobey her, relaxing her into a trance-like state as she was now; comfortable, calm, with her eyelids sagging heavily.

Creeaak

Tia shot up out of bed, hitting her head and palming it as she glanced towards the opening door, where the irritating tinkle of Anka's voice preceded her. Tia groaned.

"Tia, I didn't expect to find you here." A smile spread across her snowy complexion. "Did class end early?"

Tia ignored her, grumbling to herself as she rearranged the quilt and sat atop it with a huff. *Maybe if I ignore her she'll go away, she* thought.

But, unfortunately, it seemed her moment of peace was over as a waft of sweet peas engulfed her, poisoning her pure air with their concentrated aroma. The bed dipped beside her and the sound of ruffling pages fanned at the cloud of perfume. *Great.*

"Look," Anka insisted, shaking a glossy magazine, its pages crackling until Tia peeked at it with a heavy sigh.

"What?"

Anka raised one perfectly plucked eyebrow. "Bad day?"

"What do you want, Anka? Tell me, then just bloody piss off!" Tia glared at Anka who raised her aristocratic nose in the air.

"That wasn't very nice," Anka scolded snootily.

Tia rolled her eyes. "Whatever."

"Look, I only wanted to show you this advert—" Anka waggled the magazine again "—It's so you, Tia! You could so do this with your nails. Instead of just plain, old, boring black, you could really style it up. You could crackle!" Anka giggled excitedly.

Rolling her eyes, Tia gave in, leaning over to look at the advert. Anka's grin widened.

Tia's eyes swept from the model's clawed hand with the acclaimed crackled nails on to the tag line, *'How to Dominate Your Nails'*. Why on earth Anka read this rubbish was beyond her, most teenagers had pried themselves away from the glossy words of 'Sweet Cupcake' magazine. Especially after the scandal that went down a year ago. But that never shook Anka, she was as hooked as ever to the brain manipulating words set in their glossy covers.

Tia scanned further down the page to a dark, eerie image of a cat with sleek, black fur. Its claws scratching towards the reader with a tiny caption saying, *'Enjoy a Sleek New You'*. The cat's eyes seemed to snag hers in a thrall as they shined from the magazine catching her up in a memory Tia thought buried, dragging her into the eye of her past's storm.

The sweet scent of roses were thick on the heavy breeze, wafting over the mowed lawn of the communal garden where she used to live. A shiver wracked her body and she found herself wrapping her cardigan tighter over her chest. Another shudder vibrated her but this time it shook her very bones. She remembered this cardigan. Bile rose in her mouth as she prayed her little brother's head wouldn't appear at any second. Swallowing down the bile thick in her throat she dared a fleeting peek in her peripheral vision at *the* tree.

She remembered how happy and carefree she had been before its inconsiderate web of gnarled roots tripped her. She could feel the abrasion of its weathered bark against her grazed knee. *Oh God, please not again.* She begged, her mind's voice wet with tears. *Don't make me see this again. Please...*

But traumatic memories can more often be a stress disorder, rather than simply the reoccurrence of a bad memory, and Tia was thoroughly immersed in hers. She watched a blond mop of unruly hair bob before her and gazed into the slate grey eyes of her little brother; knowing what would happen next.

She stepped towards him, blocking any view of what lay in the root woven bed at the base of the old oak tree, which stood like an eerie guardian, looming in its shadowy grief.

She couldn't let him go there. Big sisters protected their little brothers. That's what they were meant to do right?

"Donnal no, you have to stay away." She shook her head, emphasising her point to the little blond haired boy whose brow furrowed with the warning signs of a major tantrum, his thick lips pouting as his eyes narrowed in calculation. He shot left, trying to dodge past her.

But Tia stepped out, catching him around the ribs and jerked him back. Watching, her heart thudding in time with the tears that trickled from his wide grey eyes.

"Get out of here, Donnal. I mean it, scat!" Her lungs burnt with the bellowed chastising words hurled at her snivelling brother as she released him.

"I - I'm telling mum!" he wailed, running so fast he stumbled as he sprinted to the crest of the little hill.

She remembered regretting that moment ever since. She should have been gentler with him. Kinder. At the time, she had thought she would have endless time to make it up to her brother. To explain her chilling discovery to her mother and make her understand - she had only been trying to protect Donnal.

She stood, hugging herself. A silver flecked tear in her eye as she slid the little white cardigan embellished with tiny black roses, her mother insisted she wear for church, down her long pale arms.

Tentatively, she tiptoed forwards, desperately breathing through her mouth in short pants to avoid the irony stench which had her stomach lurching in nauseous tandem.

She knelt, a frown creasing her brow as she shrouded the little bundle in her cardigan. Gulping down the bile rising in her throat from the rancid, aromatic cocktail of slaughter, she watched as the fabric stained crimson.

Tia half expected her mother to be there already, especially with Donnal coming after her. But in surveying the area, she saw no sign of her. How she wished she was here, right now. So she could tell her what she had done was right, so she could do what adults were supposed to do and deal with the situation instead of leaving Tia to contemplate an adult's actions in this disturbing situation. She couldn't just leave the poor creature veiled in her cardigan - could she? What if someone picked it up? What if a creature stole its remains to eat? Shivers raked her body, and before she knew what she was doing, her fingers scratched at the dirt, clawing and scraping - desperate to lay the poor soul to rest.

Tia never had been afraid of blood and gore, death and demise. No, she was at the age of contagious curiosity. Everything held adventure, but the one thing she did respect was laying souls to rest - just like the priest taught at Sunday school. Her mother had always taught them that a new grave was blessed in order for the spirit to live on in heaven - forever.

Nails eating through the dirt, she finally managed to claw enough earth free to encase the fluffy little body shrouded in her blood soaked cardigan. She scooped it up, her chilled, muddy hands leaving sunken marks as they squelched beneath it. Bile fought to erupt from her throat as her stomach churned. The stench all but wriggling up her nostrils like the maggots she tried not to imagine infesting the small creature.

She lay it like a babe in the dugout, for the earth to cradle, spying the beautiful black fur with disconnecting duck- egg blue eyes. Her cardigan flapped loosely in an errant breeze.

A single tear bled from her eye as she scuffed the dirt atop the broken body. Placing a mucky palm on the fresh mound, she uttered a prayer her mother had taught her.

That's when she felt it in the tiny hairs prickling on the back of her hands like balls of barbed wire stabbing into her skin. The air around her became thick. She swallowed hard, an icy heat scorched her throat, her blood vessels slowed, her head throbbing as her teeth knocked a continuous chatter.

She knew what was coming next, but she couldn't stop it, couldn't wish it away or pretend it was a childhood nightmare - she had been reliving it since its first conception.

"I - I - is someone there?" Tia whispered, wrapping her arms around her frozen bare shoulders and stumbling backwards like prey before a lion.

"I – I'm not afraid of you," she stuttered, rising on shaking feet.

Breath expelling in short, choppy clouds, Tia gazed wide-eyed at the air rippling before her. Her feet felt heavy, numb, welding her to the patch of earth crystallising with each reverberating air current.

Her heart hammered as a frazzle like ice crawled up her spine like a frigged exo-skellington. Her whole body shook uncontrollably. Her teeth chattered, and a tingling sensation accompanied a soft hue of powder blue across her pale cheeks.

With a hammering heart, Tia tried to swallow. The thick, icy air clogged her throat. The air forced shallow breaths from her lungs as it folded in on itself. Warping around her like an ice storm about to strike. Only, it did not reside in the sky, but directly before her eyes as a bubble over reality formed, encasing her alone.

Tia shivered, pushing at the folds of air. The bubble around her stretched to give way to a face as pale as consecrated ash, with large, weeping scratch marks torn down her hollowed cheeks.

Tia swallowed hard, trying to moisten her throat to scream but couldn't.

Instead, she had no choice but to stare in horror at the half forming woman with eyes as white as salt rock as they bore into Tia's soul. Her head lurched, cocking to one side slightly further than was natural. Tia cringed, her lip curled at the sight of a blistered necklace around the woman's powder pale throat.

Tia wrenched her eyes from the woman. But unable to look away completely, she saw the mottled bruises that patchworked her bare arms as they too shimmered through the veil. Amongst the bruises, score marks bled and dripped down onto nailless fingers. Nail less fingers that reached, stretching out to her.

Gagging on what little air she could muster, Tia tried to retreat, but her feet were rooted with fear. She lost her balance and plummeted to the Arctic iceberg beneath her with an odd crackling - like scrunched up tin foil - until she hit the jagged grass with a crunch before submitting to the darkness that stalked her consciousness.

Tia felt - different, wrong. Almost... evil. The semi visible woman pulled back, retracting her arms one by one back into the shimmering fold of the air.

Heathen! A voice cried out. *Soulless female!* It roared. *Kill the devil's spawn!*

What the-? Why did I-? Did I - say that? Tia questioned her own mind. She hadn't spoken those words, she hadn't even thought them. *What's happening to me?* Her mind shrilled.

A deathly growl of frustration answered as her heart started to stutter. A shell of claustrophobic ice encased her eyes blurring with frozen tears. Tia felt the bruising grip of death upon her staggering heart as, with a throat shredding roar, dark shadows oozed through her pores with the sting of a thousand jellyfish barbs. Her body sagged, its icy cage smashing with the jarring impact. Lids heavy, she watched the blurring shadows seep together, blending into another bubble like impression in the air. Another being. But this one was dark, oily. Wrong.

White glowing eyes appeared demonically; their black pupils bore holes into her as she felt the sudden spread of warmth down her leg.

Watching, barely able to stay conscious, the air around the female folded, and she vanished from sight as everything in Tia's vision went black.

Sirens echoed a warning.

Voices mingled, begging - crying.

Then a scream...

Slowly, Tia's eyes fluttered from the past conjured by the sleek cat's image, coming into focus - Anka. *What the-? Oh God, not again.*

Tia hated reliving the past. The strangest things would set her off. *Triggers*, Ms Lilly, her councillor, said. She also said they would get better. She lied. Tia's traumatic past had a way of biting her in the ass every chance it got.

Anger began to boil inside of her, mounting as she stared at the glossy picture of the perfect kitten in the magazine, hands shaking as she crunched it tighter.

"I didn't mean to insult you. Black really is your colour. I just thought…" Anka scooted to the foot of the bed, batting her heavily lashed lids over her wide sapphire eyes.

Glaring daggers at Anka, Tia wrenched the offending page from its staples, screwed it into a ball and hurled it at the bin, throwing the remaining pages at Anka.

Snatching up the remains, Anka ran from the room, sniffing delicately.

Tia rolled her eyes, stretched her arms out and rested them behind her head. Taking some deep cleansing breaths, she stared at the door Anka had slammed behind her, her thoughts stirring. "Bloody ghosts!" she spat. She hated them in all their forms. It was their fault the G-Poss were aware of her 'talent'. Tia, though, had never seen her uniqueness — interacting with the dead — as a talent. She saw it for what it really was: a curse.

Chapter 2

Tia

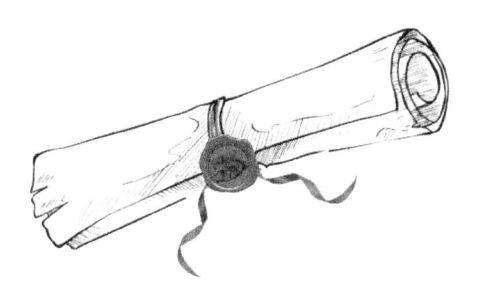

The large wire gates of the academy, intermittent with touch sensitive alarms, meant the building was impenetrable to the uninvited. But beneath the clay-like soil, buried from sight, was a fence. An impenetrable defence made up of an enchantment and protective crystals; a fence known as the ghost barriers.

Usually, these magical boundaries would pulse with strength, engorged and unbreakable. But today the lines lay dormant, hollow - as the house witch that controlled their current called the magic back to her, shutting down its power keg.

Inside the academy, Tia shivered awake with the unmistakable pass of Fiona's magic over her skin. Tia had only met the house witch once, upon first arriving at the academy, over six years ago. Tia shook herself. Now was not going to be a time when one of her loathed memories of the past pounced on her. She was too busy.

Dressing in the required uniform for once was a pleasure as she pulled out a stick of chalk from her pencil case and began etching blob-like ghosts and skulls onto it. Art was not her strong point, but anyone could use chalk, right?

Dusting off her hands, she stared at her graffiti in the full-length mirror. A sly smile crept up her pale face. *This is gonna be fun.*

Tia smiled to herself, snatched up Anka's hairspray from on top of her dresser and sprayed a plume across the blobby images. *Jailers won't get them off now!* She smiled to herself, scanning the room. She was late - as always - judging by Anka's empty bed. She took one last glance in the mirror, a deep stealing breath and left the room.

Swaggering down the corridor full of brass numbered doors to the senior girls rooms, Tia decided to take the fast route to the first floor landing - sliding straight down the bannister.

The first floor corridor was littered with mounted wall vases spewing fresh, sweet smelling flowers from the grounds. Tia stopped to stare out of a large mounted window overlooking the morbid graveyard surrounding the entire building.

The sudden *clack* of high heels assaulting the wood panelled floor had Tia grimacing. There was only one person in the whole academy who had the audacity to wander around in high heels amongst the G-Poss warriors.

Shit! thought Tia, turning from the morbid view, her heart racing with adrenaline as she launched into a sprint only to have her shoes stretch like elastic and spring her back to where she started. Frantically she pulled at her ensnarement as a huge wave of bee-like stings encompassed the entirety of her body. Scratching like a rabid dog, she hissed, "Let me go!"

"And have you go into such an important assembly looking like that?" Fiona asked, indignantly pointing at Tia's collage of chalk pictures. "I don't think so, child." She winked. "I'll fix that in a twinkle." She slid her bifocals up her long nose and began to chant.

As Fiona's magic pressed closer, Tia stilled and, to her relief, the incessant stinging ceased, leaving the bitterness of its passing assaulting her taste buds. Her body shivering with the feet of invisible spiders crawling inside her skin.

With tiny crackling pops, the chalked ghost winked goodbye and dissipated from view, followed by the rest of her graffiti masterpiece. Tia's rage grew with every pop of magic until it exploded from her mouth in a hurricane of spittle.

"Don't use your filthy magic on me, witch!" Sighing, Fiona ceased her chanting, her creepy skin-crawling magic dissipating from Tia's body, as gradually the images bled back into the fabric.

Tia found the tight coil inside her stomach unknotting, her body relaxing a little, as if fatigued, but still her anger blazed.

"It wasn't working anyway," Fiona sighed heavily, looking at her wrinkled palms. "I must be getting too old for such tricks."

"Whatever," Tia snarled, trying not to let the memories of their first meeting cloud her mind with the churning fire of negativity. Desperate for a distraction from the rattling of her ribs encasing her heart, Tia turned her eyes back towards the window.

The sky was dull and grey, odd spots of thick cloudy matter oozed about the sky . The nauseating stench of rotten eggs infiltrated the pores around the sealant of the window frame and Tia screwed up her nose. A flurry of delicately dancing feathers fluttered like a casting of new fallen snow.

Tia watched, mesmerised, as they danced atop creamy gravestones, lay at the bed of grey tombs, and fluttered through bodies like flickering shadow people as they strained to enter the physical world.

"I do regret what I did to you, child."

Tia felt her heart being crushed like a vice had stolen away inside her body and was pulverising the essential organ. Staring hard through the window she watched bright shining orbs pop into sight like the warm glow of Christmas lights at midnight.

"Sure," Tia replied stoically, a hard thin line to her lips as the lights in the corridor flicked off.

"I mean it, Tia. I am truly sorry."

"That's why you didn't reverse it," she snarled, turning to face the witch, "In what..." she shrugged, palms held open, shoes still cemented firmly to the floor. "Six years!?" Tia pulled at her feet again, her volcanic rage exploding in a guttural roar with her inability to free herself.

Fiona gently shook her head, grimaced, and lay heavy lidded eyes on her. "Come now, Tia. I -"

"You ruined my life! You bespelled me into staying here with your filthy magic! No matter how many times I've tried to escape, I couldn't. I hate you! I hate them!" she roared. "I hate all of this shit!" She encompassed the entire building in a frantic wave of her arms as she faced Fiona.

"The spell, it ceases its course today," Fiona whispered, flicking her hand to release Tia's feet as she strained to face her.

"Whatever!" Tia stormed. Finally free of the witch's hold, she ran from the corridor, her adrenaline pushing her speed past that of a normal sprinter as she fled from the dancing horrors of her lingering memories.

She stopped only when she came to the side door of the Great Hall, leaning against the dark grained wood, her lungs racked in burning gasps. Steadying herself against the door, she took a deep breath, straightened her - thankfully still graffitied - top and pushed open the finely etched door.

Instantly, the room went quiet as all eyes fell on her and her unique ensemble. Sniggers could be heard amid the bellowing voice of Jailer George's lecture. He glared over at her, shook his head, and pointed one podgy finger at the stools lining the back of the room. Tuts and sighs were the chorus to her footsteps as she strutted across the room and up the stalls, knowing full well Jailer George's piggy eyes watched her every move from the insatiable itch baring into her back.

Whatever, Tia thought, holding her head high. *Nothing can ruin today. Not even that psycho witch Fiona. Today, I unleash part one of my plan; escape the ghost fanatics.*

"W-whooo, Tia, you go girl!" Ella screamed at the top of her lungs as she made her way up to sit beside her, sending several potentials scattering to find another seat with her heated glare.

Sitting next to Ella, she smiled at the girl in thanks for her constant support. It seemed the two of them were soul sisters in everything - especially getting into trouble. It had been that way since Ella's parents had died. Tia had befriended the girl no one else wanted to know. The snotty-nosed child who went around screaming that she hated the G-Poss. Together, they were united under that flag.

"Potentials!" George's booming voice spat over the microphone. "This year we are privileged to offer Ascension to the five of you who have come of age." His huge body swamped the small podium as he directed with frantic arm waves. Tia sniggered. "Mentor Sam, will give you your assignments. If, and when, you complete them on time, you will be awarded the title of Ghost Possessor." He motioned to the young man who held up a scroll excitedly, his brown eyes alight with enthusiasm.

Then to the large burly mentors Jim and John, whom she generally called the delinquent twins. They stood dressed all in black, stationed to the side of the main entrance, where the large oak doors dominated the room.

The doors were special. *Enchanted,* the mentors said. They were engraved with witch runes which changed symbols constantly unless someone stepped close enough for them to read. It had only happened to Tia once and since the changing symbols froze, revealing a reading in glowing gold - she had never stepped near them again. Staring at the symbols from this distance, she could still see the creepy shifting eye, the lapping squiggle-like waves and the arrow that meant man.

"Potentials," George drawled, shaking her attention from fixating on the doors. "You have the three days of our house witch's holiday to complete your ascension assignment and rise to become one in our ranks. Ascend and become Ghost Possessors."

Giving the order with a wave of his podgy hand, the delinquent twins both stood before the runes at the same time, each holding a tile passed down from generations of ghost possessors right back until Death himself. A G-poss was either a direct descendant or one had diluted blood throughout the years; everyone knew only the chosen few were brought to the academy to train.

Suddenly, the large doors groaned open and the men stepped back to their pillar-like guard, moon scythe tiles firmly in palms.

Inch by inch the doors juddered inwards, opening by the magic of the runes. The sweet sickly smell of ectoplasm punched through the gap to assault their senses. Potentials groaned, holding their noses as others wiped at streaming eyes.

Suddenly, a flash of light illuminated a crypt, hovering over an inscription bordered by wild ivy. A gauzy 'typical' ghostly form melted away from the orbs' blinding flash as it spluttered out, leaving shadows to drift in its space.

The flurry of dancing feathers in the ectoplasmic clouds calmed since Tia had watched them from the window. Now a layer of them coated the fresh mown grass like fluffy new fallen snow.

The pale forms of humanised ghosts crowded the grounds, pushing and barging each other in an attempt to be closest to the rune enchanted doors.

Suddenly, a throat cleared. "Thank you, mentors," Jailer George beamed. "Now, for this year's ascenders. Li, Reece, Anka, Paul -" he called, motioning them down to stand beside his podium before locking eyes with Tia over the top of his glasses and continuing.

Tia stood, for once excited to do Jailer George's bidding, but Ella grabbed her hand before she could go. "Good luck, Tia. Don't cha go forgettin' me when ya get home," she whispered, giving her a half grin as she gazed up at Tia with dull blue eyes.

Tia could feel the sadness seeping from Ella like a blanket about to smother her. This girl had been her soul sister for so long now that the mere thought of not having her in her life was like a crushing fist around her heart.

Tia squeezed her hand. "I'll come back for you. I promise. My mother would love another daughter." She winked at Ella, whose eyes gleamed with a watery film.

"You know you've always been a sister to me, and no sister of mine will stay in this hellhole without me, okay?" Tia consoled as Ella yanked her back into a hug with a hiccupping sniffle.

"I love ya too, Ti."

"Ditto," replied Tia, prizing the thirteen-year-old off of her, taking a deep breath and continuing her descent to the stage.

"...However," George's voice boomed over the excited potentials shuffling and whispering in their seats. "The consequences of failing your assignment -" He glared at the full assembly, emphasising his warning with the raising of a single brow. "Will lead to your instant dismissal from this academy and all connections to the G-Poss WILL BE SEVERED!" He slammed his hand down in a cutting motion so fast it jiggled, eyeballing Tia.

Turning back to the crowd, he raised his podgy arms and roared, "Now, to the fun!" Rubbing his swollen little hands with glee, he turned and grabbed the pendants lined up on the 'put me up' table.

Tia watched with narrowed eyes as George placed a pendant over each of the potentials' heads before rocking slightly in agitation at Tia standing ramrod straight, unwilling to bow her head for his ease. *I'll never bow to you!* she thought venomously. *You had me magic bound to the academy so I could never escape in the first place.*

Fire flared a warning in his eyes as her own answered with a flash of lightning. He clenched his yellowed teeth and hissed, "I will not forget your blatant lack of… uniformity," he gritted out. Tia rolled her eyes. "You… will… be punished," he concluded, his smile grew tight before turning away from her and slinging her the pendant in his wake.

Dick! She thought as she tuned out his lecture. *It's not like I'll be staying any longer than I have to.* With a huff, she picked up the pendant from the cool, wooden floor. It was small and square, made from a brown alloy, maybe bronze. In the centre, nestled amongst a weave of cushioning metal, was a clear oval crystal with a slight sheen to its centre. Tia scrunched her eyes, peering closer at the object. It seemed the more she tried to scrutinise it, the more depth she discovered. *Odd*, she thought.

"Entrancing, aren't they?" Whispered a voice that spiralled like porcupine quills into her ear canal, snapping her back to reality. She quivered at the sensation of his words blistering beneath her epidermis due to the proximity of Paul's lips to her skin.

"I'm not surprised," she said sweetly, "it's the same size as that brain of yours, isn't it?" she snarked. "It must be so - disappointing," he sighed, glee swelling inside her at his hurt expression. Swiftly, he turned back into his normal suffocating arrogance and ignored her to talk to the other potentials.

"Their all-seeing eyes. Supposedly, witches can track us by tapping into their power. Kinda like a satnav. But instead of leading them to us, they can see whatever the eye sees. Cool, eh?" explained Paul, caught up in his own awe, his dark hair falling over his eyes.

"Get that out of a textbook, Scarecrow?" Tia snipped. Paul's thin lip quirked up a little, his cheeks pinkening.

Tia huffed in exasperation. *Bloody idiot thinks I'm flirting. Note to self: bitchin' is so not working on this freak!*

"Eww!" Anka shrieked, flinging the pendant to the floor and jumping up and down in her too perfect pink trainers before spiralling into a major hissy fit. "That's disgusting!" she squealed.

Li swept from his position further down the line to place a large, comforting hand on Anka's skinny shoulder and stare into her sapphire blue eyes. "Calm down, Anka. It's not real. It's just a crystal," he said in slow, rhythmic words that melted Tia's bones like a chocolate fondue.

Reece stared at Anka and rolled his eyes with a sigh.

"What, you think some ghost's gonna come in here and attack you because it wants its eyes back? Please. Even *I* didn't think you were that stupid!" Tia laughed as George bustled his heavy weight through their newly formed circle and snatched the amulet from the floor, his trousers riding down as he did so. *Oh, gag, Tia thought*, grimacing as Reece chuckled at her situation.

Tia bared her teeth when George's thick hands shoved her back into line, and once again the fire in his eyes crackled as if he couldn't wait to eat her alive. "Now!" he roared, waddling back to the stage, hoisting his slacks as he went. "Over to our first potential." He stared down at Li who walked to Jailer Sam right on cue.

Collecting a ribboned scroll, Li proceeded to the centre of the room. His biceps clenched with anticipation as he unravelled the scroll tied with red silk and rose a perfect black eyebrow over his gorgeous brown eyes. Tia sighed, her heart fluttering around her ribcage like a firefly danced along the water's edge on the darkest of nights.

Tia watched the flex of his muscles cause his polo shirt to tighten gloriously over his iron chest.

"Isn't he just perfect?" Anka sighed, pushing her blonde hair back over one shoulder, her sapphire blue eyes trailing Li's every movement.

Yeah. Tia sighed inwardly, remembering the first time they had met. It was over two years ago. She had been seeking a quiet place to dry her tears from her latest failed attempt to escape the compound when Li happened to walk by, inadvertently solving her problems with the revelation of 'failing ascension'.

"Heiress Victoria!" Li called again, his voice as smooth as chocolate as he folded the scroll and stuffed it into his tight black trousers.

Everyone fell silent, their gazes skipping over the open oak doors, to the haunted graveyard beyond. Tia couldn't see much from where she stood now, but a luminescence glowed through the huge wooden entrance and into the hall.

Potentials gasped as they saw more. Tia fidgeted irritably. It's not like she'd never seen a ghost before, but what Li and the others saw right now were the ghosts whom *they* would help cross over.

As much as Tia hated the G-Poss and their 'do-gooder' attitude, she didn't revel in the thought of dead entities suffering either. *Who cares?* she retorted to her inner compassion. She shook her head, her heart hardening like cooling steel. *No one gives a shit about me. This is my first real chance. Fiona's bitchin' spell is broken, Ascenders are allowed free rein of the academy and no one's gonna stand in my way – I can finally escape. Be free!*

The *clack, clack, clack* of heels against aged wood drew Tia's attention. Images of Fiona hell-bent on bewitching her again, flooded her mind. Sweat poured down her face and she began to tremble.

"What's going on there, Tia? You look like you've seen a ghost!" joked Paul who always seemed to catch her at her weakest. He never stopped in his pathetic attempts to charm her. He was *so* arrogant she could practically…

"Ahhh!" shouted Paul, hopping around on one foot as George yelled at him to get back in line.

Tia smiled silkily.

"What did you do that for?" snarled Paul.

"Cos I enjoyed it!" Tia snarled back. "Now shut the bloody hell up before I connect my foot with your ass!" Paul fell silent and shifted away, leaving her at the back of the line.

Shaking herself internally, Tia pushed past the ominous clacking of heels and concentrated on Li who stood in the centre of the hall, his muscles rippling beneath his shirt as a woman gradually appeared.

"Victoria?" asked Li.

The woman stood dressed in pale pink, which did nothing for her translucent complexion. Bustles cascaded from her corseted waist and fell in rivulets around her. She had the mannerisms of royalty, her posture held high as she floated up to Li. Tia licked her lips at the sight of his thick neck flexing as he tensed, unwilling to step away.

Tia heaved a sigh. *What I wouldn't give to kiss the tension from his face.* Her fingers snaked to her lips, tracing them instinctively.

Then, all of a sudden, *he* was back. It was as though he had attuned himself to her every movement. Her every thought. *Oh, for God's sake, get lost, Paul! I hate you! I bloody hate you!*

"Is it me?" asked Anka in an annoyingly delicate 'I'm a damsel, save me' voice. "Or was she a little... blue?"

"Trust you to study a ghost's complexion," sneered Tia. "You do know she's dead, right?" Her eyes glittered with sarcasm watching Anka's skin flush with a tiny smile.

Tia watched as Li swayed through the large oak doors, an arm held out gallantly, which the ghost of the countess looped her arm into as they walked out through the graveyard of ghosts. *Brave man.*

"Well, well," interjected George's baritone voice, his nose squashed against the microphone. "As always, our top student doesn't disappoint." A round of applause echoed throughout the hall, broken only by Jailer George's podgy finger tapping for silence against the microphone. "I will be expecting Li to ascend with some of the highest grades this academy has ever seen. Good luck to you, boy!" he crooned before turning his attention back to the crowd.

"Our next ascender is Reece Gwent," he announced. The boy stepped forwards, his dark as night hair hanging slightly over one eye. "Go on down to Sam and collect your scroll, Reece," Jailer George pushed.

Reece paled, flipped back his hair and wandered over to Jailer Sam. Snatching his scroll, he unwound the ribbon and dumped it on the floor. "Gwen!" Reece's gravelly Welsh twang reverberated through the room as he stopped in the centre, facing the wide open doors and monotony of ghosts waiting for their chance at 'moving on'. "Gwen!" he called again into the room's awaiting silence. "You there?"

A whoosh of wind brought waves of crisp autumn leaves mixed with a tide of soft white feathers into the hall. Orbs flashed about, their luminescence silhouetting shadow people bent over jaded gravestones. No flowers lay on their beds sparking colour against the gloomy ecto-clouds; it was not the G-poss way. No, their customs were very strict and only after the ghost barrier holiday could people lay flowers. This was known to most as the festival of flowers because so many of the G-poss lost to their jobs were buried in the academy's grounds and thanks for their service was always paid in flowers, remembering them for all time.

"Gwen!" Reece called again, drawing a bright orb flashing with turquoise highlights to the doors. It began to pulse, words drifting from within -

"Shh... the child is coming."

Chapter 3

Tia

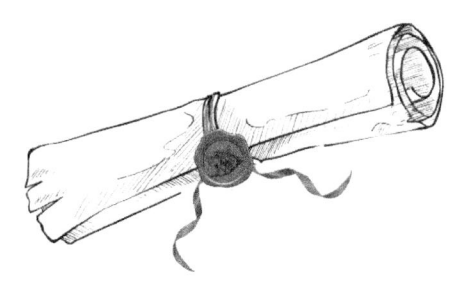

The noise inside the academy's Great Hall drained. A bone-deep chill swept through every being within. The manifested orb pulsated a blinding luminescence, and then vanished from sight. Its command for silence bounced off the old stone walls with eerie entrapment. Reece gulped, his Adam's apple rising and falling with a quiver. *Poor Reece.* Tia thought. *He's so green.*

"*Wyt it in Ffraneg?*" came a whispered voice.

"What the hell was that?" asked Tia as the softly spoken words echoed around the room and the stalls of potentials started murmuring.

"Not sure," answered Paul. Tia rolled her eyes, trying not to shiver in the sudden wash of cool air that brought with it an undertone of salt and seaweed.

Reece turned, trying to find the embodied voice's direction, responding in a soft gentle tone. "No, I'm not French." He smiled encouragingly as through the gauzy draped flesh, around the crypts and gravestones smothered in ivy, a young girl of no more than seven edged her way forwards, her delicate footsteps ruffling a path of feathers and leaves without crushing a single one. Silently, she drifted through two shadow people that twitched in agitation of her acknowledgement.

"Gwen?" asked Reece, lowering his towering frame to one knee as the ghost child approached him warily, her dark brown hair swaying in the autumn breeze.

"Well, she's definitely Welsh," Paul proclaimed starkly.

"Obviously," whispered Tia, too caught up in her assessment of the little ghost to care. Her eyes roamed over the simple black cotton dress, the white apron stained with grass and mud, and the blood-red cloak that somehow displayed her doom. *Doom? Where the hell did that come from?* Tia thought. But on closer inspection, she could make out a trail soaking the cloak's colour to a deep scarlet. She shivered.

"*Wyt ti mynd I dinistrio fi?*" The ghost girl spoke, her accent stronger than Reece's when he was messing around and so much more tuneful.

"No!" roared an outraged Reece, making the little ghost shrink back. "Gwen, I'm sorry," he sighed. "Look, I promise, I'm not going to hurt you. I want to help you," Reece consoled her.

"Isn't it adorable how she understands his every word?" Anka cooed.

"Yeah, and annoying," snarked Tia.

"Didn't you know that all ghosts no matter their age or… density—" Tia grinned conspiringly, "—can understand any language?"

"Tia's right," agreed Paul with a nod. "It's part of their transformation adjustment from physical beings to ectoplasmic entities. Still, it's a shame they can't *speak* any language," he contemplated.

Tearing her gaze from Anka's reddening face, Tia watched Gwen bound up to Reece and wrap her translucent arms around his broad body. He rocked back on his toes in fake impact. Tia couldn't help the snort of amusement as she watched the pair.

"Where are you from, Gwen?" he asked whilst simultaneously trying to figure out how to hug the girl back, which made Tia laugh even harder. He glared at Tia from over the ghost girl's shoulder, fire licking his eyes as rage all but possessed him, his muscles snapping taut.

OMG! He's seriously thinking of shuttin' me up. Like hell!

"Fishbourn," the ghost whispered, as Reece flashed Tia a warning glare before finally looking back at the little ghost.

Tia shivered. She wasn't afraid. But she knew that if it came to a fight, someone as strong as Reece would kick her ass. Even with all the G-Poss training in self-defence, she wouldn't stand a chance. Not that she'd let on to him. *Hell no!*

"I'm Welsh, too, Gwen," Reece said, giving up on the impossible embrace and smiling down at the girl. "Do you want to come for a walk with me? We can go to the library. Do you like books? I can read you one if you like?"

"*Iawn!*" said Gwen in agreement. Fidgeting with excitement and jumping out of the embrace, she turned in a flayer of her crimson cloak. A sudden gasp rent the air then more followed it with murmurs and gagging as the assembly's eyes fixed on the back of the ghost girl's head where a scarlet and brown tangle of hair matted the girl's caved-in skull.

Tia swallowed back the sickness in her throat and focused on Reece.

His eyes were wide and darkening by the second, their dark irises swirling like a whirlpool. He gulped, swallowing his Adams apple down hard and painted a soft smile on his lips as amid the raucous noise. Jailer George attempted to regain silence, Reece stood up and held out his hand. "Gwen?" he whispered, focusing the ghost girl's attention back on him.

A gentle shimmer crossed her body, her cloak whipping out with a sharp snap in some unfelt breeze as she gently rested her transparent hand in his and let Reece lead her through the back door of the hall.

"Back to business!" George clapped to gain the attention of the softly applauding assembly .

"Next we have Miss Anka Balinski." He motioned Anka forwards.

She obeyed with a shimmying sway, holding her hand out to Jailor Sam, where he placed the scroll with an indulgent smile. She took up a position in the centre of the room. Her manicured pastel nails twitched over her scroll's silk bow; within seconds, it unravelled and she called out to her ghost. "Declan Barns," she waited, twirling her blond-hair lazily around her finger and stopping the instant a male ghost manifested right in front of her. A shocking gasp came from her lips as she nervously stepped back, her eyes bulging from their sockets.

The ghost stood before her washed in sweat, his eyes sunken into barely visible skin, his lips and hands withered.

"You have got to be kidding me?" Anka turned to George, fear in her eyes, but George stared back unblinking, a thick vein throbbing in his neck.

Tia stifled a chuckle watching as Anka turned back to the ghost and gave him her sweetest smile, continuing to twirl her hair. "Sor-ry," she stumbled over the word.

The ghost gave her a knowing smile and took a deep shuddering breath. "'Tis all right, me lady." His laboured exhalation shook his fragile frame. "Me own lady would be shocked at the sight of me." He gave Anka a sad, knowing smile as she distracted him with her prattling until the Jailer twins were sent to usher them from the room. A round of applause rent the air.

"Paul!" snarled George. "Why are we waiting?"

Paul raced over to accept his scroll as his podgy uncle commanded and Tia couldn't help but shake her head in sympathy.

[52]

Sucks to be him, she thought as Jailor George started up once again, his tone becoming a monotone drone in Tia ears as he berated Paul.

"I expect great things from you, boy! My sister would want it that way. So don't disappoint me." He turned away from the microphone, but Tia still watched his bulbous lips twitch.

Harsh, thought Tia. She held no love for Paul, but she admired his intelligence – not that she'd tell him that. So, for his uncle, his only living relative, to suggest disappointment before Paul had even had a chance to call his ghost…

Paul unwrapped his scroll, anger flashing in the dark pits of his eyes. "Cain," he called, his voice laced with chocolate like Li's, but with bittersweet undertones.

The whole assembly looked on expectantly waiting for the ghost to come through the doors, or maybe pop out of nowhere like Declan, Anka's ghost. Even Paul searched the room, his vision lingering in every dark corner in case his ghost was about to pop out and yell 'BOO!' But no one was there, no ghost, nothing.

Paul scrunched up his scroll and threw it at the floor and roared. "Cain, get your lowly ass down here!"

"Now, now," George chided. "You know, as well as anyone, that it's not a good idea to anger a ghost."

Yeah, especially if you don't want them to poltergeist your ass, thought Tia indignantly.

Teeth gritted Paul glowered at the ghost people outside, his fists clenched by his sides he growled, "Hear me now, Cain Andrew Thompson, if you don't get your bloody ass out here—"

"Did someone call?" Paul jumped at the sudden over-pleasant voice coming from the foot of the podium.

Tia tried not to smirk as Jailor George jumped, stumbling back on his podgy feet, his belly wobbling as much as the ghosts did.

Clapping chorused around the room as the ghost, wearing a smart back suit barely able to button up over his rounded stomach, inspected his nails with one slender raised eyebrow.

What a jackass, thought Tia, giving the ghost a roll of her eyes. *Why doesn't Paul just strangle him with that bloody awful scarf he's wearing? Oh yeah, because he's a ghost. Duh, Tia! Duh.*

Sighing, Paul stomped to where the smarmy ghost lounged. "Nice of you to show up," he quipped.

"I thought you were never going to ask me in," the ghost snipped back.

Paul shook with rage, anger radiating from him like a fallen halo as he turned tail and stormed from the room, slamming the back door behind him, the echo reverberating throughout the silent room.

Potentials looked from one to another, murmuring with openly shocked expressions as the bemused ghost looked up at George. "Boy's sure got an attitude problem, hasn't he?" he smirked. "I would imagine he takes after you."

Red splotches of outrage soaked George's face. He spluttered indignantly, spittle flying like daggers only to cross through the ghost, who effortlessly brushed off the shoulder of his suit with raised eyebrows.

The assembly started to chuckle; some pierced their lips whilst the colour drained from some of the younger potential's faces.

The ghost sighed dramatically and disappeared with a showy *poof*, leaving George looking like a squeaky toy some dog had sat on with his eyes practically popping out of his head.

Tia chuckled, only turning her attention from Jailor George milli seconds before the ghost disappeared, catching sight of his leg which appeared more 2D than 3D. *Odd,* she recalled, the leg had been scarlet with white shards and a frill around it like a shrivelled, old- popped balloon. The glimpse she got made her stomach lurch and that didn't happen very often.

It amazed her that the ghosts could function normally even though they wore the ailments of their death. Well, as normally as a dead person could. They could all walk, no matter how zombie-horror-like they appeared. They could all talk, though some of them preferred not to. And even though they subconsciously breathed and shuddered, they had no need to. It was just a reflex; a residual essence of their life force they subconsciously wished to keep.

"For the last time, Tia, step forwards." The words slammed into her brain, lurching her from her mind's meanderings. *What would he do if I just didn't move?* she thought. As if on cue, George answered her unspoken question.

"If you don't step forward, Tia, I will simply move your ascension to next year; maybe then you'll bother paying attention." He stared down at her, fire licking his eyes. "Wouldn't that be fun?" he smiled, though his face was still red, giving it a cartoon devil appearance as a glint of wickedness laced his steely eyes.

Tia stomped forwards, snatched the scroll from Sam, and stood in the centre of the room, taking quick stock of the stalls until her eyes connected with Ella's. She gave a fleeting wink then faced the open doors, the spray of autumn leaves and soft feathers like a red carpet laid out for the ghosts of the dead.

"Go, Tia!" Ella's voice echoed around the gigantic room as Tia fixed her focus on the ghosts outside.

The sky was still gloomy, ecto-clouds casting dark spots of frigid temperatures wherever they cast their gloom. A shiver snaked its way down her spine as her eyes ran over orbs shining their luminescence down on translucent ghosts. Some sat like refugees seeking asylum, others whispering to faceless shadow people, young, old; it didn't matter. Death didn't discriminate. Race was unimportant. Death wasn't prejudice. But Death was, in Tia's mind, a collector. A collector who didn't appreciate his prized trophies defying him. So when ghosts appeared in the earthly realm, because they stayed behind for a loved one, or they were very, very bad, Death wanted them back! Although, the animal ghosts remained an enigma. But she supposed there was a whole other secret academy to help them or the world would be overrun.

Tia's eyes darted from the ghostly image of a shaggy old dog lolloping across the graveyard, to a young boy sat upon an old, weathered crypt, his legs swinging to an unheard beat, his slate eyes shining.

"Tia!" George's exasperated voice bellowed over the microphone, making the stalls full of potentials, along with her, jump.

Tia's attention snapped back to reality, her body shivering with goosebumps even though the hall's ambiance was set at a comfortable heat.

"Call your ghost," Jailor George demanded with a thump of his meaty fist against the podium stand.

Slowly, Tia untied the beautiful, red, silk ribbon. Her palms sweated slightly as her heart galloped. This was her moment, her time.

She could taste the bitterness of magic as she unravelled the scroll; the parchment's aroma hit her like a shot of ghost chillies – scorching a warning in her senses. She sank her teeth into her lower lip, bruising the tender flesh as she remembered scenes from her past.

Her fingers shook like they had separate consciousness of their own, wanting to run their own way. Sweat dripped a rhythm from her forehead and pooled in a loop around her collar bone.

Her knowledge that the parchment would spellbind her into a contract to either help or dispose of a ghost didn't make it any easier to read the name calligraphed in magic by the hand of Death himself.

"TIA!"

"Okay, okay."

Jailer George is really getting a sweat on, thought Tia, smirking. *Good, maybe he'll fail me right now! Then I can go home. Maybe I'll ask mum to make that hot cocoa with squishy marshmallows she always used to give us Christmas eve. Or maybe we could cook dinner together for Dad and Donnal.* Tia smiled to herself, took a deep, calming breath and read out the name scrawled in fine, slanting script, "Yule…"

Everyone in the hall waited in silent suspense straining to hear Tia's barely audible whisper- she theorised that Paul's ghost didn't respond until his full name was called, so maybe hers wouldn't either. "Oh, Yu-le," she sang, eyes locking with Jailer George, as leaves blew in from the open doors, crunching as they aimlessly smashed into each other and feathers gently soured like wisps through the hall.

Tia's smile broadened. The ghosts outside milled around the graves, still waiting, hoping to hear their names called. A partially transparent man looked expectantly around him, pausing on a faceless shadow that drifted closer. Tia held her breath. But thankfully the shadow person didn't enter the hall. No orb, gauzy ghost, or transparent one, entered. Tia's smile grew wider as she stepped back, raising an eyebrow at Jailer George.

"One last time, Tia. Call your ghost and use their full name. If it doesn't appear then you have your wish; I will dismiss you from the academy and the compound forthwith." He flourished a swollen hand.

Tia smiled, her heart skipping a beat, adrenalin surging through her. She crossed her fingers tightly beneath the parchment before whispering the ghost's full name. "Yule… Winter." Her voice did not waver from the hushed tones she had purposely adopted in an attempt to abate the destiny cursed upon her. Her smile spread inwards when no movement caught her eye.

"There is no one there," Tia announced haughtily. *This is it,* she thought. *I'm gonna be dismissed. Then… then I can go home. See my mum, my dad and Donnal. I can't wait! I wonder if mum will even recognise me? I've grown so much and I'll have to get out of these clothes first. I knew I shouldn't have packed already. I'll have to unpack, to repack, to change…*

Drip.

Drip.

Drip.

A blood-curdling scream wrenched from the lungs of a young potential, who raced from the stalls, her face as ashen as a newly cremated coffin.

The stalls of potentials stood, the whole assembly veering back like ripples from a stone-struck pond. The Ghost possessor warriors fanned out, forming a line to search and flush out the ghostly culprit terrorising the potentials. Another ran down the steps, barging past Tia and slamming into her shoulder, sending her into a full-on spin.

Lilly hit the floor, striking her face, tears rushed from her eyes. "Mentor George, it's awful, she's… so awful," she stammered as George pushed his way through the crowd.

"It's okay, Lilly." He bent down and helped the sobbing girl to her feet. "I'll take care of this. Sam, up here now! Twins, bar the doors! Tia!"

"What?" Tia sighed dramatically and turned to face George. Lilly, clung to mentor Sam's toned arm.

Tia glared at George. *What the hell does he want now?* She watched uneasily as George wiggled his stomach around. *Oh God, eww!* She closed her eyes, unable to look.

He finally unfastened the pouch from his belt and took hold of Tia's hand, shocking her into opening her eyes. He prised open her hand and slammed the velvet pouch inside. The tiny cord strings dangling over her splayed fingers as she inhaled a shaky breath. "It is your ghost, Tia. The choice is yours."

"Choice? What choice?" she asked blankly.

George sighed, shook his head, and muttered barely coherent words about listening in class. He glared at Tia with exasperation. "The - pouch, Tia. Inside - is - salt."

"Obviously," she snarked, irritated by George's slowed speech. *I'm not stupid, asshole. I – clever – human. Human – girl – understand – stupid – man. Duh!* "Why did you give it to me?"

George blustered, his face heating like a blistering pork rind. "Decide whether or not you will exorcise the ghost you have called," he spat. "And do it now!" Tia's eyes flicked, her mouth opened and shut before she burst out -

"What?!"

"*It's your ghost, Tia,*" he spat, causing her to cringe back to avoid the debris from his dinner. Her nose wrinkled. It smelt like he had eaten liver to her.

Talk about disgusting!

"...Your responsibility. Decide!" He bellowed as a wave of young potentials rushed past them.

Decide? Everyone's terrified and he's leaving this down to me? Bloody coward. Well, she shrugged. I suppose it's my ghost so I guess I have to do the dirty work.

Rolling her eyes, she huffed, trying to hide the fact that a creepy tingling of web-like prickles were meta morphing through her internal system, leaving her mouth as dry as a thousand year old mummy's .

She turned back to George. "If I salt... it, can I go home?"

"Tia, if you choose to destroy your ghost, you will fulfil your assignment on the level of exorcism and be graded accordingly..." he prattled on.

Great, so I would become a ghost possessor. Tia sighed inwardly. *So, my only option is to accept that... that... ghost as my assignment.*

Tia opened the drawstrings on the black velvet pouch, her fingertips caressing the prayer Death himself had handed down through generations of G-poss warriors. Tia mumbled the words etched into the seam –

"Exerce hoc malum ex oculis meis,

sal purgatum,

nunc in limbo resident."

It seemed so final. So cruel. Sending a ghost to limbo where they would spend centuries being punished for their crimes before they took the next step. *Whatever that was,* she thought.

But who cares – this is my chance. I have to take it. But mother would never forgive me if I sent this ghost to limbo and it was an innocent. But then again, what she doesn't know - Tia shoved the salt-filled pouch into her chalk-graffitied slacks, her eyes hardening.

Step by step, she ascended the stalls, eyes constantly shifting for a glimpse of something ghostly as the remaining potentials scuttled past, not one stopping to direct her, but then again, from the pungent stench of waste she could tell the way. She wrinkled her nose, her eyes watering as they smarted and slowly she crept left along the benches. Suddenly, she slipped, her heart raced, her body spun as she tried to avoid toppling down the stalls, narrowly missing a landing against a bench and toppling to the floor. A half frozen puddle of water greeted her palm, she frowned, noticing more patches of iced water. Shivering, Tia pushed herself back to her feet, careful not to step in the iced patches again. She shut out the chaos of potentials, the orders of G-poss warriors, and the blatant hollering's of Jailor George to hone in her sense of hearing.

Drip.

She crept further along the bench, the air shifting to cold as her lungs felt the bite of ice.

Drip.

A figure, barely visible, fuzzed in and out of view like an old movie on the blink. Tia stilled, slowing her racing heart with deep breaths, the taste of mossy wet earth and something irony on her tongue.

Cautiously, the figure configured before her like a swarm of pixels coming into focus. She watched as first sodden blue-tinged feet appeared, their toes dancing on icy shards.

Tia's heartbeat thundered a deafening battle cry in her ears. She watched water rivulets drip from its mutilated garments before hitting the floor where they vanished.

A memory danced around the edges of her mind, taunting her with a familiarity she sensed was a warning.

Oh God. Oh God no! This can't be happening. This can't be bloody happening! Tia's breath caught in her chest. Her heart rose so fast she could feel it climb into her throat. Nausea spiked its way from her stomach turning her saliva to bile. Her hands shook as slowly the ghost raised its glazed eyes to hers. It was female. A ghost woman just like… *No. It couldn't be.*

"*No!*" Tia screamed for the little girl inside her whom the ghost woman terrified. Screamed for the loss of her old life and then screamed in savage anger at the ghost whose manifestation had incited the loss of her family.

Drip

Drip

Drip.

Her mind flickered like a film on rerun. An image of her brother, Donnal, running from her with tear-filled eyes engulfed her, pulling her back into *the* memory she loathed. A black kitten lying open, a splay of innards visible as it rested beneath the canopy of an old oak tree. A ripple in the air, a blur, a shimmer and then, the - the ghost.

Scrunching her eyes shut, she counted to ten and blinked. But the ghost woman who haunted her past still sat before her, knees gripped tightly to her bruised chest by arms covered in weeping scratches. Tia cowered, her shaking spread the stomach wrenching aroma of mould ridden damp mixed with the pungent tang of faeces. Tia's eyes watered and she clasped a hand over her mouth, pinching her nostrils together.

The ghost tilted her head, her filth-ridden hair hiding hints of the golden corn colour it once was, splayed back revealing a morbid necklace of rope burns. Tears streaked the complexion of her bloodied face as she slipped to her knees before Tia. "I beseech thee, help me!"

Tia's heart raced like a firecracker had exploded in her veins as she frantically tore at the velvet pouch in her slacks, wrenched it open, and scooped out a fistful of salt. "You! I will destroy you!" she screamed into the face of the ghost who haunted her every nightmare. Her fingers bleached white with rage as her grip locked onto the salt.

The apparition faded in and out of view, a pitiful shadow of the ghost that had terrified her as a child. Seeming but a stain in the air, a forgotten ripple in time.

Tia shook her head, her black braid whipping fiercely at her lower back as she turned from the begging woman.

"He *shall* return," the ghost warned, fear crossing in a shadow of her sightless eyes as she flickered in and out of focus before vanishing completely.

Tia turned back to where the ghost had sat and stared at the water-soaked bench. Fear stemmed through her body with her muscles recalling her past memories. Her heart thundered, punching bruises into her soul. Who was the ghost talking about? What did they want? Could it be the darkness that had bled from her body all those years ago when the deathly woman first appeared to her?

Chapter 4

Jinx

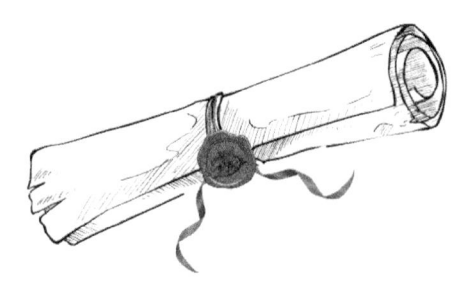

"Eye's shalt not see," chanted a boy with earthy green eyes, a chilling mist coiling within them. "What beneath the mountain hides?" The scent of damp moss soaked his nostrils. "So mist cover, blind," he roared, tilting back his head, his gem-strung corn braids whipping at the dark skin of his face as he concluded, "our enchantments we must hide!"

Mist shot in streams from his out stretched fingers with a whoosh, blanketing the picturesque Welsh mountain of Carnedd Llewlyn. He stood back admiring his handy work wondering; *why do we bother casting a concealing mist when we live inside the Goddess-given mountain?*

As if reading his thoughts, his grandmother replied, "Tis more discreet this way, Jinx. We wouldn't want the humans seeing us cast now, would we?" she purred.

Jinx sighed, sweeping the braids from his sweaty face, his heart thudding sluggishly with the cost magic had upon it. Casting always took its toll and although Jinx was powerful, he was no exception to the cost of magic.

"Grandmother, I…" he began his long-suffering quest to modernise the way his grandmother thought.

"That's High Witch Elder to you," she snarled, turning on him with eyes that reflected his own, set in a withered face he had come to love as a child should a mother.

Ever persistent, he continued, "No one can see us High Witch Elder, please-" He took her frail hand in his and whispered, "We're inside a mountain." Jinx felt his lips bow into a wide smile as his grandmother snatched her hand from his, sneering. They had been over and over the same argument for the last three years, yet still the old woman would not sway her outdated opinion.

Jinx turned to her old oak cabinet stocked full of the aromatic herbs, thanks to her assistant, Yarik, and began reorganising her aged labelling system.

"That is no reason for negligence, Jinx. Do you want to bring back the witch trials?" she asked with a deep sadness lacing her mellow tone.

He sighed. He knew his grandmother worried; she was paranoid about the witch trials, as most witches were.

If they were going to kill us, they wouldn't be supporting us as a government faction, that's for sure. They're using us – like weapons in a war, thought Jinx. Not that he could get his Grandmother to understand. "Of course I don't want to bring back the witch trials, Grandmother, I mean High Witch Elder. But that happened centuries ago." He sighed.

"There is no *but*! If they see us, they will hunt us and we- will- burn!" She smacked her desk with every syllable. "Not even a witch of our standing can escape being burnt at the stake- Jinx."

He ran a hand over his corn-braids in frustration, their crystal-beaded ends clanking angrily as he huffed, "I know, I just—"

She threw her wrinkly hands up in the air- "Enough! Be silent so that I may begin my casting."

Jinx quieted, knowing to well the punishment his Grandmother bestowed to the witchlings in their coven who didn't listen; and he had never enjoyed supply counting. Finishing off with the last label he turned and busied himself making a fire in the open hearth of his grandmother's private casting room, instead of observing the spell she cast so that he could practice it later- repeatedly. But he had always found himself having an aptitude towards spells. They just came easily to him- like walking.

A flashing icon on his grandmother's open laptop beeped to signal a Skype link requesting an audience and he couldn't help but snigger as she harrumphed, trudged towards her desk, slumped down into the plush computer chair and sighed in comfort.

Jinx tore his eyes back to the open fire and busied himself stabbing at it with a poker whilst eavesdropping on the conversation.

"Merry meet," said a woman's voice from the laptop.

"Merry meet, sister. What can I do for you?" his grandmother asked in her no-nonsense tone as she shuffled in her chair. Her silver hair bounced in crazy ringlets like the dance of storm clouds on a thunderstruck day.

"A...a spirit visited me last night when the ghost barriers were down."

Jinx threw another cedar log onto the fire, causing it to crackle and spark. A pungent perfume smoked around the room, filling it with a calming aroma.

"Pray continue, sister. If this is important enough to interrupt my private casting session with my grandson, then get on with it." Jinx's grandmother was not known for her patience. But amongst the covens left, most witches chose to ally themselves with hers and simply ignore her imperfections. Whereas, Jinx was merely biding his time until it was his turn to take over leadership.

"High Elder..." began the woman.

His grandmother sighed in irritation and held up a finger in a bid for silence. She turned her large, green eyes towards Jinx and stared down at him. "Well, you might as well come up here and listen instead of pretending you're not," she snapped.

Jinx rushed to his feet, obeying his grandmother as he would his parents, if they were still around. Striding up to the wooden desk he peered over her bony shoulder, down at the Apple Mac laptop. He stared at a woman stood blocking the screen, her black polo shirt added a stark contrast to her petrified skin.

Clearing her throat, she began again, her voice quivering as she spoke, "High Elder Shannon—" the woman bowed her head in response "—last night I woke to the persistent sound of dripping inside my apartment. I thought I'd left a tap on or something, but then the dripping got louder and... Oh, Goddess..." She gulped, her thin bottom lip wobbled as she continued, "It hit my skin, drop after drop. I scrunched my eyes shut as tightly as possible, but the putrid smell of waste and... Oh, Goddess...my eyes stung so much that I had no choice but to open them. Through the blurry sting, I saw the blind eyes of the dead looming over me. I screamed, wiped the water from my eyes and realised the dripping had not been the tap, but blood that fell from scratches scored into the ghost woman's face. My face- it was covered- in blood!"

"Sister, calm down. Breathe deeply and tell me what the spirit wanted," commanded the High Witch Elder.

Jinx watched sweat pour from the woman's brow as she fought to collect herself, her bottom lip still tremoring out an s.o.s.

"That's what I'm trying to tell you, I don't know because just as she opened her mouth..." The woman on the screen shivered in repulsion. "She...she was... I don't know!" She threw her hands up and then wiped them over her face as tears streamed from her eyes. "The room suddenly grew cold, icy, and there was this…darkness. An evil matter crawled up her skin. She screamed as it dragged her away from her bed, onto her knees and then…they just disappeared! It was so fast, so fast I—"

"You should have called me straight away! Why didn't you, Fiona? This dark matter is obviously dangerous, and you are responsible for the safety of an entire academy of Ghost Possessors – with whom I wish to remain on good terms to push my petition.

This situation could have ruined my chances if it had got out of hand!" She admonished Fiona through the screen.

Jinx found himself shaking his head in disgust at the way his grandmother was abusing her power to chastise an obviously traumatised woman. He placed a hand on the thick shrug wrapped around his grandmother and channelled a calming restraint of power through to her. His fingers pricked like tiny needles as she sighed and reached up to clasp his hand.

Patting it in gratitude she took a deep breath, her nostrils flaring before returning to talk calmly to Fiona who was hysterically trying to explain her actions that night.

"So, let me get this straight," Jinx interrupted her nonsensical prattle after his grandmother's commands to calm down had not proved fruitful, "you're from the Ghost Possessor Academy. The one near Hereford," he said after noticing the Skype location app, "and yesterday you let down the ghost barriers for the three-day ascension ceremony. In that time, the spirit of a woman – obviously tortured – visited you. Before you could find out what she wanted, a dark matter attacked her and dragged her away. What did you do next?" Jinx was still channelling calmness into his grandmother whilst simultaneously lacing his voice with a hypnotic sedative until Fiona visibly calmed.

Fiona answered with slow measured breaths, her voice cracking as she spoke. "I grabbed my candles and lit them one by one to invoke the elements, and that's when I noticed the…" Her voice began to quake, its tone becoming shrill. "The letters, Elder…" Her eyes once again rested on Jinx's grandmother as she added, "The letters, they were written in blood spiked with ice. High Elder, it was ghost blood." She burst into sobs.

"Ghost blood?" Jinx questioned, unsure of his standing on the topic; he wasn't a Ghost Possessor, after all, or an 'answer to everything' e-book.

"Jinx, bring me my grimoire," ordered his grandmother, pulling him out of his thoughts.

He turned, searching the bookshelf at the back of the room, his hand gently skimming across the only picture of his family that his grandmother had kept. Being High Witch Elder of the Pren Ceri Coven, she was used to loss and disappointment and constantly reminded him. That's why she kept the photo here in the confines of her private casting room.

Jinx stroked a finger over the pale face of his mother, his silver chrysoberyl ring clanking against the frame. He gazed longingly at her as she stood locked in the tattooed arms of a tall, sharp-faced man. Jinx felt his eyes water and quickly blinked back his tears. It had been years since their sudden disappearance, but he still missed them. He stared at the tall, dark-skinned man, Samuel Pren Ceri, his father. Jinx and Hope, his younger sister, were both coven-born like their father; but unlike the two males, Hope was born without magic.

Jinx sighed deeply, the loss of his mother and father was a stain on his soul. He missed them dearly. Jinx ran a finger over the image of his mother, her cheeks were flushed with pregnancy, her stomach just beginning to swell. The slight smile curving his thick lips soon festered into a frown as he once again wondered why his sister had to be banished. *Why couldn't she have stayed with me? She could have been protected by the coven.* It's not as if his grandmother couldn't bend the rules slightly, or even break them; after all, she had written them- once upon a time. But no, his grandmother followed the rules she wrote as the young High Witch Elder and did not deviate.

Even in the case of family. So Jinx's little sister was cast out a year after their parents' disappearance, and Jinx was left alone with no idea where his grandmother had sent her.

All he knew was that the letter he wrote to her every month since they were separated was delivered by Yarik, who covertly made sure Hope got them and his grandmother knew nothing about them.

But to his hearts disappointment he received a very factual letter every December in response. She refused to answered his questions. She shut him out of her life. He only kept trying because his mother would want him too- Goddess bless her.

"Jinx," scolded his grandmother, forcing him to push his thoughts from the past as he skimmed the titles lining the highest bookshelf to the left of the fireplace, finding the engraved spine of his grandmother's grimoire.

Jinx placed the book of magic before his elderly grandmother knowing she would find some way to help Fiona. His Grandmother was like an apostle in her knowledge, so even the most dire of situations seemed to blossom hope under her scrutiny. Jinx admired her – but deep down he knew when he succeeded her- the coven *would* change.

"Ghost blood is rare, I know that. But I can't quite remember..." She thumbed through the pages of her grimoire. "Ah yes, here it is. Once a ghost's blood is spilt it creates a recurring phenomenon known as 'ghost blood'. Unobvious to most is that the ghost blood is sent as a warning of a great evil amassing. Remember that, Jinx," she commanded before waving him away and burying her face back in the screen again. "Blessed—"

"Wait!" Jinx shouted and stalked back to peer over his grandmother's shoulder. "The letters, what did they spell?"

Fiona looked confused for a second before comprehension dawned. "Wait a minute." She grabbed a scrap of paper. "I wrote the letters down before they could disappear. The ice it was spiked with remained, melting into stinking pools of water on my floor."

"The dark presence must be powerful to have ice form at its presence," said the High Witch Elder aloud. "Be careful, Fiona. Be very careful."

"Yes, High Elder," She replied, and then turned her large worried eyes back to Jinx. "The letters, they spelt 'HUNTA'."

Hunta? Jinx strode back to the fire lost in thought as he swiped a notebook, tapping a pencil rhythmically against his temple as if to spark ideas, before scribbling down notations.

"Blessed be." The High Witch Elder mumbled, her mind caught in thought as Fiona signed off, swivelling to look at her grandson.

Lowering his head Jinx hid behind his curtain of braids as his Grandmothers gaze sent prickles down his neck. "Jinx, my dearest grandson, I think you are ready- at last."

Oh Goddess. Those words were the most ominous Jinx had ever heard out of his old grandmother's mouth. *Ready for what exactly?* he wondered as he remembered the last time she announced him as 'ready'; on Jinx's thirteenth birthday several years ago. 'It was an important age, an age where he would begin his journey to manhood.' She had smiled down at him, gently tousled his hair and retrieved a small cardboard box tied with a dust stained ribbon.

The only one he had known who used pale blue bows on gifts was his mother. He remembered the itch that had begged him to rip open the box, the excitement pumping adrenalin through his veins.

Delicately he had unslipped the bow, revealing in the tiniest scent of the perfume his mother used to spray on every bow she tied.

But when he had noticed his grandmother's eyes staring greedily at the box, he found himself secreting it away into his room where he could open it in privacy.

Inside the box had lain an assortment of gifts from his naming ceremony. He had riffled through them one by one pulling them out and setting them aside without reading their notelets or taking time to enjoy the gifts. Jinx had known that somewhere in the box would be a gift from his parents, a connection to them he so deeply needed.

Then his hands had finally found it. He had picked it up and held it in his palm. It was a small handsewn dove, as white as mountain top snow, with big beaded eyes and a miniature key around its neck. He had stared at it for hours before reading the card, tears streaming down his face. He picked up the notelet his mother's fine calligraphy print like a gentle caress:

Son, we pray you find the key,

Love and blessings,

Mummy and Daddy

XXX

Jinx shook his head to dislodge the memory of his mother's handwriting on the recycled banana paper she used. He smiled. He missed them terribly.

Steeling his heart against the flood of memories drowning his soul he took a deep lungful of fire tinged air and turned to his grandmother, his expression guarded as he asked, "Ready for what exactly?" His eyes narrowed.

His grandmother turned in her seat and smiled at him knowingly. "A trip, Jinx dearest, a trip."

Great. He thought as he made his way out of the cavernous room. He walked inside the mountain's centre, the cool rock smooth with repeated use beneath his feet. He followed the winding path, hunching slightly when the mountain dipped, until he arrived at the common room where most of the coven were gathered in a circle chanting. The smell of candle smoke and cedar encircling them.

A lone body stepped around the massive circle and headed towards Jinx. "All right, boyo?" asked a man slightly older than him.

"Yes, I'm fine, Yarik. You?"

"The High Witch Elder said you might need a hand packing for a trip?" Yarik smiled, his crooked teeth visible. "That true, boyo? Going somewhere nice?"

"Yes, you're right. No idea where she's sending me, though." Jinx rolled his eyes and shrugged.

"Don't matter. Come on, let's get you packed before she starts screaming orders again." He chuckled.

Jinx smiled glad of the company as he led the way to his alcove room. Inside was a bed, magically built into the wall, a small desk complete with laptop and a stumpy bookcase, on top of which sat a tiny ornamental raven.

"Where do you keep your clothes, bud?" asked Yarik, his heavy frame squeezing through the magically hinged doorway.

"Over there." Jinx motioned behind the door with a teasing smile, watching with a glint of amusement in his eyes as he fumbled about.

"Right," mumbled Yarik, his dark hair flopping over his deep brown eyes as he hunched to retrieve the splayed clothes. "S'pose we'd better get on with it."

"I suppose so." Jinx sighed. *I wonder where in the Goddesses name she is sending me now.*

Chapter 5

Tia

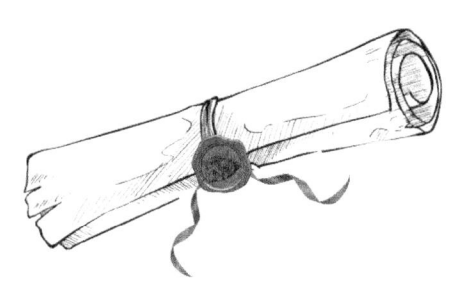

Tia nearly jumped out of her skin when her haunting nightmares were interrupted by the academy's shrill wake up bell. Stretching until her bones popped with delicious relief before refreshing herself and dressing, she rummaged around in Anka's drawer in search of a hair brush and ties before checking out the spindle weed on top of her head.

    With a deep sigh Tia began raking the bristles through her raven hair, tugging at its snagging ends. *Not long now.* She assured herself. *Then I'll be home with them. I've just got to-* A flicker in the mirror caught her attention and she found her fingers rising to poke at the bruised semi circles beneath her eyes. Another flash shined over them like the light of a printer upon gloss photo paper. Swallowing she pulled the brush free of her long hair and leaned into the full length mirror, one hand examining her eyes whilst the other pressed lightly against the reflective surface.

A shine, this time so bright it blinded her, her world going dark. Heart thundering so loud in her hysteria, it became a white noise as she fumbled about her hair frizzing in a cage around her.

"Tia, what the hell" Anka moaned, snuggling deeper under her fluffy pink comforter as Tia flailed, smashing into the mirror.

"Aah!" Her heart thumped a parry against her ribs. Tia hissed as the bite of crushed glass beneath her palm sliced a burning cut alone one slender finger. "Tia!" Anka moaned. "what is wrong with you?" She reached out blindly to her bedside table, patting around for her giant tatty teddy that sat there spookily staring at nothing all day and plastered it over her ears.

Gritting her teeth hard enough a pulse jump in her temple Tia stood, plucking the glass from where she felt it in her palm. "Get out of me!" She roared as all at once the darkness bled from her eyes, slowly forming a manifestation infront of the door. A clout to her head had her rage rivalling a poltergeist as she watched the tatty teddy die upon the mirror spikes. She turned, glaring at Anka who at the site of her smiled nervously and ducked back beneath her comforter. Tia's shoes ground on the mirror glass, sending up a puff of glittery cloud. She spun to the doorway at the sight of a manifestation in front of it, barely making out the outline of a woman as the lights flickered on and off with static orchestral accompaniment.

"Tia Morgan... *Help me...!*"

"Seriously!" Tia snapped, stamped up to the incoming manifestation and punched her hand right through the ghost's forming chest to the doorknob behind, viciously twisting, before yanking it back through the dissipating ghost.

She stormed out, her hair still netted over her face like a funeral veil, the pull of her blood drip, drip, dripping as she walked making her finger throb in time with its rhythm. She stalked down the hall and into the nearest bathroom, a stream of mumbled curses falling from her mouth. It had nothing on her as she staired through the raven strands curtaining her vision. Huffing she pulled the band from her wrist and scraped the strands back from her face, taming her hair into a frizzy french braid. A stream of crimson streak glinted in the florescent lights. Her heart pounded so hard she could barely register the pain as she turned on the tap and stared at her finger dripping blood into the communal sink, curdling with the glistening water.

Suddenly the lights flickered, their humming grew louder and in a split second it turned dark. A gush of water caressed her injured finger. Instantly she snatched it to her as the lights simultaneously flicked back on, the humming ceasing.

"Get lost Yule!" Tia screamed, wishing she had Jailor Georges exorcism pouch. "I hate you!" She raced out of the rest rooms and along the staircase, bowling straight into Reece.

"Idiot!" Shrieked his ghost at Tia as she floated over him, gazed down at him with her doe brown eyes. "Byddwch chi'n dal I fynd a mi adref?

Wyt t'in iawn? Oedd hi'n brifo chi?" He replied as tears beaded in the ghost's eyes, she floated back allowing Reece to clamber to his feet.

"Whoa there! Seems little Welsh lamb's found her voice." Tia laughed as she untangled herself from the floor, frowning, she noticed the absent throbbing in her finger. She gazed down at its smooth surface glittering with excess water. *What the hell*? She thought.

Reece stood up, dusted off his long, lean arms and shot a glare at Tia. He turned to the little ghost girl and in a soft voice said- "It's all right, Gwen, Tia didn't see me. Did you, Tia?" He glared daggers at her.

"Of course not! Like I'd purposely barge into you and your little girl friend. Oops! I meant ghost friend." She chuckled, feeling the tension of the morning lift slightly.

Reece harrumphed, then turned back to answer Gwen. "Yes, I will still take you home. It would take more than a premenstrual Tia to stop me." He smirked at Tia as the little ghost giggled.

"Checkmate," grumped Tia. "I'll leave you and your little fan club alone. Maybe you can do us all a favour and stay the hell wherever you transport back to!" She growled, her mood sinking.

"Damn, Te! You sure got a loada shit in your mouth today. Maybe you should go wash it out before you see anyone else!"

"Beats having shit for brains!" snapped Tia as she watched a light dance through his milk chocolate eyes, like it always did when they had one of their 'snipe fests'.

Tia tracked further down the magnolia corridor aware of coloured flashes in her preverbal vision as landscaped pictures trembled on the walls as she passed. Paying no heed she glared straight ahead, sliding down the old oak stair cases banister, as was her custom, to the first floor where potentials rushed about clutching books, chatting and attempting to contact ghosts. Tia huffed at them, fully aware that they parted for her like she was the devil itself. All except the pathetic third year with books piled so high she couldn't see over them.

Suddenly a frozen breeze brushed past knocking her into a spin, her books flying everywhere to smack open on the floor, notes and pages spewing around. A chorus of laughter drowned out the chortling voices as the straggly haired blond scraped around on her knees collecting up the books littering the floor before Tia.

Huffing Tia bent and snatched up an essay tarnishing her boot. "Here blondie." She held out the paper, blinking as the words shook, the ink bled into a roaming blot before dripping; forgive me. Tia hissed, her blood boiling as she scrunched up the paper and threw it at the floor, storming along the corridor, she kicked the books in her way before descending the staircase to the ground floor and storming into the pigpen.

She surveyed the range of piping hot breakfasts, the delicious smell of hot cocoa swirled inside her nostrils and her stomach instantly growled as she found herself pushing past the queues and diving in front of the cocoa machine.

Grabbing her drink and cramming it full of marshmallow toppers, she made a beeline for the booth at the back of the room, the one with the awful green faux leather and graffiti-covered table. The one she and Ella called theirs. She slid into the long seat, her gaze drowning in her molten vat of cocoa.

It wasn't as good as she remembered her mother's being, but it was still comforting. The calorific mallows sweetened the world back to reality; the bitter chocolate smoothly stroked the fear from her insides, abating the anger it produced, the heat of the cocoa warmed the fractured pieces of her broken heart.

"Hi Tee." Ella spoke as she slid into the booth, her tray crammed full of Hawaiian shortcrust pizza.

"How the hell did you get that?" asked Tia, ogling the tray.

Tia watched Ella grab a piece of pizza, the cheese stretching to the tray. She waggled it dramatically in front of Tia's solemn face. "Sally saves me somma the leftovers."

"Sally the kitchen bi-a-tch?"

"Uh-huh," mumbled Ella through a mouthful, winking- "feels sorry for me, ya know."

"I suppose something good's got to come from your loss." Tia shrugged.

"Pizza for ya thoughts?" tempted Ella. Tia smiled indulgently at her, straightened her posture and lifting her gaze from the swirling meanderings conjured by her drink. "Come on…" she enticed, "it's Hawaiian, your favourite." She waggled it again, causing a swollen chunk of juicy pineapple to catapult straight onto Tia's polo top. "Oops!"

"Ella!" Tia berated, swiping at the chunk that left a slimy glistening trail like a slug would. She leant over the table and attempted to wipe it off, only to add to the destruction.

"Sorry, Te," she said as she slammed her behind back onto the faux leather seat with a deafening squeak. Her face reddened at the unwanted attention when other potentials shot revolted looks her way.

"Ignore them, Ell. And don't worry about the top, Jailer George said they were gonna burn all my uniform anyway. He thinks they're no good to anyone, what with all this graffiti." She looked at the top, stroking the calked images lovingly as her heart swelled with pride. She had finally gotten under the old jailors skin.

"Aw, no fair," Ella whined. "I wan'ed them." She frowned in consideration. "Maybe ya can give me 'em before he takes 'em?" she pleaded, eyes as big as LOL dolls.

"They're too big for you, Ell." Tia sighed whilst snatching another slice of pizza from Ella's over stacked tray.

"I'll grow!" she defended, her face reddening with bluster. "I'm *so* not staying this small forever."

Tia chuckled and drained the last of her, now cold, cocoa.

A shadow darkened their booth, blotting out the light and sending fearsome memories of dark spectres floating through Tia's mind. She took a deep breath, regaining her equilibrium, and rose her eyes to glare into the awesome brown depths of…Li's. *Why is he here? Not that I don't want him to b,e but damn how those muscles flex beneath his shirt. Delicious… OMG, Tia, you're drooling!*

Li leant both his hands on their table with a thud making the whole thing revibrate whilst Tia gorged her senses on his chocolate aroma.

"Te." He nodded, then faced to Ella. "Ellzy." He gave the girl a killer smile before turning his attention back to Tia. "You, Morgan," he said pointing a large finger and wagging it in her face, "are one hard-nosed bitch if you can't find some compassion inside that shrivelled heart of yours for your ghost assignment."

Tia's mouth dropped open, her face grew red and her heart thundered in her ears

"Are you really that self-centred that you can't leave the past where it belongs and help her?" Li motioned to his booth where a beautiful ghost Victoria sat, dainty dabbing a lace handkerchief at her nose, barely tolerating the presence of Yule who sat opposite.

Tia smirked at Victoria's blatant discomfort, jumping as Li banged a fist down on her table, shaking it and startling Ella so much she shot out of her seat.

"Later, Te!" she shouted, racing from the room.

"Damn it, Morgan, look at her, really look. She trembles every time a shadow passes. She apologised for the past! She's even begged you to help her. Have a heart, Te."

He softened his approach, leaning closer to Tia whose face imitated the shade of her heart as its rhythm echoed through her bones. "I know you want to go home. But seriously, do you want to spend the rest of your life hanging out with freaky stuff over there?"

Tia smirked. But all too soon her mirth was gone. She played with her fingers under the table, unable to take her eyes off of them. Her beat red face flamed under his scrutiny She had so badly longed for Li's attention and this is what it took to get it.

She slumped dejectedly in the booth whispering- "I'm sorry, Li."

He let out an exasperated sigh and glared at her. "Don't apologise to me, Te! Apologise to Yule." He snapped, pushing away from the table and striding back to where Victoria and Yule sat. Once there, he extended a hand to his ghost and together they left, leaving Yule sitting uncomfortably alone.

Chapter 6

Tia

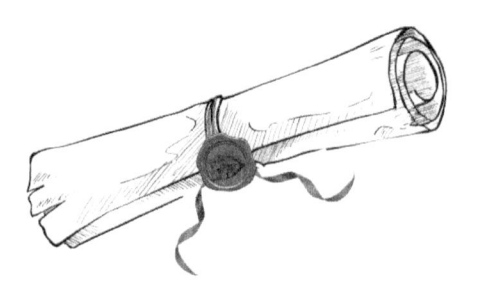

Tia had spent the night tossing and turning, waking up in a super sweat early. She decided to take a walk and clear her head. last night had convinced her that Yule was as determined to haunt her as she was to escape the academy.

The sky was grey with a subtle hint of white that signified a likelihood of early snow, even though the sky bore the heavy burden of ecto-plasmic clouds.

I have no choice. she thought as she wandered aimlessly through the maze of tombstones and crypts, surrounding the academy. The gravel beneath her boots crunched despite the layer of frosted feathers that made her nose itch to sneeze. *No choice. If I exorcize her ass then Li will never speak to me again. Then we'll never take long walks on the beach. I'll never have my first kiss.* She kicked at a clump of leaves and feathers, sending them in a spray through several shadow people. Honestly. she thought. we've called our ghosts already- why don't these hanger on's just disappear already.

Tia shivered; her polo top was starting to become a little too cool. *If the weather keeps deteriorating like this, I'll need a new sweatshirt before the month is out. I might even need to wear a woollen coat.* she groaned at the thought. Wool always made her skin itch. Thinking of itchy skin, she wondered why Yule, the ever-present peeping ghost, hadn't appeared yet. Not that she was complaining. After all, it gave her time to figure out how Yule had managed to write on the mirror and exactly what type of ghostly creature she was, after all, ghosts couldn't write.

Caught in the cacoughany of birdsong Tia stumbled forwards, with a huffed cuss, across the stone crypt where she had seen the young ghost boy swinging his legs yesterday. Something about him seemed familiar. But no matter how hard she tried to place him, she just couldn't.

Suddenly a shadow crept over her, freezing the blood in her as a deep sense of foreboding slithered its way over the tiny hairs on the back of her neck.

Her eyes darkened as they darted around, focusing to see the perpetrator's form. A familiar cocky grin met hers, but beneath it lurked something cruel and hard.

Pauls usual doe brown eyes sparkled with primal desire as he swiped Cartier shades from his bloodshot eyes. Tia retreated a step and then two, every fibre of her being on high alert as what felt like ants patrolled her skin. She stared up at him but his eyes were hollow, soulless.

"Are you following me, Tia?" he asked in an unusual sultry drawl, backing her up into an ivy-smothered crypt.

What the hell is going on? She placed a supporting hand on the rough stone, the ivy snagging her fingers like a chain trying to keep her in place. Her body began to shake like a Queen bee's when signalling her hive of emanate doom. *What the hell is going on?* Her mind stammered. *Why is he acting so-weird?*

"P-Paul, what are you doing here? I-I thought I was alone." She had meant her voice to come out strong, authoriteric; but instead, it sounded meek, timid even.

A slight smile curved his lips as he pressed closer to her, raising one fawny eyebrow. Tia frowned, looking again at his odd coloured eyebrow, noticing the addition of a piercing; the cause of the fawny colour. *When the hell did he get that?* Tia thought as she attempted to slide sideways across the crypt and out of his range. *Its new, defiantly recent but there's no redness or anything- what the hell?* She flicked her eyes away from it, instantly the feeling like she'd swallowed a nest of ants? Paul took a quick step to the side, blocking her escape.

"Where did you get...?" Tia began to ask but changed her mind as his eyes darkened with malice.

"What?" He purred, running his tongue over his bottom lip.

"T-the-" her mind screamed at her to change the subject, she flicked her eyes up and down desperately hunting for something she hadn't seen him wear before. Something that wasn't giving off creepy vibes. "The jeans?" Normally Tia would have pointed to emphasise the direction of her question, but her fingers would touch the material of his polo if she had. He was so close.

"Why?" he asked, staring down at his jeans, as if not realising he was wearing them. Then he rose his head slightly, a sultry smile tilting his lips. "Are you jealous?"

Jealous – ha! thought Tia. But she kept silent, her body still quaking, aware of the primal predator lurking beneath Paul's exterior.

His voice softened, his eyes sparking with silky smoothness he said, "Do you want a pair, Tia?"

Her name on his lips sent shivers down her spine. She sucked in a deep breath, willing her nerves to calm but everything about him seemed off somehow. His scent was off somehow, a bitterness hit her nostrils before she could process it and she scrunched her nose up in repulsion.

Oh God help me!" she tried to slip sideways again, only this time she lost her footing and hit the stone crypt hard, wrenching the breath from her lungs as she lay sprawled across it.

Oh God, no!

The sound of his button popping shot like a firearm in her mind. The scuff of the zip froze her. She knew what was coming, but all of her training was useless in that instant. She had never expected to be in this situation; she trusted the G-Poss and never thought Paul, of all people, would be capable of... *Oh God. No!*

At that moment, heavy panting sounded. She scrunched her eyes shut in silent remission as a single tear leaked from her eyes.

"I can't. Shit no! Tia, I'm sorry... I can't help my..." He pulled away. "Tia, don't cry. Shh... It's okay. I'm back now."

But Tia was locked in a casket of fear. Her disbelief and emotion so raw. When she felt the first touch of his hand upon her face, she found herself screaming like the child she had been six years ago. Her hearing drowned out by the racing of her heart and the rush of blood zooming through her system.

"Paul. No." Her voice choked. She could feel his smooth skinned hand upon hers and shuddered. Shaking her head to ward off his advances Tia couldn't help but jump as a rougher hand clasped her shoulder harshly, shaking her back to reality.

Her eyes shot open to see a tall, butch man with shaggy blond hair and mud-stained clothes. *What? Who?* The man leaned in closer, his mouth forming words she could not hear. *He's gone. He's really gone.* She consoled herself, trying to calm the rapid beat of her mousy heart.

"…Gone… You're…you're safe." Blinking twice, she stared at the man before her. His scent was earthy and helped calm her racing mind as she realised the man before her was the academy's grounds keeper.

She sighed, her breath quivering as he pulled her to her feet and dusted the soil from her arms. "How did…? How did you…?"

He smiled kindly down at her, and then turned as if listening to someone over his shoulder before nodding and saying; "A little ghost told me. You should report this straight away. I'm sure Mentor George will deal with it severely."

Tia let the bite of his fingers in her shoulder ground her back in reality as she fought with her mind on what she should do. *It's not like anyone would believe me if I told them what happened. I don't want everyone to know I'm a coward. I shut my eyes in the face of danger. I should have fought.* "No. I can't. I won't. Please don't- please don't say anything." She begged, her cowering heart desperately hoping he would comply.

The man harumphed, guiding Tia back through the maze of gravestones, past a crypt lite by several orbs and into the back entry of the academy, right next to the canteen. It beckoned with the smell of fresh bread all yeasty and warm and her senses floated away on its compulsion.

"You sure you don't want to report him?" the gardener asked, his voice strained with concern as he beat at the soil dusting his own clothes.

"Yes," Tia snapped, not wanting to talk about it anymore. But still he didn't drop the subject.

The large man caught her attention, eyeballing her softly. "Look, I'm not sure my report would do any good with George being his uncle and all, but I'll set him straight, if you like?" He raised a fluffy blond eyebrow in question.

Tia's heart squeezed and a rush of anger drowned her cowerdice away. "I'm fine. I just wanna forget it." Tia sighed and swiped a loose strand of hair from her face.

"Yeah, I bet. I'd offer you a beer, but you're still a little too young for that I think. Never mind. I'll talk to Ms Lilly," he said turning away.

"But nothing happened," whined Tia.

"I'm still talking to Ms Lilly." His curt voice deemed the conversation over.

Ms Lilly. Her counsellor. *Great.* "Fine, whatever." She shrugged, sinking into her usual bravado and walked into the pig pen. Ladling her tray full of bolognaise she grabbed a drink set it on her tray and mechanically walked to her booth, sliding in opposite Ella.

"Wow, Te. Bolognaise? What's happened?" The girls brows furrowed as she leaned in, diagnosing her mood.

Tia quirked a lip. "Nothing, I just hate this hellhole." Her mousy heart cried, beating so slow she could barely concentrate.

I can't tell you Ell, I'm sorry; I just can't put this on you.

Plastering a smile on her face like a clown at a little kids party, Tia abruptly changed subjects. "How was class?"

"Oh. Class. Yeah, well, when I finally got there after sortin' out the muss ya put in my hair, I was ten minutes late. So jailer Jennifer gave me a detention. But I didn't think that was fair, so I told her it was your fault – and she made me stay even lata!" she whined, helping Tia to sink into Ella's problems instead of wallowing in her own. "That's why I was late down to lunch. Not that ya noticed what with being late an' all too." She took a deep breath and beamed a mega what smile at Tia. "Oh, and I stopped to see Reece transport!" Ella waved her arms around for dramatic impact, making Tia chuckle.

"He transported? Already?" Shoving her dinner aside and leaning closer over the table her attention fully focused on Ella.

"Yeah, I saw the whole thing. He was in the corridor, the one by my room, and it sounded like he was having an argument with that ghost of his. I'm not surprised. If I was Reece, I sure as hell wouldn't be caught dead in a dress! Not even for my assignment!" Ella snorted, her long bangs falling into her face.

"A dress?" Tia questioned, unsure if she'd heard right.

Ella did her best not to snort with laughter as she pulled her fringe from her eyes and elaborated. "Yeah, a red one with a frilly white apron and silly black hat. He looked so stupid."

"God, I wish I could have seen that!" roared Tia, finally able to bury her feelings under a rock of denial.

"I just wish I had my iPhone. I could've earnt a fortune! No way Reece would've wanted anyone to see him!" She cackled. "Anyways, they were talking all funny, a different language or summat." Her pigtails bobbed dramatically as she fidgeted in her seat peeling an orange.

"Welsh," Tia offered, screwing up her face in disgust as Ella stuffed so much orange in her mouth that juices spurted down her pale chin.

"So," she talked whilst chewing. "they were arguing, and then the ghost girl, ya know, what's her name…?" She paused for Tia to fill in the blank.

"Gwen." Tia rolled her hand encouraging Ella to continue.

"Yeah, well Gwen just vanished! She just disappeared right there in front of me. Like she was never there!" Ella clicked her fingers together. "Reece kinda looked funny after, he got all…weird. He was holding his head and shouting in…Welsh. I tried to see if he was okay. But then he disappeared too. Aaron said Reece had transported, and he'd know because his brother Moreno transported last year." Ella took a breath. "Cool, right?" Suddenly the bell chimed lunch officially over and the class bells began to ring. "Oops. Gotta go. See ya later, Te!" She slid from the booth, dumped her orange peel in the bin and ran from the room.

What now? Thought Tia. *I don't have any classes and I seriously can't face that bolognaise. Even my personal haunter hasn't made an appearance today!* Sliding out from the booth she decided to escape to her room and set about packing up the six years of her belongings so she could finally go home when she failed ascension.

Chapter 7

Jinx

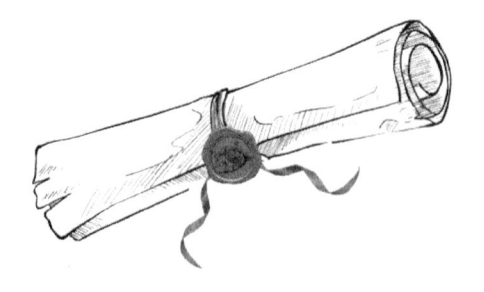

So now I'm heading into ghost central, thought Jinx. *Great. As if I haven't done enough of Grandmother's dirty work to prove my worth already. Obviously not. Because now I have to go and granny-sit another old witch!* Jinx ran a hand through his braids. *Argh!* He sighed. *I just wish she wouldn't treat me like such a child! I guess I am being just a little over sensitive.* He thought, chewing his bottom lip. *They do have a 'haunting' problem, after all.* Jinx chuckled lightly, his nerves about riding on a train calming a little at the release of endorphins into his system. Deep down he knew the G-Poss needed help with this ghost. He'd even suggested his grandmother sent them aid. But he just couldn't comprehend the motive behind his grandmother always choosing him for missions and saying he would represent her, when she treated him like a child at home.

For once I just wished she would do it herself or choose someone else.

Jinx sighed, his breath catching in his throat. *Goddess, I hate trains.* He thought, taking deep breath and boarding the nearly empty train as it pulled into Llangernyw station. He had a job to do, a mission to undertake, a chance to prove himself worthy of his grandmother's position – and he would- again.

He slumped down into his window seat just as the train took off, weaving across country and around wet hillsides destined for Maloroy Station. It would take him over three and a half hours riding the uncomfortable public transport to get there.

He shoved his overfilled black rucksack between his hard-muscled legs, cringing at the tightness of the space. He moved his numb leg and the contents of crystals, candles, clothes and essential spirit-related books scraped against his shins. *Don't break. Don't break.* He prayed. They stopped at yet another station, the train now filling to uncomfortable levels. His chest tightened like his skin was possessed by a boa constrictor, his shallow breaths rattled as his mind feverishly chanted a calming spell as sweat seeped from his pours.

An old man sat down next to him mumbling incoherent complaints under his foul eggy breath as he rustled the morning paper.

Jinx closed his eyes, inhaled through his nose and exhaled. *I got this.* He told himself. *I've got this. Oh Goddess why am I doing this?* he wondered. *Because Grandmother asked me to...* he answered himself, grimaced. He hated trains. Hated them.

The moment the doors slid shut, Jinx found himself fighting his own anxiety. He wiped the back of his hand across his sweaty brow. He sighed, his breathing a little shallow as he rubbed his shaking hands into his weathered jeans.

His grandmother would say 'how odd it is that your claustrophobia is only triggered in man-made contraptions'. He winced. His grandmother had an answer for everything. She would say; *'As a Pren Ceri, it is your responsibility to take control of unruly situations.'*

He just wanted a chance to prove to his grandmother that he could cope alone. That he wasn't the little witch orphan anymore. He could do this and when the time came, he would take his rightful position and replace his aged grandmother to become the faction's High Witch Elder – and lead them into the future- his way.

Leaning his arm against the window, Jinx stared out at the rolling hills, the mottled colours calming his claustrophobia as he unfurled and re-read the crinkled report he stuffed into his pocket that morning.

Emergency meeting

called by High Witch Elder- Pren Ceri of the Welsh coven

Coven attendee representatives

- High Witch Elder McGriffin of the Scottish coven aon

- Witch Elder Hatt of the London coven

- High Witch O'Brien of the Southern Irish coven

Merry meet.

As in previous years we have disgused the importance of extending our reach within the paranormal community- especially as far as the government academies are concerned.

Because of this our sister Fiona Ivy Reed of the Pren Ceri coven volunteered to become the Ghost Possessor Academy's, House Witch, we are here now.

A situation within the academy has our sister concerned. A warning of amassing evil was sent to her.

As disgust, it is of immense importance to keep our position within the academy and so it has been decided that we will send assistance to our sister.

Keeping this alliance is of the utmost important to our future. For this reason we have agreed that sending my grandson, heir to my coven is the best cause of action.

Thank you all for your attendance.

Blessed be.

H.W.E Shannon Pren Ceri

Jinx felt his heart racing along with the trains thrumming engine it thundered so fast its beat became a static tempo in his ears; a hypnotic beat that lured him into an exhausted sleep, the crumpled letter floating from his hand.

He hadn't been dreaming long when a movement caught his attention, snagging him from his oblivious comfort and back into reality. *What in the Goddesses name?* He thought as the pounding vibrations of the train began to slow, when the lonely brick station of Maloroy crept into view. *Deep breath.* He instructed himself as he felt the train jar to a stop. His whole body tensed as the miserable old man rustled around next to him, flapping his paper and grabbing his leather satchel as he fumbled out into the long line exiting the carriage.

Kneading the muscles in his neck, Jinx rose from his seat and swung his heavy rucksack onto his back, waiting in the little space he had until he was the last one left. *Okay, let's go.* He thought.

Looking around the platform, he watched people greeting their friends and loved ones. Jinx hated that; the last time he saw his parents, was at a station just like this. They had said what all parents say to their children when they were going away for a 'little while'. "We love you, Jinx. Be good for Granny. We'll see you soon, okay." He remembered his mother messing with his shirt tie as his father patted his corn braids affectionately and shoved a tattered old book into his hands.

"It's magically locked," he had confided. "When you're ready, it will open." His father had been sure, but to this day, Jinx had carried around the tattered old book, but no matter what spells he cast or the faction teachers he approached, no one could open it! No one knew how. Not even his grandmother!

The musty stench of smoke and morning dew on metal snapped him back to the present as he searched the platform for Fiona. *Where is she? She should be here by now.* Jinx thought, slumping back down against a platform column and pulling out his phone. He checked the time, surveyed the platform again and shoved it back into his rucksack. *She should definitely be here by now.* His brow furrowed and he chewed his lip as he watched the crowd clear.

A space on a nearby bench was vacated and he made his way over. "Do you mind?" He asked, indicating the empty seat.

The woman gave him a small smile, inclining her head in a nod as she returned to scrolling her phone.

Suddenly a powder puff of skirts popped from beneath the bench like a newly blooming rose.

A small angelic looking girl emerged in her flowing white dress. Her hands cupped enthusiastically around a palm full of beautiful crystals as she jumped up and down with excitement.

"Mummy, Mummy. Look what I found," she said with a giggle as her mother stopped scrolling to attend the little girl.

The energy around the girl caught Jinx's attention as if something was compulsing him to look at what the little girl was holding.

Those are crystals infused with magic – witch crystals. What in the Goddesses name are they doing here? Jinx thought, a sudden darkness polluting his thoughts. *I've got to find out what's going on.* He thought, his senses tingling like the spluttering of a sparkler. As he tried to focus, but with so many commuters bustling around the platform his attempts were short circuited. Sighing he leaned back on the bench, resigning himself to wait until the platform emptied.

Time ticked by slowly and in all its seconds he didn't spot a glimpse of another witch let alone the House Witch supposed to meet him. When the last man had cleared the platform, a porter came, broom at the ready as he swept up the dust of many a traveller. The thought of it was quite magical really Jinx concluded, taking a deep breath and beginning to chant as the man wandered from view.

"Time ripple, unwind,

On this platform seek not to hide,

Fiona from my witch's eye."

The wind at the station picked up, whipping his crystal-strung braids against the dark skin of his face. Trees bent in savage bows as they grovelled before it's majesty. Suddenly the air beside him splintered, tearing a seam through time. Jinx watched as events of the day rewound on the platform at sonic speed until, alone near the edge of the platform, a figure caught his attention. His senses buzzed like livewires sparking at the recognition of another witch. *Fiona*. He thought, recognising her from their Skype conversation.

Although he could tell instinctively that it was the same woman, this one seemed void, like the very soul inside of her had been sucked out. Her eyes were dull and trans like with the knowledge of whatever haunted her. Knowledge Jinx longed to know.

Her image in the time tear was still, awaiting Jinx's command to forward itself, but he faltered with the thought as an awareness of something within the tear, something he had not seen, niggled at him.

Rolling his eyes at his own distraction, he began to study the time tear anew; within it stood Fiona at the edge of platform. He couldn't quite see the number behind her, but it didn't matter as his focus was on her. Her pallor was insipid like newly cleaved bone, her blue eyes wide with terror. A thick pink-tinted goo ran slowly from the golden crescent earring in her left ear. Like him, the wind had whipped her hair around her face.

He let the time in the tear move forwards a little, watching with woven brows as a fist of wind knocked her handbag from her grip, smashing it to the floor, spraying a mottled confetti of crystals everywhere.

"So that's how the crystals got beneath the bench," Jinx mumbled as they were shoved along by the wind, dragging his attention back to the bench where he sat.

Suddenly, an old woman touched his arm, shocking him from his concentration. She was slight of build and stood at his elbow; a mere five foot if he was guessing, against his six foot two.

"Sorry, darling, were you talking to me?"

"N…" Jinx began to reply, but the old woman was already chuntering on.

"I'm getting a little old, you see. You'll have to speak a little louder if you want old Shelly to hear, my darling," she said cupping an ear in Jinx's direction.

"No, no. I was talking to myself," he insisted.

"Strange, youngsters these days. Would have been thrown in the loony house in my day." She tutted and shook her head before walking away, pushing a trolly full of stuffed bin bags a flag of fresh ones flowing behind her like the train of a wedding dress.

Watching the old woman leave, Jinx decided to scan the platform for any more staff he might have missed, before he bid the time tear back into motion.

He viewed the time tear like a cinema screen on fast forwards, shaking his head as Fiona scrabbled to retrieve her mobile peeking out from the mouth of her open hand bag. A sudden gust of wind had her stumble, the mobile in her hand slipped from her grip and onto the tracks as she hit the platform hard. Cuts opened up on her palms following her attempt to lessen the impact.

Fiona's mouth opened wide... *In an angry curse? A scream?* Jinx didn't know. But at that moment, she began to shake like a flea-infested dog.

Prickles of warning stabbed like tiny needles up Jinx's spine. The lights at the station flicked on and off, the wind howled like a lame dog left to the elements. All the while, even though the distance of time, he could feel the heavy thrum of energy buzzing inside the crystals tying his cornbraids. Their warning imminent. Lost to the thoughts entrancing his mind Jinx suddenly noticed the lack of static prickling at his spine. His glazed eyes focused as with a huffed curse he noticed the time tear moving.

Jinx knew he couldn't afford to lose it so hefting his backpack, he sprinted after the tear, following the tingling feeling in his gut that something, if not everything was wrong.

His feet slammed into the concrete, his heavy backpack slapped at his spine, urging him to go faster. Heart slamming, adrenalin to pump his limbs. Jinx ran faster and faster but the tear up the metal stairs to his right, coaudened off by police tape- not that it made any difference to the spell. It sped up to the platform above and out of sight behind a strip of chevroned yellow tape.

Cursing softly under his breath, Jinx raced for the nearest elevator in a panic. He counted under his breath as the heavy metal doors closed shut with a resounding boom that echoed the thundering beat of his heart. A thick sweat broke out of his pours, causing a tremor to shake his frame.

One – breathe. In…out…in…out.

Two – trust in the Goddess; she will deliver you safely.

Three— DING!

Agonisingly slow the elevator doors slid open, a pale faced Jinx spilling from within. With his hands on knees, he stood hunched, his lungs filling desperately with oxygen as he fought to maintain control of his pounding heart. *Got to…* He took a deep breath. *See what- happened…to Fiona.* He gasped, righted himself and sucked in one last calming breath before he shot down the expanse of platform separating the elevator from the stairs. He stared wide eyed into the time tear hovering just inside the police tape at the top of the metal stair case on the opposite side of the track.

The energy around the tear crackled and popped, static had his hair standing on end, his clothes standing crisply to attention. *What in the Goddesses name-?*

At the bottom, bloodied, broken and barely conscious, was Fiona sprawled face down on the platform. She jerked trying to wrestle her broken form into a sitting position. Desperately clasping her head as blood gushed through her fingers and streaked through her hair a sickly crimson. Her brown-flecked eyes sparkled with pain, frosted tears leaked from their ducts and her nose ran thick with gore.

No one ran to her aid. Why? Jinx wondered, his brow furrowing as he moved with the time tear, keeping his eyes glued to Fiona as she wobbled to a stand and hobbled forwards. His gut clenched, bile rising in his throat as he watched her drag her left foot at an unnatural angle behind her; the gleam of bone visible through its shredded flesh.

"Are you okay?" interrupted a young woman with a soothing voice.

Jinx swallowed down the bile in his throat, catching a reflection of himself bouncing off the windows of a café as he turned to face the concerned woman.

"I'm fine." He smiled at her broadly, forcing blood into his paled cheeks. "Thanks."

The woman looked unconvinced, but moved on all the same, shutting the glass door and pulling the cafes beige blinds down.

Jinx took off, searching for a way down to the base floor where the time tear stood still- for a moment. By the time his feet clanked down the staircase the tear had shifted, pushing him until his throat burnt, his breath scolded his lungs and he tore through the ticket office where he was suddenly snatched aside by a large, rough handed police officer. "Now there, young sir." The man's moustache twitched over his thick lips.

Jinx cringed. The officer reminded him of a mouse with his short build and wiry hair poking out beneath his hat. He stroked his moustache obsessively.

"What?" growled Jinx, his witches magic rialed by the sudden approach of the man.

"There's no need t'snap and no reason t'be pushing peoples outta yer way. In case you ain't noticed, there's been an accident 'ere." The man dressed in traditional black police atire motioned around himself.

I don't have time for this- Jinx thought- something terrible was happening this very second, he could feel it in the thrumming magic inside his bones.

He peered around the officer, catching a glimpse of the time tear beyond another string of yellow tape. Inside it, Fiona jerked as if smacking into something hard, before convulsing and disappearing from his line of sight.

Damn it! I can't see a thing. The officer who contentedly stroked his hair back beneath his hat sidestepped into his view. *I have to get rid of Officer Twitchy.*

"Ere, now ya listen lad- no more pushin'!" He kept eye contact until Jinx conceded to lower his in respect. "Alright, its best if ya just press on now lad."

Jinx stormed from the building tracking the pull of magic the time tear exuded as fast as he could, running around the outside of the ticket office. Everything was eerily quiet until he stepped into a side car park.

What in the name of the Goddess is going on? he wondered at seeing a large crowed formed, a low chatter of confusion emanated from the crowd.

"Hey, watch it!" Shouted a man as he bowled past him, shoving his way like an arrow through unwilling to part flesh.

Before him a small white tent stood erected behind and the team of people dressed head to toe in white overalls. *Forensics*, he thought; but his attention was snapped away as he caught sight of the time tear bleeding across the tent's surface.

Deep in his heart he could feel the truth rising. The pull of magic was fading and so, he knew, was Fiona's life force. Taking a deep breath and trying desperately to ignore the repugnant smell sifting through the gap in the tent as it mixed with a thousand different anti perspirants and perfumes. Jinx began a soft chant, but before Jinx could shut down the flow of magic, he saw Fiona.

Her eyes were a startling blue, shining with clarity, as flames ignited in her car. They licked at her skin like the vilest lover as her silent screams echoed through his heart, the car exploded.

Jinx recoiled automatically and people stared as he gazed at the magic they couldn't see. The black sludge seeping through the flames ate Fiona alive. The time tear rippled and spluttered catching up with itself – then faded into nothing.

Stumbling back out of the crowd, white noise screaming in his ears. Fiona, his sister witch, had been burnt alive. His grandmother's fears of being burnt at the stake suddenly seemed less of an old woman's rantings, and more of a realistic possibility.

What the hell is going on here? First a ghost appears to Fiona, then a dark spectre attacks it and now Fiona is dead! Jinx sighed. *Somehow these events had to be connected- didn't they?*

Chapter 8

Tia

[120]

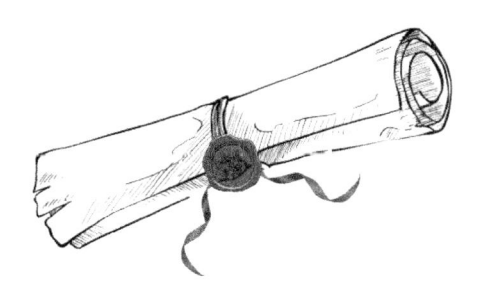

That night, tendrils of compulsion tore Tia from her usual nightmare and into a new one. She tossed and turned; engulfed in fire lapping at her tender flesh, burning and melting as two large eyes stared from a body stiff with rigour mortis. She shivered in her sleep, her mind convinced that somehow she recognised the body. As the flames roared thick with scarlet, a screaming voice bled a warning through her ears- "He's coming, child!"

Tia shot bolt upright in bed, her comforter bunching at her knees, her breath thick with fear. She squinted in the fluorescent light of her room and ran a shaky hand through the trail of perspiration sticking her hair to her forehead. *Eww!* Taking a deep shuddering breath she forced her eyes to focus on the blinding swirl of colour bobbing before her. "What the hell are you wearing?" she shrieked, pointing at Anka's absurd choice of- Victorian dress.

"Good morning to you, too," snapped Anka, breaking into a smile as Tia flipped her the finger and proceeded to blot out her tinkling voice by smothering her head with a pillow as she flopped back down, exhausted. "So, did you want to talk about what happened? You know, last night?" asked Anka now perched on the end of her bed.

Tia rolled around to face her. "You look ridiculous," she quipped, "why the hell would I want to talk to you when you're dressed in that…?"

"Corset and bustle," Anka stated matter-of-factly, arching one delicate eyebrow.

"It looks more like a waterfall of pink candyfloss." Tia sniggered beneath her pillow and peered out at Anka.

"Oh really?" Anka stood and swirled, a grin spreading across her face. "You like it that much?"

With one side of her lip quirking grotesquely, Tia snarled in response, "I just told you it was a—"

"I know, I know. Back to bad. But really, Tia, I know when you're trying to give a compliment." She giggled bouncing back down onto the bottom of the bed, her cheeks flushed with rosy perfection as she continued to chirp happily.

Shut up! Tia's mind screamed as she wrenched back her leg and booted Anka's butt off the bed.

Anka screamed, and Tia rolled over to watch her fall on her perfect little ass – but instead- she vanished.

"Holy shit!" She leapt out of bed, the comforter flung to the floor, her pillow shot against the wall with a loud puff and Tia fell to the floor, crawling around the surface. *It has to be a trick. It has to.*

Suddenly her bedroom door flew open with a crack, rebounding of the wall as Ella skipped in. "Te, what the-oh-" she began to chuckle and snort, her black-polished nails clutching at her stomach as she doubled over in overzealous giggles.

"Aww, Te." She sucked in a deep breath bouncing up and down on the spot, her eyes watering with delight. "She gotcha, didn't she? She gotcha good!"

Tia spun, pushing herself up from the floor and meeting Ella's eyes with a dark flash of her own. 'what the…?' expression. "What the bloody' hell is going on?" roared Tia, spittle flying from her mouth.

"Eww Te." Ella snorted, trying not to hyperventilate as she giggle- hiccupped- "she transported. I mean. She said she'd make it all dramatic an' stuff t'get ya back for being such a…um…" Ella twirled a strand of hair that had slipped loose from her pigtails. "Ya know." She smiled guiltily.

"A bitch." Tia stood up, wiped down her pyjamas and grinned at Ella.

"well, yeah. But that was epic!" Tia laughed and drew Ella into a loving embrace "I'll get her back. Don't you worry." She grinned, muzzing Ella's hair before releasing her.

"Aww, Te!" She frantically tried to smooth down her hair as a bell sounded over the tannoy. "It'll be ya fault if I'm late, Te!" She rushed from the room like a hurricane moaning- "I gotta fix this. I jus' gotta."

Shaking her head, her hair whipping her pale face, Tia chuckled, kicking the door closed with a bang before heading to the bathroom.

Emerging refreshed, she was suddenly conscious that her defiled uniform had been confiscated while she slept. *Bloody jailers!*

Having no choice but to pilfer Anka's stash of uniform from inside her cabinet, Tia swiped a pair of slacks and a polo shirt.

Loosely braiding her hip-length hair, Tia tugged at the skin tight polo for the third time but it still plastered itself to her curves, giving sneaky peeks at her abdomen thanks to Anka's short stature. *God, I look like a wannabe swimsuit model in a Lycra onesie*, she thought, *except models are sexy and perfect looking, like Anka and Li.*

Tia made her way down to the pigpen, Anka's too-tight polo digging into her small biceps when she wrenched open the large oak doors. The line was not too long yet. Not that she cared as she gave a snort at the only potential to make a fuss about her que hopping.

The smoky aroma of fried bacon and scrambled eggs greeted her as she took a huge lungful of air. Wrestling a plastic tray from its precariously balanced stack, Tia proceeded to fill it full of the delicious offerings. She delved into the stainless steel bread bin on the side, riffling through until she found the wholemeal bread she loved. Popping it into the toaster, she continued her stalk of the counter to survey the delicious medley of cooked, chilled and fresh foods. She scooped creamy scrambled eggs onto her tray, along with a slice of crispy bacon and tucked an apple securely in her pocket for later. Finally grabbed a steaming mug of coffee from the dispensing machine. With tray in hand, Tia whipped around to the subtle sound of a knife rolling over a coarse surface. How she could tell, she didn't know- but her senses were becoming more attuned.

Paul. Oh God!

Her throat went dry; she gulped profusely trying to moisten it. As always, he looked like a business prodigy rather than a potential. *Ascender*, she mentally corrected herself. But the new eyebrow piercing he had adopted stained his smart appearance.

He stood there, one hand stuffed in his trouser pocket and the other lifting her wholemeal toast to his crooked, grinning lips.

Tia's herculean rage erupted like an ultra-plinian as memories of him cornering her in the cemetery wove a trail of fire through her mind. The way he had… *No! You can't let him do this to you.* she thought, her, She didn't need to go there, not now when his royal egotistical ass was stood right in front of her. Her good mood turned sour as she rammed her tray full of breakfast roughly onto the rail, causing a tidal wave of coffee to breach its mug and flood her scrambled eggs, staining them brown. *Perfect*, she thought.

Anka's tight polo dug into her biceps as she angled her fist towards Paul's cocky jaw, preparing to smack the ass's sneer right into the back of his throat.

"Ah, ah, ah," he chastised, wagging a finger inches from her steaming face. "You wouldn't want our old witch to see you hit me now, would you?" A smarmy smile spread across his face as he leant a hip against the tray rail and stroked the crumbs from his bottom lip; her toast finished.

Absorbed to the brink in her rage Tia could barely stave off the modeless compulsion to shatter Paul's jaw.

Surveying the room full off knocks and corners was easy with the florescent lights glowing like beacons in the fog. Kitchen staff shuffled around the food line. *It's not like they're gonna rat me out to the jailors when they never bothered to report the fight between the Jonses last week.* She thought, finally getting her brain into motion. But the resident witch, Fiona, was nowhere to be seen. The tell tale clack, clack of her heels were unheard. Tia felt a wicked smile split her face. "We're all alone, asshole," she corrected, glaring her cobalt blue eyes glairing into his.

Tia cranked her arm back another inch enjoying the horror on his face as his fingers fumbled around his collar. "What's wrong, Paul? You think I'm just going to forget what you did?"

Quickly Paul pulled the eye pendant from beneath his shirt and grinned.

Her heart rate slowed to a screaming stop, her breath hitching in her throat as she choked so as not to collapse. Reluctantly she lowered her raised fist to her side and watched Paul smile in overtly cocky delight. "That's right, Te. You're smarter than you look," coaxed Paul.

She shook her head, he had it all planned out. All of it! There wasn't a move she could make that he wouldn't counter- was there?

He stepped closer, close enough for her to see the pores on his tanned skin, close enough to smell her toast on his breath and close enough for her to lay her hands on his muscled shoulders. *Where the hell did they come from? Muscles like that can't just pop up overnight!*

"That's right, Te, play nice, or I'll tell Uncle George what you did." He whispered, his chocolaty voice all sour. She stiffened, her brow furrowing.

"Good girl," he crooned while tucking a fallen strand of hair back behind her ear. She shivered in disgust, her eyebrows knotted, above her sparking angry eyes. "Oh, Te. I've waited, longed, fantasised for so long about you and now, now I have you. Don't I? Just tell me, why did you do it?"

Tia, her hands still gripping his shoulders, moved as close as she could without their bodies physically touching. *I have to know.* She told herself. *This is the only way he'll tell me.* She swallowed down the rising bile in her throat and looked up at him from beneath her thick lashes, batting them delicately before linking her hands behind his neck. She could feel the blood racing through his thick pulse, see the hunger in his eyes as he licked his dry lips. "What did I do?" she purred.

He sniggered and pulled back a little to stare straight into her eyes. "Nice try, Tia. I know you. You burnt her."

Tia pulled him down to her; his eyes took on a note of surprise, his eyelids heavy. The bone piercing in his brow seemed darker as his head levelled with her neck. Quickly, she secured his body to hers and raised her knee, straight into his groin. He slid down to the floor with a shriek of pain, cupping himself and spluttering- "Fiona...she...would have..."

"What? Seen? How?" Tia circled his hunched form, glee swelling inside her like the glow of water in a desert.

"The pendant-" He gasped. "its active-" Paul moaned, gasping for air as he rocked himself on the floor "She's linked, to them. She sees- everything."

"Whatever!" Tia raged, a shiver raking up her spine at the sound of his manic cackle- "One day, Tia, I'll tame that fire of yours."

Tia stormed out of the pigpen and slammed through the doors to the sound of Paul's arrogant vow.

One day, thought Tia, pushing past noisy potentials and a tutting chef- *I'll silence that mouth of yours! Touché.* Her mind called the draw. But her feet took over as she stormed down the corridors. bounded up the staircases and slammed open the door to her room.

Closing the door on the world, she leant against it sighing as her knees crumpled beneath her and she slid down its surface to collapse in a ball at its base. Her head in her hands, her heart in her throat and an errant tear forcing its way through her duct.

Just get through this. You got this. Only a little longer- just a little and we can go home. Home. She felt the word sober the adrenalin pumping her depressed emotions like an alcoholic forbidden a drink. She had no choice. She had to fight. Fight for her freedom; her life.

Lifting her head, she swiped at her eyes, shaking a little as she stood, letting out a trapped breath in a bubble of fear. *You got this. You got this!* She nodded to herself suddenly noticing the wet tred of a footprint forming. "What the hell?"

Tia crouched down to examine it, just as the floorboard sucked the image from sight and a resounding creak eerily sounded as the bathroom door peaked open. She felt her eyes dilate with anger, grinding her teeth together like a plain sanding wood. Tia stalked with heavy thudding feet to the door.

Ripping open the door she stepped in, her heart beating fast despite the exo-skelington of steel unfurling as her metaphorical shield.

Inside, the walls were slick with water, the damp scent raining from clouds of condensation filled the small room. *What the bloody hell does she want now?* Tia wondered, rolling her eyes almost as hard as she ground her teeth.

A sudden shadow of motion flit behind the bath curtain. *It's never left like that*, thought Tia, her heart racing the seconds as time ticked by. She held her breath and edged her way forwards, her hand curled around the edge of the clinical curtain. Heart pounding in her throat. She counted to three and tore open the curtain too; nothing.

Harumphing Tia stalked, to the sink with her hands clenched. "Bloody ghosts." she cursed.

That's right, breathe. It's Paul's fault banging on about all this 'she's watching you' crap. Deep breath Good-okay. Calmer, Tia raised her head, automatically gazing at her reflection in the mirror, only there amid her face was her name- dripping in crimson.

Tia gasped, jolting back and banning into the wall as one by one the letters reversed their dripping trail before vanishing. *Yule*. Tia seethed. *It had to be Yule. If the bitch thinks scaring me is going to make me help her, then she's haunting the wrong girl. But if she wants to play games, then I'll play games.* Tia smiled wickedly. Her reflection mimicking her like a disembodied evil twin.

Chapter 9

Jinx

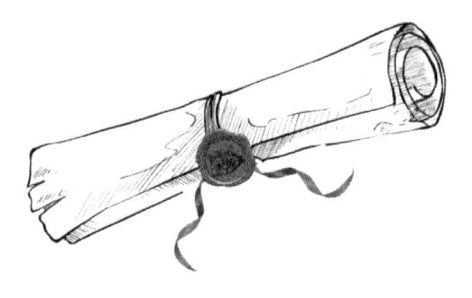

The academy stood in the heart of the compound surrounded by gravestones of all sizes. Standing like stalagmites, fingers up to the world, they displayed their impervious strength, laying in wait for someone to make the wrong move

Jinx had arrived that morning by taxi, which stopped at the well-guarded security gates. After Jinx had got out and paid the cabbie, he watched the driver zoom off. He got the feeling that the locals had been scared away from there by some ghostly means or another. He had no idea what. But something made the man check his rear-view mirror every few seconds as they drove to the compound. A magical buzz of protection seeped through him as he passed through several ID checks and began to walk towards the academy.

Suddenly a security guard stepped out from a box office, halting him in his tracks with a large out stretched palm. "Uh, if you would like to wait here Mr Pren Ceri Sir- I can uh, get a car?" Warily he stepped aside and motioned to a large rock where Jinx could wait. His eyes twitched nervously but didn't leave Jinx's.

A tingle of amusement bubbled in Jinx's mind and he couldn't help but wonder what he would do if he suddenly began to chant? He had to suppress a wicked smile at his thought.

"No worries, I'll walk. It'll give me a better understanding of the layout of the place anyway."

"Oh, uh-I-yes sir." He stepped aside, hand twitching over the leather purse at his belt.

Jinx chuckled internally. The man could throw as much blessed salt at him as he wanted but it wouldn't make him magically vanish like it did the ghosts they dispelled.

Stepping past the nervous guard Jinx was careful not to make any fast movements, although unafraid of the salt, he was well aware of the extensive self defence training all recruits underwent before become a fully fledged G-poss warrior.

His large boots ate up the gravel as his mind wandered the conundrum of this dark entity wreaking havoc. His strides were long like his patients in executing an effective plan, which was considerably difficult considering the distraction from the shadow people curiously following his every movement. His skin crawled like the maggots he imagined infested their bones. Taking a deep breath, he prepared to utter a shielding spell just to get them to back off enough so that he could clear his head of their presence.

Beeeeep! A shock shot up his spine like an electric shock and he turned just as he prepared to deal with his ghostly audience, grateful to see a young man with shaggy blond hair speeding up to his side in a golf buggy.

"Hey there, I'm the groundskeeper here. My name is Garth. Garth Smith. Jump in, and I'll give you a lift." Slinging his rucksack onto the back seat, Jinx settled himself in next to the driver who warmly shook his hand.

"Nice to meet you. I'm Jinx, the new...assistant."

Garth frowned at him. "I thought Fiona was going to pick you up from the station? I'm only here now because security called saying you'd arrived in a...taxi. And trust me— walking the miles to the academy alone is a prime time to be mobbed by all of these ghost asylum seekers and once you get caught in their troubles- you'll never get away- not unless your one of the G-poss anyway."

"Yeah," Jinx replied, thumbing a calming crystal sewn into the end of one of his braids. "I get it- they all want to move on."

"You got that right." Garth agreed, driving steadily through the landscaped gardens and on through the surrounding cemetery towards the academy's front doors.

Garth skidded to a stop outside the overtly large building crafted of dark stone walls in an almost gothic appearance. Ivy tangled its way down the coarse bricks creating an enchanted fairy tale feel, like the Grimm's gingerbread house. But this was real!

Jinx shivered. This is the sorting house of the dead. In his beliefs the dead should be cremated and their ashes scattered to the four winds, not buried beneath the earth to rot and remain still chained to the earth. Their empty husks then potential conduits for those wicked enough to use them. He rubbed his arms staring at the building that loomed ominously, like a promise you didn't want to keep. But the Ghost Possessors believed different and somehow, he had to deal with that.

He stared up at he academy's turreted roof that gave that classic 'happily ever after' facade. But it didn't fool him. He knew it for what it was– to lure children into thinking that the G-Poss would make their new life perfect. Jinx shook his head in sympathy.

Staring back at the graves he wondered why people who dealt with ghosts every day would surround themselves with the buried dead. *Wouldn't they want a break from them? Or were they really trying to build an army of ghosts like McGriffin of the Scottish coven claimed at last month's meet?* Jinx dislodged the disturbing thought and entered through the large reception hall, admiring the building with its unique periodic charm.

The four large walls held electrically lit sconces like a medieval movie, adding an eerie scene of discomfort to a place where he knew ghosts often tried to linger. Shivering slightly at the thought, Jinx continued to admire the walls and the large bay windows with stained glass depictions of what he could only assume was Death. The cloaked figure was stained black and breaking something over people who slept in beautiful beds of silver and opal. The depiction was strange, but Jinx thought back to his knowledge of how the G-Poss was born. He realised these stained glass windows must be their past. Jinx chuckled disbelievingly.

Tearing his gaze back to the hall, he marvelled at the large Victorian chandelier looming overhead. The sparkling rays from the crystal teardrops against the stained glass resembled disco ball at a nightclub. Delicate coloured spots danced over the tiered seating to one side of the hall, whilst a small portable stage equipped with microphone and stand stood nestled in a darkened corner. *Obviously used for assemblies or such*, thought Jinx as he made his way to a door at the back of the room and quickly skirted through. The last thing he wanted was to be found lurking around after all, the G-Poss hated witches and he didn't need to make an unsavoury situation worse– and have everything blow up in his face Or incite the annoyance of his Grandmother.

The exit led out to a magnolia painted corridor. To one side mounted opposite a large landscape was an intricate 3D map of the building.

Memorising the route to the head mentor's office Jinx began his track, head held high and an unquestionable intent glairing in his eyes

George was sat in his office thumbing through papers as Jinx walked in. "Don't knock, then!" he scolded, glaring over his reading glasses which sat precariously on the edge of his plump little nose.

"I apologise," said Jinx, taking an opposing seat at the desk and raising a single eyebrow.

George lowered his papers, stacked them neatly in a pile and harrumphed. "I suppose you're the witch's new assistant?"

Jinx, uncaring of Georges's prejudice, replied, "I am. My name is Jinx Pren Ceri, and I bring greetings from our faction's High Witch Elder to you and your people."

"Warrior boy. *We* are warriors! We fight to rid this planet of the earthbound spirits that plague it! We have a noble cause, unlike others who merely stay in their government-funded compound and leech on the whole of society!"

Jinx raised an eyebrow, determined not to be caught up in the pretentious propaganda the G-Poss was famous for. "That is why the faction has sent me. I am the High Elder's grandson, next in line to lead our people, and I would like us to be friends."

George stood and shooed Jinx out of his office with a parting snipe. "For now, that remains impossible. I will reconsider if Fiona upholds our alliance by getting rid of this evil spirit. Not before!"

"Then, I am afraid there is a problem," Jinx replied smoothly.

George slammed his podgy palms on the desk, which shuddered in distress. "And what would that be, witch?" he spat, his eyes lit with fury.

Jinx ground his teeth together, gritting- "Fiona. Your house witch- is dead."

George sunk back into his amply cushioned chair, spluttering obscenities, his face flushed a putrid red. "How do you know this?"

Jinx grinned wickedly "I'm a witch." He turned to leave, but he only made it a few steps down the corridor before George was whispering threats at his back.

"I will investigate this alleged death. Until then, stay out of my academy, witch, or you're fair game to me and my colleagues. Understand!"

Yeah, I understand. Jinx thought. *You predgudice pig.*

Jinx understood completely. This man's threats were driven by fear – but even so, he meant them. He would come after Jinx if he entered the building before he learnt the truth of Fiona's death, by mortal means.

Great. so where am going to stay? He didn't fancy invoking the wrath of George, so he decided not to ask; after all, it was obvious he wouldn't be staying in the building.

Maybe Garth knows of a place I can stay? he thought, striding through the long stretch of corridors, his anger stiring the magic within him as his crystal braids tried to negate his animosity.

His only encounter was with a young girl who stared suspiciously at him from the doorway of a classroom. Her long dark hair reminded him of his sister, Hope. The sister whom his grandmother had sent away when their parents disappeared, leaving them orphans. He hadn't seen her for years, and the old witch would act as if she never existed whenever he asked about her and why she sent her away. He prayed to the Goddess that she was happy.

Striding past the young girl and feeling his temper calm he gave her an indulgent smile before exiting the building to crunch the gravel road beneath his boots once more.

A deep sigh escaped his lungs, freeing his remaining anger to the cool ecto-plasmic air around him. Jinx spotted the golf cart cruising amid a volly of glowing orbs. *Maybe their not all bad after all.* he thought as Garth pulled up. Jinx shook his head, a slight smile playing on his lips as he approached and lent an arm on the top of the buggy. "So, you met George?" asked Garth.

"Seems quite the reception. So warm and heartfelt," said Jinx sarcastically.

"The man is the top in his field – but other than that, he's a dick." Garth chortled.

"Good to know. I'm guessing his prejudice against witches is warranted somehow?"

"Yeah," Garth replied with a sigh. "It's warranted. Get in and I'll tell you all about it."

Jinx sat back in the passenger side of the buggy, took a deep breath and waited patiently while Garth backed out of the car park and continued driving through the extensive gardens littered with gravestones and spirits. The wet autumn leaves made it difficult for the little buggy to get traction, but Garth expertly manoeuvred the vehicle as he told his story.

"It happened quite a few years ago when George's younger sister, Yazmin, was pregnant. She came to the academy - George and Paul are the only family she had left.

She wasn't carrying well. She was in a lot of pain. The doctors found out the baby was breech and needed turning. They booked her into the antenatal ward but two days before the appointment everything went wrong. Yazmin's pain got worse and George had to make some hard decisions." He pierced his lips into a sad smile.

"What about her husband? Why didn't he help out?"

"Yazmin didn't have a husband, not even a boyfriend, just a one-night stand with some guy who claimed he was a Ghost Possessor," He leaned closer to Jinx, lowering his voice. "Although, between you and me, I have my doubts. Anyway, George took care of her. She lived here at the compound. When she needed treatment for the pain, he suggested the services of the in-house witch – Fiona." The buggy's wheels screeched as the back tyres slid sideways on the dewy path. "Fiona knew it wasn't her speciality, so she suggested a friend, a...headwitch?" Garth glanced at Jinx for confirmation of the unfamiliar terminology.

"Hedgewitch," Jinx replied automatically, lost in thought admiring the beautifully sculptured Buxus as they pulled onto a narrow path.

"Well, the hedgewitch tried to help, giving her all these remedies and things, but that night she went into labour."

Jinx could guess what happened next. It was obvious, but he listened on silently as Garth confirmed his suspicions.

"There were complications. George called for doctors, but the doctors, unknowing of the remedies she'd taken, used drugs to combat her pain. The drugs reacted badly with the hedgewitch's remedies, so the doctors ended up performing a caesarean to get the baby out."

"And Yazmin?" Jinx held the top of the buggy as Garth slowed to a stop in a small shed adjoining a bunkhouse.

Garth turned to look at him, sadness bleeding from his eyes. "She died."

"I understand. But I wish to change his view of my people. Do you think it is possible?" Jinx asked, sliding out of the buggy and wrestling his bag free from the well.

"Anything's possible." Garth shrugged.

"And how do you feel about witches?" he asked, staring him straight in the eye, his expression blank as his heart thundered in his ears.

"Well, Fiona is a beautiful woman, but uninterested in me and you mate, so no dates there, sorry to disappoint!" Garth quirked a smile at Jinx, clapped a firm hand on his shoulder and chuckled deep in his throat.

"About Fiona," Jinx began his voice solemn as his heart rate slowed. "I didn't know whether to mention it before, but now I know George doesn't give a damn, I—"

"That's just the way of the G-Poss. They're all taught from being young potentials never to trust any of your kind." He smiled sadly.

"They trust us enough to keep the spirit barriers up," he retorted haughtily.

"Yes, but even that doesn't stop some of the spirits getting through. I've been watching. It seems to me that any spirit with a strong emotional tie to anyone in the compound can weasel through."

Jinx considered this and muttered under his breath, tugging at a braid of hair. "Loopholes."

Garth nodded, searched his jeans pocket and pulled out a rusty iron key. He shoved it into the bunkhouse lock and sighed in exasperation. "Welcome to your new home!" he switched on the lights and the small bunkhouse lit up. "Fiona asked if I had a spare bed, she said George wouldn't let you stay in the main house – too many witches under one roof, and all that." He gave a slow shrug.

Jinx couldn't believe it. Fiona had already sorted his accommodation. *Poor Fiona. Goddess bless her.*

"Thanks man." He clasped Garths shoulder inclining his head. "It would have been a nightmare to come all the way here and have nowhere to stay". He strode over to the neatly made bunks and eyed them speculatively.

"Top bunk's yours. Hope you don't mind heights." Garth chuckled. "I'm gonna leave you to settle in. Don't mind what you do, just no blood sacrifices or anything gory. Might stain the carpet." He winked and backed up. "I'll catch you lait—!"

But Jinx had moved at the speed of light to clasp the man's large arm before he exited the door.

"Garth," he said as confused eyes met his, "I hope that you'll believe me, that I say with deepest sympathy, that Fiona is dead."

Garth slammed the bunkhouse door. "No. No! I don't believe you!"

"Garth, please."

"No she can't be!" He advanced towards jinx, shirking the hand from his shoulder and snarling- "we were supposed to-"

"Garth- she's gone. " His heart bled as the words poured from his mouth and he begged that they were faulse. But he was a witch and he believed in the Goddess and she never steered him wrong.

Garth fell to the floor, his knees curled tight to his chest, sobbing.

Chapter 10

Tia

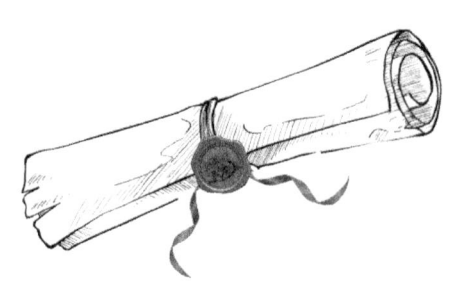

Tia stood in her room on the second floor of the academy slowly packing what few good memories she had. The locket in the shape of a key with a small photo of her family rolled up within its heart was one of the most precious. She no longer wore the piece as it weighed on her heart knowing she could not escape to be with them. So instead, she wound its chain around the neck of a small knitted mouse Ella's parents had gifted her one Christmas-long ago.

Tia sighed. *Not long now, Not long now. Then I'll be home and I won't need some stupid crumpled, outdated photo to remember my family by.*

Placing it safely in the bag she ferreted around for the plastic wrist band she had stowed beneath Anka's dresser, knowing that no one would go through her things as she actually wanted to be in this hellhole.

A snick rang out. "Ah ha. Gotcha!" Even though she could barely stand to look at the thing she could not part with it. It was a reminder of the worst day of her life.

The day she woke up in the tiny hospital on the academy's outskirts the first day she was taken away from her family. *More like abducted* she snorted, shoving the bracelette inside a sock before shoving it into her bag. She had kept it all this time, needed it really as it was the only thing she had with her parents home address on. H*opefully they still lived there* she thought. *But any where is better than here. It has to be. This place is surrounded by a graveyard.*

That had really bothered her at first, especially being ten and knowing about things like zombies and vampires. The very thought that people lay dead beneath the earth on which she trod gave her nightmares for months.

She remembered peeking through her dark navy curtains just in case one of them rose from the dead. *Not that it could happen, technically.* Or so she thought. But after a while of having practical 'hands on' academy trips to visit with a few trusted ghosts, who merely wanted to stay close to their loved ones, Tia's fear had disappeared. Either that or the whole 'ghosts are real' situation had desensitised her.

She threw a few more effects into her bag, making sure to add enough of her uniform that she wouldn't smell when she reached home. *Well, that's that done.* She thought zipping the bag before surveying the room for anything she might have missed. Nothing seemed to stand out. But as her eyes took in the room for the last time she couldn't help but remember some fonder memories, even that first day when she remembered being dragged through the academy by a G-Poss warrior. He had repeatedly mumbled about her being an inconvenience: he was supposed to be on a mission. Tia had barely been able to keep on her feet as he marched her up two flights of stairs and along a boring looking corridor with a few framed landscapes. She remembered he had stopped abruptly and she had slammed into his side.

They had stood before a large door, the number thirteen was bolted on by screws around which someone had stuck diamante hearts. Tia had curled her lip with distaste when the door was shoved open.

She remembered inside the room was a young Anka, swaying like a will-o'-the-wisp to foreign string music. She was beautiful – and that had made her mad. She remembered wondering- *Why should anything in this place be beautiful ?It isnt fair! I'm* alone. They abducted me! Ever since that witch Fiona had visited her in the hospital, she seemed, even to herself, cold and uncaring.

Tia shuddered. She'd had all she could take of the past. And as her Granny Penny used to say, "To think bad thoughts of those who have newly crossed over- or transported Tia adjusted- is to invite them to haunt you for the rest of your life."

The comforter was the only other sentimental item she had packed. A gift, of sorts, that Tia just couldn't part with. Again, it had come from Ella's parents. The Jones's were very kind. They had said she could keep the fluffy patchwork blanket after discovering her at the compound's fence. She smiled, remembering yet another failed attempt at escape.

She remembered how badly here leg had hurt when she fell from the fence. It was so high and she had only managed to climb half way. But then she looked down. She remembered sobbing when Mr Jones- the Ghost Possessor on duty that night had found her, taken her to the guards office and bundled her up in the comforter before tending to her leg. Thankfully it had been nothing but some unsightly bruising and a sprained ankle.

The next morning Mr Jones's daughter had appeared with his breakfast and the two girls had fast become friends.

Tia cleared her mind, deciding there was nothing more she could do in her room. She'd packed away what little belongings she had accumulated over her six years at the academy; her own personal hell. The room was cleaner than she'd ever seen it, looking almost lonely without her comforter spread over the lower bunk.

Tia decided to stop by the pigpen for dinner. She'd already missed lunch, just snacking on the apple she'd crammed into her pocket at breakfast, and now the whole academy smelt spicy with the scent of chillies. Sniffing a large lungful of the aroma caused ravenous gurgles to erupt in her stomach. The dinner line was almost non-existent, but two jailers stood at the doors posted to 'keep an eye' on everyone. Stuffing her food quickly, Tia exited the room determined to avoid anywhere where Paul might suddenly appear.

The corridors were strangely empty as Tia shot out through a side door and out into the maze of graves, ignoring the shadow people and orbs that fussed over her, desperate for her attention. *Oh for Gods sake- just piss off!* she thought as she stomped over the buried mounds, past brick, marble and ivy gobbled headstones.

She strode past shaped Buxus and into Georges private garden, where she sat at the edge of a lilly spotted fountain. She knew George wouldn't be there, after all he she had only ever seen him in this place once; when Yazmin was staying at the academy. *She was nice.* Tia thought as she stared vacantly at the two marble statues preforming a ballet lift in its centre. She stared at it often, her thoughts racing like her mind as she imagined her life as if she never met the G-poss and was never forced into their academy.

Her mind heavily engrossed in what *could* have been. *I could've learnt ballet if I hadn't been brought here*, she thought. *I might have even liked it.* She smiled to herself wondering if her mother would have been one of those pushy mums or a silent cheerer. *Maybe I'd have a boyfriend*, thought Tia, then she scrunched up her nose and snorted. *Yeah, right. Boys are a pain in the ass.* Even Li had a talent for getting on her nerves. *But if I was normal, I would be picking my classes about now, ready for sixth form college. I would have liked that: to have a choice.*

Her mind ceased its pointless wandering when she spotted a translucent shape glide across the gardens. It headed straight towards the gardener's bunkhouse where it was promptly rebounded by some unseen force. Brows furrowed over narrowed eyes, Tia watched with curiosity as the spirit once again attempted to enter the bunkhouse, to no avail, before it just disappeared. *What the-?*

She lifted her body off the gravelled path and dusted off the tiny stones stuck to her numb behind. *Was it Yule trying to get into the bunkhouse?* She had a mind to get the truth out of that ghost about her 'writing' on the bathroom mirror. Harumphing she wondered- *is she even a ghost? Or something else? Ghosts can't write, they don't possess the ability to manipulate an object long enough to be able to write. But somehow, Yule can! And I have to find out why.*

Tia's internal autopilot kicked in. She walked forwards making her way through the beautiful gardens towards the dilapidated little bunkhouse where the gardener resided and the spirit orb had disappeared.

It's Yule. It has to be. When I find her I'm gonna make her pay for that little mirror trick. Her thoughts grinded from her mind as she set her sights on the dilapidated old bunkhouse.

Knuckles as white as new carved bone, Tia wrapped them against the wooden door. Brow furrowed she waited, one foot tapping at the dirt as she contemplated the existence of a barrior she had not encountered- which kept the spirit orb at bay.

Suddenly the door flew open with zest. Startled, she stepped back, eyes wide as a young man with a well-built body filled the doorway.

He was broad chested, wearing a long-sleeved white vest that clung to every solid pectoral. She gulped, but nothing could stave the dryness of the Sahara taking up residence in her throat. She raised her gaze to his face; her cheeks flushing as she caught his eye. *O.M.G!*

The young man smiled indulgently, his earthen green eyes shining with mischief as Tia caught sight of the smudge stick pluming smoke from his hand. Giving a delicate sniff she inhaled the relaxing aroma. "Lavender?" She questioned.

"Impressive. You know your herbs," he replied. His chocolate brown braids whipped his neck as he nodded. Tia stared at the precious gems wound into his braids. Jinx turned his attention back inside the small bunkhouse continuing to wave his smudge stick around, nodding as though in agreement.

Interest piqued, Tia tried peering inside but she couldn't see anyone inside. Suddenly he turned back to her, a small smile playing on his lips. "Can I help you, Tia?" he drawled with a deep welsh twang that made her body shudder.

Tia regained her momentum, pushing her sudden heat into spiky anger and propelled herself into the room, her body coming way too close to his in her adrenaling soaked stupor. "Where is she?" Tia stormed, taking note of the miniature rainbows cast by hanging crystals in the windows adjacent to neatly made bunk beds. *Weird*, she thought, *a guy's room that's tidier than mine. And I have Anka to clean up the place.* She shrugged. *Go figure.*

Sizzling anger had her spiky attitude shedding sparks of burning anger as she pushed past the man. "You don't have chairs." She hissed, clearing a space on the only cabinet in the room, its dark old oak groaning at even her slight weight as she heaved herself to sit atop it with a satisfied thump. "I'm not leaving until you get out here Yule!" She sang, a wicked smile on her face.

The young man raised an eyebrow, pushed the door shut and continued his parade, the smudge stick smoking happily as it cast out purifying plumes.

"Seriously get out her!" She yelled, her blood pumping so hard she was sure she was about to errupt- that was until comprehension dawned; Tia stopped. Took a slowly shaky inhail and began chewing the inside of her thick bottom lip.

She watched the young man began to chant, making his way slowly around the room until he came to the cabinet where she sat.

She squirmed uncomfortably fighting the desire to flee, but a strange contentment began to rise slowly inside her; a calmness. She watched him intently, stubborn as always as the young man assessed her back. Suspending his actions he asked, "Who is Yule?"

Tia slid off the cabinet, uncomfortable with her central position, and slowly backed towards the door. "Why? Are you the one who's chasing her?" She stuck her chin out defiantly, her eyes gleaming with brevado.

"No," he replied forcefully, smirking slightly at her retreat. "I am here to help the G-Poss stalk their ghosts." He grinned while Tia eyed him warily.

"Yule is the nightmare that haunted my childhood. The nightmare that's haunting me now. Not some joke for a 'wannabe know it all' like you. You're not even a Ghost Possessor. You're just the cavalry, here to mop up behind us." Tia smiled cockily.

Jinx rose an eyebrow at the dramatic smackdown and stifled a smirk. "Is that so?"

"Yes. And Yule's my bloody bitch of an assignment," she sniped. "She's ruined my life!"

"I'm sure she's not that bad," he placated, a show of magic playing across his eyes in a subtle mist.

Tia took a quick step back.

"Are you afraid of me, Tia?" He stepped forwards and placed the smudge stick in a candle tray balanced precariously on the windowsill.

What the hell does he think- i think? That he's gonna shoot me with the smudge stick or something? Tia slowed her retreat to a stop and glared boldly into his vivid green eyes. "I'm afraid of no one! Nothing on this earth can scare me anymore!" she yelled at him over the thunder of her heart beating in her eardrums.

He rose his hands up and opened his palms in defence. "I didn't mean to offend you, sister."

Tia's veins boiled with rage. She slammed her hand down on the nearest surface, grabbing an ornament and lifting it to throw. "I am not *your sister*!" She roared.

Suddenly the rage filtered out of her like someone had just pulled the plug. Gently she placed the small object back down on the shabby, old book where it had been sat and looked at it properly. It was a raven, with enthralling dark wings. She stroked their swooping arc, entranced, her finger scraping against the tatty old book beneath which began to glow with a green-tinged smoke.

Tia's heart raced, sweat pooled across her forehead and her eyes darted around fearfully as the young man stepped closer. "Stop it! Stop it!" she shouted, her voice quaking with mounting fear. "Stop it!" she screamed. He stepped towards her but Tia instantly recoiled, backing up so quickly she knocked her head on the door with a resounding thump. Her body shook uncontrollably as she struggled to catch her breath and regain her senses.

Hands outstretched to placate her, the young man cautiously approached her. "I'm not trying to scare you, Tia, I didn't—"

"Please!" she begged, her body shaking with terror as she unsuccessfully tried to unlock the door behind her. Oh God, he's a witch. A witch! *What is he going to do? Hex me?* Bespell me? Worse-? She gulped, her throat so dry her tongue ripped layer of skin from her pallet.

Her skin had never felt this aware of someone before. It was like she could feel his magic crawling all over her like army ants out to strike. He's powerful. I can feel it. Sense it. I would stake my life on it. Oh God, I have, haven't I? No one knows I'm here I'm-"

Two warm hands pressed against her shoulders as the young man stepped closer. Then it was too late. The crystal ring on his right hand was already digging into her as slowly he began to chant.

Chapter 11

Jinx

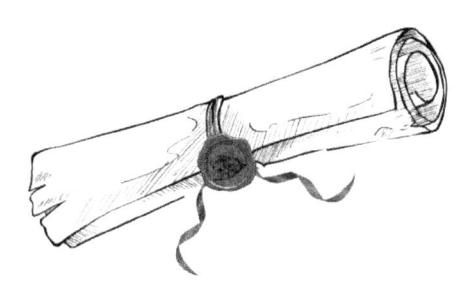

The air whirled around him, enhanced with his soul's magic as it gently caressed his skin, and flicked tendrils of loose hair from Tia's plait which hung seductively down one shoulder. How he longed to tuck it neatly behind her perfect little ears. He shook himself mentally. *I came here to do a job, not flirt with the G-Poss.*

Jinx, being Jinx, had no lack of admirers back home in the Welsh mountains. He was well known for his 'gift' with the ladies. After all, he had status, power and good looks; he had everything. *So why does this girl captivate me? Why does she make my heart flutter?* Jinx ran a hand through his braids, which clanked together like maracas. Slowey began to chant:

"Calm Tia,

Be at ease,

Feel the Goddess,

Rest in her peace."

Before Jinx tore his gaze from Tia's beautiful deep cobalt eyes, he felt the erratic tempo of her heart slow to a delicate, enthralling drum. *Hypnotic.* With his grip unyielding, so she wouldn't fall, he tried unsuccessfully to convince himself. His earthen green gaze roamed over her.

Goddess, she's beautiful! Her raven hair splayed in unruly locks from its plait. Her black polo shirt stretched tightly over her chest that rose and fell, showing a tantalising amount of perfectly toned abdomen in time with the caresses of magic air upon her skin. *Goddess, she's sexy!* Jinx watched with rapt attention as goosebumps broke out along the length of her bare arms.

Shivering with delicious awareness, Jinx slowly sucked the magic back into his soul where it settled as content as a cat in front of a warm hearth. He watched entranced as Tia's bottom lip quivered beneath its black gloss, making him long to lower his lips and cover hers; to drive away her fear with passion.

Jinx shook his head, his braids whipping around, and he centred himself. *Strange*, he thought, that *after all these years, the book has reacted to this girl. And why had a little ghost given him her name? Was it connected to her somehow?*

The ghost sat swinging its legs from the top bunk. A possessive glint in its eyes as it met Jinx's questioning glare. Suddenly the spirit leapt into the air and gently floated down to the floor. *Could the ghost have just inadvertently proven Garth's theory about the ghost barriers having 'loopholes?'* Jinx wondered, returning his concentration to Tia.

She was calmer now, but her breath was shaking from her lungs in rattled gasps as she pushed through his magic to command- "Let. Me. Go!" Abruptly a force as strong as iron shoved his hands from her shoulders. "Now!" she demanded.

Jinx leaned around her, her natural aroma of sticky-sweet oranges slightly accented by lavender wafted up his nostrils, and he let a hand gently slip from her shoulder. He just had to know if her skin was as soft and tender as he was imagining. His fingers skimmed the bare skin of her arm, stroking gently. A trail of goose bumps appearing in their wake. *Yes, yes. It is.*

Jinx smiled wickedly, moved around her and blew a breath of magic into the door lock, his lips lightly skimming the pale skin of her arm. *Ummm...* his mind purred.

He felt more than heard her sharp intake of breath as the door clicked gently open. Stepping away, he gave Tia the space she needed to flee from him- but she didn't. He stared at her, incredulous.

She just stood there, hands fisted on curvy hips, head wobbling slightly with attitude as she raged, "You will never do that again!"

"And what exactly is 'that'?"

Tia's finger mimed a magic wand, her finger swirling around in the air, a sharp flick of her wrist indicating a spell had been cast. He chuckled, his eyes sparkling with mischief as he caught her wrist in his palm. "Oh, is that right?" he continued mercilessly.

Tia's eyes narrowed, darkening, an angry flare sparking in their hypnotic depths as Jinx, knowingly pushing his luck by stroked his other hand up the smooth underside of her pale wrist. He smiled seductively, his eyes transfixed on hers. "Because I thought you were referring to my touch."

"Noticed the goose bumps, did you?" Tia snarled.

Jinx smiled slyly before releasing her and retreating to Garth's bottom bunk a safe distance away. He reclined on the plush white pillows with his arms stretched up behind his head.

"How did you expect an ascender to react when a witch," she spat the words, "has her cornered?"

Ouch! That hurt. But he knew deep down she was lying. He'd felt her breath hitch and heard the near silent sigh from her succulently glossed lips when his hand slipped silkily across her forearm. *Ascender? Now why had the ghost failed to mention that little nugget?*

Tia stepped back, her steps faltering slightly.

Before turning and quickly marching from the bunkhouse, her hips swinging with rhythmic attitude. The little spirit followed closely behind her and exited with a childish poke of its tongue. Jinx flinched when the door slammed shut, ricocheting like his heart.

There's no way she has any idea that she's half-witch, he mused. But the book's reaction had proved it. *I wonder what she'll do when she finds out.* He chuckled to himself imagining Tia's face frozen in shock. Then amending the image to one of her exploding like the nova bomb she was. *How was it that she had been trained by the G-Poss anyway? How had they discovered her and not seen her witch magic? Were the G-Poss really that arrogant they couldn't even entertain the possibility of cross-species?*

Jinx walked over to the book his father had gifted him before his disappearance and moved it back to the centre of the cabinet. He remembered that day nine years ago. His grandmother had escorted his family to the train station; she was looking after him and his sister while their parents were away on official coven business, bringing a dangerous warlock to justice.

Jinx was proud of his parents, and he had been that day when his father gave him the 'precious' book.

"This," his father had said, "holds the secrets of the universe. Be careful with it, Jinx." He ran his fingers affectionately over the cover, recalling the look on his father's face,

"The universe?" Jinx had said, his mouth hanging wide open as he looked to his father.

"Yes, Jinx." His father winked and then embraced him, before turning to watch his mother's exchange with Hope as she gifted her a crystal so clear that it sparkled a prism of rainbow light in the early April sun.

That was the last time he spoke to them before, hand in hand, they stepped onto the train; his mother blowing them a parting kisses.

Jinx's mind slammed into reality with an enlightening thought; *What if Tia is the key to Grandmother's plans of integration? By uniting with the G-Poss, witches will become less vulnerable to spirit attacks. We won't need to petition the G-Poss to exorcise the power-leeching ghosts drawn to us because of the use of our magic. They would be...safe.*

Gently he caressed the books spine, still caught in the entrapment of his thoughts.

But Jinx had to wonder how Tia would come out in all of this. *Certainly not unscathed. Not with George, the prejudiced dictator as head of the Ghost Possessor Academy, and certainly not with his cantankerous old grandmother being their faction's High Witch Elder. Tia was a nexus – a bridge between species integration.* And an enigma that pulled at his heart. *I will make sure she is okay. I feel...compelled to.*

He paced to the window staring out at Tia's distant form stomping between the graves that littered the compound and felt his heart thump an extra beat just for her. "We will meet again Tia," he promised, "and next time you will want to stay."

Just as she slipped from his view Garth rounded the corner of the shed with a look of desolation bleeding from his face. Jinx opened the door, waiting for him to step inside.

Garth's footfalls were heavy, and immediately Jinx felt guilty for the delayed way he had revealed Fiona's death. Obviously, despite the age difference, Garth and Fiona had had a lot of history, and Jinx suspected a very close relationship, once upon a time.

"Just tell me one thing." Garth ran a hand through his dishevelled blond hair. "Her spirit, will it be okay? I mean, it will go to the 'light' place. Right?" He slumped onto his bunk, his eyes red and puffy.

Jinx looked at him curiously. "Why do you ask that?" His eyes narrowed on Garth as he whispered the door to shut and lock itself.

"She… We… I… Argh!" he roared, slamming a fist into the wall. "I…can't…do this…right now. Just tell me. Please!"

Jinx coaxed his magic from its eternal fireside within his soul and let it burrow through his body. Vibrations stormed his veins like sparklers being lit, fanning out to encompass his entire being.

Taking a deep breath to calm his heart he let his body relax fully into a meditative state.

Willing his magic to elevate his awareness, out of his pores, up through his crown chakra and into the atmosphere and the realm beyond, praying for the Goddess's help as he searched the hereafter for Fiona's spirit.

"She is safe." He sighed contentedly as a fluttering feeling lifted his heart like the embrace of a mother. "It's alright Garth, she is sleeping in Summerland." He smiled, letting his awareness sink back into the confines of his body.

"Summerland?"

"It's a place of rest and reflection before a soul chooses to move on to reincarnation or to become a spirit guide. Its eternal summer there, it beautiful Garth. And she is safe with the Goddess."

"She's with your Goddess?" He confirmed.

"So to speak," replied Jinx.

"So, she's alone? That's good. That's good."

"No, Garth she's not alone, an…" Jinx paused, unsure of how much he should and could reveal. *Sod it! He needs to know.* "An angelic being watches over her. She is safe."

"Really? They're real? Angels, I mean. Can you see it? What does it look like?"

Jinx noticed Garth's interest had finally broken him out of his sorrow for a few seconds. He wanted to cheer him up, rather than letting him wallow in his grief and knew he shouldn't be talking of such, but he couldn't help but indulge his new friends curiosity when he saw the wonder in his friend's eyes.

"Bright. She's very high up in the angel hierarchy. Her skin is smooth and tantalising, it shines like newly polished black diamonds. Her hair is long, down to her waist and curled. It looks like fine-spun silver. It's beautiful." All of a sudden, Jinx felt a jolt like fire racing through his body as the angelic being pushed at him with a chastising glare of her burnt amber eyes.

Suddenly his arms felt heavy like lead and he slumped in exhaustion. A weary, drained feeling encompassed his soul and his magic stalked it, attempting to heal him.

Garth suddenly bombarded him with more questions. "Does she have wings? A...halo?"

Jinx sniggered.

"What?!" Garth yelled in outrage.

"Halos are just make-believe. A symbolic creation meant to capture all that is 'right and pure'. But the reality is that no one's that good! But yeah, I saw her wings when she shoved me out."

"Jinx, you're killing me here," Garth whined.

"Okay, okay." He chuckled. "She had huge bat-like wings; they only reveal them when they use their powers. Hers looked leathery, but the undersides sparkled like blue fire and got brighter when she used her power to check who I was. That's why I'm so tired now. "She was…"

"Intoxicating?" Garth supplied, a smile edging his lips.

"Scarily so."

"Thanks, Jinx. I've just been so worried what with-." Garth's face blanked. "Never mind." He sighed.

The atmosphere was thick with tension. Jinx knew he was hiding something from him, but he hadn't the energy to press him.

"There will be a passing ritual. I can make it so you can attend, if you wish to," Jinx muttered, climbing onto his bunk, his limbs heavy and clumsy.

"Uh, yes, no. I… I'll think about it. Not many people knew we were, are… I don't know." He sighed, his breath heavy with choked sobs.

"Get some rest, Garth," Jinx said with a yawn.

"Tell me about Heaven. Please?" Garth whispered.

Jinx rolled to his side, threw off his shirt, trousers and shoes, and slid beneath the thick quilted duvet, his eyes already blurring from fatigue and his mind numbly quiet.

"We call it the Summerland." he replied sleepily. "When you get there, the first thing you notice is the smells, they're thick and heady, disorientating, but in a good way – like having one too many beers at a festival." He smiled. "It smells of warmth and citrus. Luring in its sweetness, but with sharp undertones; but that's only because my soul doesn't belong there yet. I imagine it's just sweet and comforting to the souls of the dead." Jinx yawned again and stared at the ceiling, his eyes watering slightly. "The grass there tickles your legs like silken fingers as you glide through it; the ground was soft and spongy beneath my astral feet.

Then you see the sky. It is beyond all imagining. Ripples of pinks and blues swirl in a calm tornado, like ice cream in a candy shop that has ever colour syrup possible – like a rainbow. *Beautiful.* Sometimes you can see newly made angelic beings fly. They radiate power, their wings of all different sizes, textures and powers. They fly with grace, yet their speed is unnerving. The whole realm sounds like it's full of excited children. The noise hums through the land like a welcome chorus."

"Yes," Garth said in equilibrium, "I remember. The way they cast light down like a hot summer sun. You can't even look at them if they don't want you to because their power is so otherworldly."

Jinx heard the smile in Garth's tone and furrowed his brow. "How do you know that?" He leaned over and stared down at Garth's guarded face.

"Uh... I saw it in a dream." Garth shrugged, feigning nonchalance.

"Sure," Jinx replied. *I'll question him later-when I'm not so tired.* He thought.

"Jinx, how often have you been there, to Summerland?" Garth replied solemnly.

Jinx, rolling over and pulling the duvet up to his head, replied, "I had to know if they were dead or alive." A tear leaked from his eye. He clenched a hand to his heart and his voice cracked. "My parents, they disappeared when I was just a kid, and I...I just didn't understand how they could leave me. So, at first I snuck my awareness into the realm of the Summerland for an hour every day, searching. Until I was sensed by some being and shoved out. The next time I visited, an angelic being was waiting for me. He told me he was an archangel. He was terrifying. He had long feathered wings that sparked like lightening on the underside, crackling with power. I don't remember much else, but he told me I was not to visit anymore.

He said that my soul would crave to stay a little more each time I came, until one day it would finally leave my body. So I left. Not that I was going to do as he told me, but... I don't know." Jinx's throat suddenly felt as raw as his heart. He hadn't told anyone of his visits to Summerland, and he had never planned to. He just hoped Garth may trust him with his innermost secrets one day and they could remain friends. But Jinx had a feeling that Garth's secret was much, much worse than Jinx's unauthorised visits to Summerland.

"God, I'm sorry, Jinx," Garth whispered.

"No worries," Jinx mumbled beneath his covers.

"Jinx?"

"Mmm."

"Does every soul go to the Summerland?" asked Garth.

Jinx frowned wearily unsure in his lethargic haze if he'd answered Garth or not. But a few seconds later, he was conscious of Garth's energy calming until he could hear faint exhausted snores rising up steadily through the bunk like a soothing lullaby, luring Jinx into sleep.

Jinx slept deeply dreaming of Summerland's beauty, how the willow trees had bowed gracefully to the earth when new spirits arrived, and the sky swirled hypnotically, lulling everyone into the peaceful realm. He turned around, suddenly sensing he wasn't alone. No longer did he run his hands playfully through the soft caress of the grass, but he stood still, shocked into silence. There was someone else there. Someone he felt with a shiver of recognition he knew, watching him. His heart rate doubled, swelling with hope.

Jinx rolled restlessly in his bunk, a thick sweat breaking out on his brow as his spirit self screamed broken-heartedly, "Mother!? Father!? Show yourself!"

An instant later, the grass stopped its friendly wave, the hypnotic sky seemed to freeze, the tousling willow branches stilled and the powerful angelic being with skin like newly polished black diamonds appeared.

She touched one dark finger to her lips, and Jinx's dream-self barely took a breath. A wave of peace and tranquillity swept over him as he fell gently into a mist. Then he could just about hear the angelic being whisper, "Not yet, Jinx, it is not time. But soon, I promise, child. Soon, you shall learn the truth."

Chapter 12

Jinx

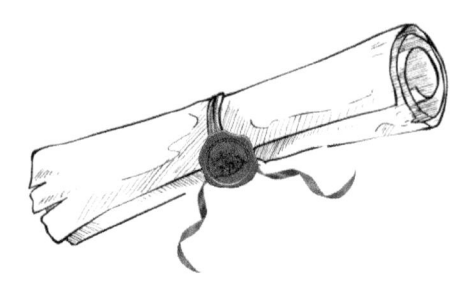

A few hours later, Jinx was suddenly awoken by a flurry of persistent knocks rattling the bunkhouse door.

Jinx sighed a huge lung rattling breath, he slid down from the top bunk trying not to disturb Garth who was busy snoring heavily below. The poor man had woken and sobbed in the night until exhaustion stole him to sleep.

The knocks on the door loudened. Jinx pulled on his faded, low-slung jeans that rested just below the branded elastic of his boxers. He glanced at the alarm clock Garth had set earlier and frowned. It was four a.m. *Who in the Goddess's name calls at four a.m.?* thought Jinx wearily.

He reached for a band and loosely tied back his dark brown braids, stuffed his mobile into his pocket and wedged his bare feet into the comfortable surroundings of his old trainers.

At this hour- it has to be an emergence. He thought. *A potential probably injured themselves or maybe a G-Poss warrior has transported back to the academy with a broken bone or bloody gash.* Jinx cringed at the thought; *transporting with any injury is a bad idea- it would be extremely painful. Not that waking me up for first aid will help much- I'm not a hedgewitch.*

A hedgewitch, herbal healer or a crystal healer could help. But those people were not considered witches, just highly talented humans. He braced himself for the worst. Whatever that was, placed a hand firmly on the door handle and opened it.

Two huge men stood blocking the entrance. One with a chubby fist raised, his knuckles about to strike the shaking door again. The men stared at each other, their blond hair rustling slightly in the early morning breeze as their cold eyes met his.

"Yer coming with us, witch," ordered the bulkier of the two otherwise identical men. He reached out a rough hand and grasped Jinx's upper arm, propelling him unexpectedly out of the bunkhouse doorway.

"What in the Goddesses name!" He roared, adrenaling hitting him as fast as the crisp, frosty air on the skin of his bare chest. Quickly he planted his feet firmly on the gravel path outside, his eyes narrowing on the twins every movement. "Get lost!". He yanked his arm free of the big brute, turning slightly as he did so, and positioning himself in a power stance. Dodging to avoid the striking fist of the second man, who moved faster than he predicted, knocking him from his feet to the frozen gravel with a thud. Instantly his teeth punctured his bottom lip leaving the bitter taste of blood on his tongue as he stared up at the two delinquent twins.

"You really wanna do this?" Jinx asked calmly, feeling the air around him beginning to stir with his mounting anger.

One of the twins screamed in shock, his tenor voice rattling through the air as he flew back towards the bunkhouse and slammed the open door with his thick form.

Suddenly Garth rushed out, his hair tousled and feet bare. He ran through the thick sparking air with forced slowness to where Jinx lay sprawled out on the ground, his swollen lip dripping blood down his dark-skinned chest and a fist indentation blackening his toned abdomen. He took shallow breaths, the pain in his chest radiating heat like a fire.

"What the hell do you think you are doing?!" Garth bellowed, holding a hand out to help Jinx.

"Mentor wants to see the witch," the closest twin drawled, his thick accent hard to understand beneath the furious roars of his brother charging like a rhino at the two younger men.

The air around him suddenly thickened, slowing his movements with its sticky hold until he could no longer move, his fist retracted ready to strike a clean path to Garths eye. "Whoa," hissed Garth. "Did you do that?"

Jinx nodded in affirmation.

"Impressive!"

Jinx took the offered hand, letting Garth pull him firmly to his feet. "Yeah, I did, you okay with that?" He asked, holding Garths gaze as he quickly side stepped the motionless airborne fist.

"Y-e-s," Garth stumbled over the word. "Definitely okay. A shiner really wouldn't have gone down well with Fiona!" He chuckled, then in a sombre tone added, "But I guess that doesn't matter now. Does it?" He stood back and distastefully admired the immobile twin suspended in a rhino like charge by the congealed air around him.

The second of the twins prowled, caught between enacting revenge for his sibling and fear of Jinx.

"I hope you can reverse it? I really don't need another statue to weed," Garth joked, a small chuckle escaping his lips.

Dusting himself off with frozen hands Jinx slid through the thickened air like a blade arcing at its enemy. Voice low and hypnotic he commanded-

"I'll let you go. But from now on, neither of you touch me! You wanna talk- you ask me. And treat me with some damned respect- I am the heir to the Pren ceri coven and soon to be Hight Witch Elder. As for this" he motioned to the slowly purpling stain bruised into his chest and then back to the twins- "I'd say we're even. Your brother—" Jinx motioned to the statue-like twin "—is gonna have one hell of a headache. Remember guys- It's not a good idea to piss off a witch, especially a tired one." He rubbed a hand down his weary face.

"Now, why are you here?" he asked before whispering to the air around him- "Thank you, Goddess. Air, please release him."

The air quaked around the suspended twin before ripping and sending out frozen shock waves. Finally released the twin hunched to the floor, shaking like a newborn pup and hurled his stomach's contents to the ground.

"You'll. Pay. Fer. That!" he spat before choking and collapsing onto the frozen gravel.

Garth stared back at him. "You know, he could've left you like that. Just think of all the cats that would have stopped by to pee on you." A wide grin spread across Garth's face as he pointed to the hunched twin. "That's Jim. Just so you know which twin will be holding the knife next time." He pointed to the other brother. "And that one's is John. Watch him. He's the brains."

Jinx nodded, turned and headed back to the bunkhouse, Garth trailing behind him.

"Oh and you can clean that up when you've finished too!" Garth rumbled. "Uh and don't yer be going anywhere John, Jinx will be back in a moment."

Inside the bunkhouse Jinx feverishly sponged the blood drops from his face and chest, surveying his newly forming bruise before slipping on a long-sleeved vest. It fit snugly over his chest, insulating him against the cold morning frost -- but more importantly, it hid his obvious brawl mark.

I guess I've got somewhere to be, he griped to himself, a deep foreboding settling into his skin as he passed Garth and headed back outside to the twins. Jinx motioned to Jim, who was still crouched on the ground with one hand holding his head, the other hand dragging a uniformed sleeve over his bile-covered mouth, and said, "He'll stay here. You—" he turned to Jhon "—can take me to see George – now."

John sucked in a breath, his cheeks reddening. He raked a hand through his wayward blond hair causing it to stand on end as he muttered curses Jinx ignored.

John led the way along the gravel path, through the gardens and into a side door of the academy, uncaring of orbs, spirits or shadow people he passed through. Jinx however, sidestepped them as necessary. They walked silently down empty corridors decorated with endless depictions of landscapes framed on the old magnolia painted walls. Finally, they came to George's office.

Inside, George was hunched over endless paperwork whilst listening to a violinist playing through his laptop. "About time!" George grumped, raising his head from the papers.

Pushing his reading glasses back up his fat little nose he stared furiously at John. "What took you so long? And where's Jim?"

"The wi... I mean the, uh, assistant, sir, he froze him. He's all right now, though. Well, not really all right, but he will be all right, I think." John glared at Jinx who merely smiled and nodded his reassurance that Jim would indeed be 'all right'.

"What is it you want?" Jinx asked at the sight of George's raised eyebrows. He obviously hadn't expected Jinx to come out on top of his little invitation. George motioned to a wooden seat opposite. Jinx stared, blatantly ignoring the commanding gesture.

"It's bad news about Fiona. You were right after all. She really is dead."

"I told you that yesterday," Jinx droned. *When will anyone bloody listen to me?* He thought, rolling his eyes.

George sighed. "Yes, but you are a witch and witches lie. Now listen, we've had a call," George continued as he leaned his withered elbows on the desk, his fingers steepled above them. "The police department in Maloroy found one of our vehicles." He stared up at Jinx as he added, "It was the one Fiona took yesterday. When they found it, it was burnt like a tinder box." Jinx watched the Adam's apple in George's throat bob uncomfortably beneath the neckline of his black polo shirt.

"Fiona was…inside…when it blew up," George concluded. He sighed dramatically. "In light of the current situation, I feel it is beneficial to first offer you the temporary position of in-house witch. Although you will remain bunking with the gardener."

"Temporary?" He didn't want the job full-time, but even so, for a trainee High Elder to be offered the position temporarily was an insult. There was no other witch in the vicinity, so they would have to discuss securing a more permanent member with his grandmother. Jinx had had enough, he was a Pren Ceri, a trainee High Elder, a witch of high ranking who had come to help these miserable Ghost Possessors in their futile cause. And they, in return, treated him like this!

He slammed his hands down on the desk and lowered his head to lock eyes with George. Spittle shot through his teeth at the same rate his blood spat from his volcanic heart.

"I talked to the High Witch Elder, **my grandmother,** yesterday evening. She insists that *I* take over Fiona's position within the academy." *For now*, he added mentally. "You have no idea what's going on. The death of Fiona was premeditated!"

George's eyes were glassy with the adrenalin of pre-battle as the warrior within him rose to the surface, demanding details. "what makes you think that?" He growled, slinging himself back into his wooden chair, before running a plump hand over his exhausted, reddened face.

"Residual energy," Jinx stated before continuing to explain the particulars to George. "Fiona was supposed to meet me at Maloroy Station yesterday afternoon around three thirty. When she didn't show, I cast a time reflection spell. The spell locates a person's residual energy and replays their actions back, like a film."

George leaned closer, his eyes glinting with the fire of the warrior he was. "And what have you deduced from this time aberration?" He demanded, his eyes never leaving Jinx's.

"I have reason to believe Fiona was murdered. My prime suspect being the malicious spirit haunting these grounds."

"A spirit, you say." George laughed. "Spirits cannot KILL! I see them every day- have done for years. None of them *kill*. You are over exaggerating, boy- affected by the death of one of your own, perhaps. None the less, mistaken."

Jinx slammed his hands onto the large oak desk. "No ghost you've ever met! But I hate to remind you, George, that your little G-Poss unit here hasn't even reached maturity yet! There are things- things you can't even imagine- that walk the night alongside us. I strongly suggest you open your eyes!" Jinx had no idea how he kept the lash of his temper from exploding while the Head Mentor sat there criticising his theories. "Most dangerously of all, you are undermining the ghost's potential."

"Ha! Not possible, witch."

"It is not unheard of, for a ghost to turn poltergeist and become active enough to commit murder."

"Ah, now there is where you're wrong. After all, you are not a Ghost Possessor, so how could you possibly know the specifics of a poltergeist's activity?" George raised an eyebrow. "Hmm?"

"Then, tell me," Jinx gritted.

"Poltergeists do not murder their victims, they thrive on a person's fear, and their terror drives the poltergeist to become more active, and then *bam*!" He slapped his hands together. "A slightly accident happens and the poltergeists are blamed for them."

Jinx stared wide-eyed at him. "So you're trying to tell me that poltergeists are... innocent?"

"Not entirely, no." He sighed. "I don't expect you to understand. You're a witch – everything is good or evil to you."

So. Not. True, thought Jinx. But they were steering away from the subject, and he wasn't going to let that happen. "All species evolve! And all species have the ability to produce rogue megalomaniacs with barely unstoppable powers,". He clarified thinking back to the time when his grandmother had caught him with her grimoire.

He had been thumbing through the thick magnolia pages when a pencil sketch of a classic cartoon ghost caught his eye. Intrigued, he had stopped to look at the page, reading its entry;

Ghosts, Spirits and Spectres.

The word 'spectre' refers to a more aged spirit from around the seventeenth century. Where as, the term 'ghost' is more modern, the universal term would be 'spirit'. But beware because all have the potential to turn into a poltergeist! Or, if they continue to cross the line between unseen forces, they may become a Cacodaemon – a malevolent species of spirit that will surpass the boundaries of even the most fearful of poltergeists.

Cacodaemons do not feed off fear like poltergeists, Jinx remembered, *they feed off the evil deeds they enact.* Their race barely classing below that of a born demon. "It could be a Cacodaemon," Jinx suggested quietly.

George clenched his side and roared with laughter, tears springing to his eyes. "Aw, boy." He grabbed Jinx's elbow, propelled him outside of his office, "Cacodaemons are just nonsense. We tell the potentials to keep them in line."

Goddess why won't he listen to me? He sighed. *He won't even entertain the idea.* As rare as Cacodeamons were, they were still real and were not to be underestimated. If undiscovered, they would continue to haunt, terrorise, madden and eventually murder their victims. He tugged at his braids, their crystals clanging.

The spirit that murdered Fiona was already a killer, and Jinx was determined to find out who it intended to prey on next.

Chapter 13

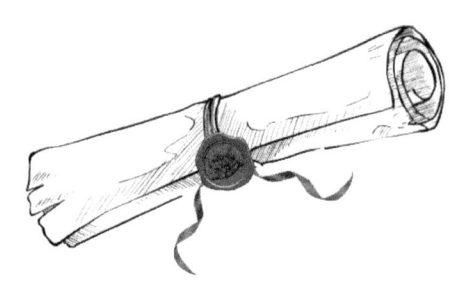

Jinx

Jinx found himself lost in an expanse of overcrowded corridors with potentials swarming like bees around a hive, giving him an enormous headache. They clattered around opening and shutting bent out of shape lockers as they armed themselves ready for classes. He rubbed at his forehead, grimacing.

Older potentials gathered in a circle, entrapping him. *Are they intending to attack or intimidate me into submission?* He chuckled, earning a spasm from his searing headache. *Goddess I'm too busy for this.*

I have to attuned to Fiona's duties, look in on the already transported potentials, and arrange the passing ceremony for her spirit. Not to mention I have to locate and destroy a poltergeist whom I suspected was quickly ascending into the category of Cacodaemon. Is it any wonder my head is splitting?

Jinx levelled his eyes to the largest potential heading the circle infront of him. "Do you have a problem?"

"I'd say we do," the boy taunted, sticking his index finger into Jinx's solid chest.

"And that problem is?" Jinx asked, one eyebrow climbing.

"You! Witch!" spat the boy, stepping back amongst his group, before edged them forwards in an attack formation. Jinx stood calmly, his rage already palpable in the air whipping around him.

Drawing the natural magic from his pores to join the already disturbed air, he formed an air block around him. The boys piled into it one by one; their fists punching out against its congealed shield.

His head swam with the intense pregdudice of the g-poss. His brain felt like a race circuit with the car accelerater peddle stuck on- he was just waiting for the blow out.

Jinx brought forth his magic,stiring the air into a cyclone he sent his petulant young attackers back into into the crowd. Shrieks and sobs echoed from the younger potentials at seeing his fury power the elements. As his magic swirled around him tugging at his braids. His dark hair contained swirls of white mist as his natural ability of air magic rose from within him and chilling his bones, he caught sight of his reflection in a dented locker.

A tug on his hand made him look down. A young girl with badly dyed hair stuffed into pigtails stood before him, her hands planted firmly on her hips.

"You're totally scaring Mimi! You need to stop!" she yelled. "You're being a *bad* witch! Te doesn't like *bad* people."

Jinx looked at the young girl, her words quaking with fear, but she didn't relent as she chastised him. *Who in the Goddesses name is Te?* He thought. It seemed everyone here hated witches, so what was one more witch hater on a hate list so big.

His magic began to simmer, calming from its storm thanks to the girls distraction. Slowly he centred himself, restoring his inner equilibrium, the torrent of air around him ceasing its volitile momentum. Only the white mist swirling in his eyes was an indication that he had not yet relinquished the air from his aid.

He projected his voice with the air's assistance, encompassing the potentials who crowded the corridors around him.

"I am Jinx Pren Ceri, your new house witch. You will show me the respect my position deserves! Now, one of you will lead me to the reception hall. I have business to attend to."

Jinx looked around surveying the dried tears staining some of the younger potentials' faces.

True, he had taken it a bit far; but luckily, he had invoked air. The element he had the most affinity with. Otherwise, there could have been dire consequences. Consequences only an experienced witch or Elder could reverse, resulting in banishment-. *Grandmother will not be pleased.* He thought. *I lost control of my emotions and my magic seeped through. Although, I haven't got a head ache anymore.* A slight smile tweaked his lips.

Taking a deep breath, Jinx surveyed the few potentials who hadn't scurried away, one being the young girl who had brought him out of his fury.

"Follow me." She walked slightly ahead of him, leading him through the blockade of Open-mouthed potentials and through the maze of corridors.

The girl stared up at him, her blue eyes unfazed as they took in the power pouring from Jinx. "D'you think you can turn that off? Please?" she asked. "It's kinda creepy," she added as an afterthought.

"Says the girl who's training to possess ghosts," stated Jinx with a grin. He thanked the air for it's aid and felt his magic surrender it's hold before pooling contentedly back into his soul.

The girl stuck out her tongue defiantly from blackened lips and asked, "So, what's a Pen Cre? It's supposed to be impressive, right?" She bobbed up and down with excitement.

"Pren Ceri," Jinx corrected with a snigger "it's my family's name, the name of a High Witch Elder."

The girl smiled, glad that she got the gist of importance from his words, even though she hadn't fully understood.

Jinx knew potentials were not taught about the other government paranormal factions. They were only given evasive information the year before their ascension in case they required aid after an assignment. "What's your name?" he asked the girl.

"Oh, I'm Ella. But my friends call me Ell. Well, my true friend does."

Jinx could feel her sadness infiltrating his senses and emulating his own.

"And this Te is your friend?" he quizzed, only half interested in her response.

"Yeah, she's my best friend. My soul sister." She pointed to her bad dye-job. "See, just like twins."

Jinx couldn't stop the laughter bubbling up his throat as the tension from the previous few minutes rolled away.

Suddenly Ella paused, produced a mobile from her trouser pocket and swiftly flicked through her photos. She held it out to him, the face of a girl with raven hair and cobalt blue eyes stared back at him. "That's Te?" he asked as she shoved the mobile back into her pocket.

"Yeah, Tia."

. Jinx thought. "So, what does Te think of witches?" he asked, fascinated by the Ella's nonstop banter – with a witch, none the less.

"She doesn't like witches. We're not supposed to." Seeing the hurt in his eyes, she quickly added, "At least she doesn't hate 'em!" followed by a goofy smile.

"That's good, seeing as she is one," Jinx mumbled, but too late to catch the motion of a tall, dark-haired boy in his peripheral vision.

The boy's head tilted towards him in interest.

Did he hear me?

Ella stopped him in his tracks, her eyes wide and mouth hanging open. "Just remember not to tell anyone. It could put her life in danger- you people here dont seem too keen on witches." Jinx smiled sadly at the girl- hoping she understood the severity of the situation her friend was in.

"Right, so this is one of those 'if I tell, ya'll have to kill me' moments?" Winking, she finger shot him. "Gottcha."

The girl continued to make him chuckle with little quips about G-Poss life in the academy as they made their way to the large door that led into the reception hall.

"So, do ya think I'll get in trouble if I tell my menta I was escorting ya?" she asked cheekily.

"Definitely," Jinx retorted. "Probably best to say I kidnapped you. They might actually believe that." Ella smiled and with a parting wave, she turned away and raced back through the labyrinth of corridors and out of sight

Heading to the stage near the centre of the room Jinx saw a desk had already been erected, a simple sticky label deeming it–property of the house witch-. On the plush little cloth coating the fold out desk was a large crystal ball.

With a deep bone wrenching sigh Jinx sat down to his adoptive work. His hand rhythmically caressed the surface of Fiona's crystal ball as it balanced precariously on a stand of human bones. Most would think it was unethical- but to witches, the bones of deceased ancestors held great power. A stack of yellow files sat adjacent it with a square clock that ticked by the seconds with the most irritating pleasure. *No doubt they want to make sure I do my time.* Jinx snipped. Reading the glowing hands that pointed stiffly to seven.

Taking a deep breath Jinx cleared his racing mind, relaxing each and every muscle until his body felt like jelly and he finally managed to centre himself.

Staring deep into the depths of the crystal ball he watched as random images began to appear. *Here we go.* He thought, concentrating on tracking the power of the ascenders pendant, whilst sending his awareness into the crystal to be sure he tracked the correct person. A tiny image began clearing in the crystal. Jinx willed it bigger with his magic, tuning it like the reception ariel of an old T.V whilst simultaneously thumbing through the ascenders' file before him.

In the crystal's image he saw two young ascenders walking hand in hand wearing Victorian-style clothes. Eyes flickering back and forth from the crystal ball to the files, Jinx deduced that the male was Li.

Li led the way through the cramped streets, a wary eye ahead of him. With an indulgent look on his face, he listened to the prattling's of the female ascender; Anka walking alongside. Her beautiful flowing skirts and lace bonnet were swept back by the thick smog of- he willed their pendants to whisper their location- London.

Interesting, thought Jinx. It was obvious the two had figured out that their ghost assignments were lovers, and, like the two young ascenders, they hadn't yet confirmed their unrequited love to each other. He noted the date, time and general information on a sheet inside their files, Expecting that their assignments would be fulfilled rather quickly as they were off to a great start and teaming up could only make it easier – even though Jinx considered it cheating.

"Crystal clear." He bid it, watching as the ascenders dissipated from view in the rolling mist, another image filling its place.

Sighing heavily, Jinx stared at the new image embedded in the crystal. A raucous, throaty laugh welled from the pit of his stomach, his toes involuntarily curled, his large ring-bearing hand clenched at his ribs as he willed the torrent of hysterical laughter to end. Swiping tears of amusement from his face, he refocused on the crystal ball before him. At first glance stood a tall and lean woman, her dark hair spilling out of a high velvet hat and her traditional Welsh dress of black and red swayed in the breeze.

She climbed large rocks along a clifftop, the pendant hissed into his mind that the place was called Fishbourn. At this moment, she turned around and revealed herself to be not only an ugly woman, but the ascender Reece.

Jinx chuckled again as he noted the date, time and general details in his file. Reece seemed to be doing okay, but Jinx couldn't help but wonder what he would do next. Engrosed in Reece's assignment Jinx felt his heart stop as the lunch bell rang out, severing his connexion with the crystal.

He bid the crystal to rest and covered it with a protective felt sleeve so that its power would not be disturbed. He knew very well that all crystals were powerful and the more a crystal was used, the more likely it would take an impression of that person and they could become very dangerous indeed. Just like the crystal his grandmother had in her casting room. The one she said dated back to the first Pren Ceri. A man of legend, power and no mercy. A man called- Sigtrygg.

How he'd found that out was a pure accident. He remembered his grandmother popping out of one of his many lessons. She had left Jinx alone in her casting room to study what he found to be a very boring herbalism text. Like most young children spending hours upon hours studying, Jinx had been restless and took the opportunity to nose around.

Initially, he thought he'd play Minecraft on her laptop, but the old witch had secured her precious tech with a password Jinx couldn't break. Defeated, he had spun in her computer chair and caught a glimpse of something hidden in an alcove above the bookcase. Intrigued, he made his way over and climbed the bookcase. He shoved his hands into the alcove and pulled out something heavy shrouded in a black silk hood. Cradling it in a sling he'd made from his T-shirt, he clambered back down and eagerly set it on his grandmother's desk. He pulled at the black silk to reveal, to his surprise, a crystal ball.

Jinx remembered the crystal in detail. It had been a gift to the first Pren Ceri for helping a man with Brazilian bloodlines to heal his sick daughter. Sigtrygg had grown extremely attached to it, or so Jinx was told a few years later.

The crystal itself was beautiful. A rare phantom crystal that had been brought to England with the man's relatives many years previously. He had said it was mined in Minas Gerais by his ancestors who had thought to sell it, but then they couldn't bear to part with it.

Jinx remembered staring at the crystal, a smaller crystal giving a ghostly appearance as it grew inside. It sat elegantly on top of a witch's knot. The four points holding it like superglue in their grasp. At that young age, Jinx had wondered why the stand appeared to be made of silver, real silver. But now he knew that this represented the Goddess.

He remembered being mesmerised by the crystal and stroking a finger gently over its curved surface, before a voice suddenly boomed, "Thy dares to summon me, child!?"

Instantly Jinx had snatched his finger back from the crystal ball, stuttering "I…I…I didn't." He remembered peering around it, perplexed before tapping the surface with his knuckle.

"Are…are you in there?"

"If thou dare touch my crystal ball again, child, my wrath shall enfold upon thee!"

"From in there." Jinx had chuckled impetuously as his hands clasped the crystal ball; his body began to shake with waves of visions sweeping through him.

He saw a young girl with long corn-coloured hair, dressed in a dark woollen dress, petting a little black kitten.

His head hurt.

He then saw the girl and an older version of herself stirring a small black pot over an open fire. Their faces were alight with smiles.

His head pounded and his stinging eyes felt dry. Sweat dripped down his brow and his hands shook feverishly, but he could not let go of the crystal ball. Panic rose within him as another vision took root.

He saw the young girl who was now a woman. A man was with her, holding her hand, and he placed a small old-fashioned key in her palm and smiled… Smiled… Teeth bared… Snapping…

Then a voice roared from inside the crystal and shot sparks of fury from its depths. Jinx was blasted from the crystal's surface. His head cracked against the bookcase and books rained down upon him.

Not long after, Jinx remembered waking with his grandmother crouched in front of him. Her gaze concerned and yet furious as she stared from his charred hands to the crystal ball sitting innocently on her desk.

"Thy may be of Pren Ceri blood, child, but I remain the first," shouted a man's voice with a chuckle from inside the crystal.

Jinx had watched his grandmother raise an indignant eyebrow and cast a banishing spell, before reapplying the silk hood to the crystal.

He had never forgot the lesson he learnt that day: to never underestimate a ghostly essence when it's haunting an object, because you just might end up singed.

Strange, he mused, *I haven't thought about that incident in years.* And yet for some reason the last vision in his memory kept replaying across his mind, as if he was missing something – something important. And then it clicked. *The key… She had the key!*

Chapter 14

Tia

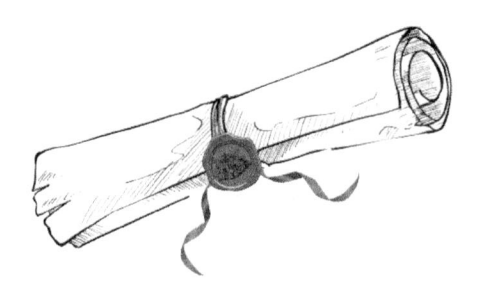

That night, Tia dreamt herself a bystander to her awful memories as they slowly replayed through her nightmares.

Ten year old Tia stood beneath the old oak tree, the fresh mound of dirt at her feet, trembling as before her Yule appeared, her pale skin haunting, the scratch-like marks down her cheeks bleeding and her glazed eyes bulging from bruised sockets.

Beneath her long corn coloured hair, she wore a necklace of rope burns.

Tia hadn't recalled Yules full appearance before and in remembering it so long ago that her subconscious ingrained it in her nightmare, was unnerving.

Yule's shoulders were mottled with bruises of every colour, scribbled like a child's drawing. Scratches etched her bare arms.

She tugged at what once resembled a dress; before it's niceties were torn and splatter stained by the polution of refuse and grime. She floated closer and unveiled a hand like a zombie breaking free of the earth.

Tia couldn't help but tremble as her younger self let out a blood-curdling scream.

Yule stretched out a hand, and the young Tia tumbled backwards. That's when things got strange. The face of her ten-year-old self focused, but the features were all wrong. Her eyes were suddenly dark, her chin pointed, and her lips were thin and sneering with malevolence.

Malevolence directed at Yule as she cursed, "Yule Winter, I damn thee now as thou were damned in life!" Raw masculinity dripped from the gravelly voice that spilled from the lips of her ten-year-old self. "I sentence thee to eternal death, for the crime of…"

The words trailed off as she ripped herself from the horrific nightmare of her past. Raking her hands through dishevelled hair, her frustration palpable, she tried to remember the sentence, the sentence the malevolent spirit made her younger self enact. *What crime had Yule committed to deserve eternity in limbo?* A place where she would forever be tormented by her deeds.

Tia looked at the little blue alarm clock nestled on a pile of Anka's beauty magazines. It was two a.m. She sighed, a thick sheen of sweat coated her brow and she wiped it away with a corner of her sheet. *What the bloody hell just happened? I must find Yule. I have to find Yule. I have to know if what i saw was the truth.* Tia rolled to face the little blue alarm clock Anka has propped on a stack of beauty magazines. *2AM- its too early.* She decided to wait as the hours ticked down into minutes, the minutes were eaten up by seconds and the ascension bell chimed noon. Then, finally, she would be free!

When the clock finally ticked around to a decent hour Tia washed and dressed before searching out the only room she had yet to visit in the academy; the G-poss wardrobe. Stepping inside was like opening the doors to Harrods; they had everything from catwalk styles to Victorian bustle panniers.

A large wooden desk stood in the centre manned by a silver haired women slumped over a clip board.

"Name?" She crowed, sucking on her teeth as if they were uncomfortable.

"Tia Morgan. I'm here to-"

"Ascender or G-poss?"

"Ascender, I'm here-"

"Assignments era?" Tia paused, chewing her lip when the old woman raised a wirery eyebrow and looked up at her.

Well I;m certainly not planning on going back to my ghosts era, so what do I want to wear? If i go too fancy like the prada stuff in Anka's magazines then she's sure to suspect something. I know she thought. "Modern- but like jeans and t-shirt." She added quickly.

"Size, favourite colour and hat."

"Medium, turquoise and no thanks although a hoodie would be cool."

"I suppose you will be wanting trainers as well." She snipped, jotting the information down.

"That would be awesome." Tia smiled, unable to help the twinkle in her eyes; today was the start of her new life; her freedom and reuniting with her family.

Unfortunately for Tia things hadn't gone the way she planned. She stormed into the hall, all eyes slamming on her as she entered, dressed in a plain cotton skirt that itched. It stretched from her waist to her tattered trainers peeking out from beneath. There was no way, dead or alive, she'd be caught wearing the little stumpy black things the wardrobe wench had given to her while trying to pass them off as shoes. Her top half was covered in a tight-fitted, long-sleeved matching waistcoat.

The women had tried to bully her into a corset, but she told her that was never going to happen in what her mother used to call 'colourful language'. So they had stuffed her into an abomination they called a shift. They had tamed her raven black hair into a tight teacher-like bun at the back of her head, much to her disappointment. A wicked smile slid across jailor George's face, his eyes shining with mirth.

Enjoy your victories while you can jailor. Tia thought, pissed off that when she returned to her room to change her bag with everything in it was missing.

"Stand over there, Tia," George commanded as he sauntered towards Paul, who was smirking devilishly at her through the form of Cain, his half-manifested ghost.

Tia walking stoically to the far side of the hall, sat cross-legged and watched Paul with his ghost through half-lidded eyes. *He's so different lately-dark. I never know what he's thinking.* She thought. *His comments and jeers always gave me whiplash before but now they're malicious.*

He stood wearing the same outfit of faded jeans and T-shirt he had been wearing the last time she saw him. With one hand on his hip and the other raking through his thick black hair in frustration as he yelled at the unresponsive ghost before him.

Paul turned to his uncle, Jailer George. "There's no point in me transporting him back three years ago just so he can hit 'send' on some bloody blueprints for a car that doesn't even exist!" Paul raged.

Cain stood stock-still, his weight held slightly to one side as he roared back, "It doesn't exist because I never got to send the blueprints, you infantile idiot."

"Oh yeah, why was that, then?" He stopped pacing and glared at the ghost, his cheeks alight with rage, his eyes sparkling dangerously as the piercing in his brow appeared to darken.

"The handbrake on the car slipped, it rolled, my leg got trapped, and then I fell. The next thing I knew, I'm dead! A stupid accident! Least I didn't give up on life like that no good boy of mine. He had it all, but he just never listened!" he shouted as the glass of water George held exploded, sending sharp shards splaying across the room.

"Bloody hell!" George yelped. "Paul, go cool off and bring back something to clean this up." He motioned to the spray of fractured glass around him.

Strange, Tia mused. *There's no glass by Paul.* Tia watched Paul stop to glance at her and hurl a curveball that made sure she kept her eyes firmly stuck to the small table in the centre of the room and her mind far away from him.

"There's plenty of me to go around, Te. Don't worry." With a step towards her, he added, "Damn, you look so fragile in that outfit. So delectable. I can almost taste you."

As she flicked her eyes up to him, she was caught in a momentary trance at the faint flicker of darkness over his left brow. Tia shook her head, dislodging the compulsion to stare. *God I'm losing it!* "The only thing you'll be tasting is a knuckle sandwich if you get any closer to me," she spat, her rage barely contained as the large hall door slammed open.

Paul sniffed the air dramatically scrunching his nose "Witch." He turned and stalked from the room with a parting of, "Later. Te Bee."

Tia grimaced at the affectionate nickname. Why was it she attracted moronic psychopaths who thought 'no' meant 'yes'?

Her eyes spun back to the door as it slammed shut, revealing the young man she'd bumped into in Garth's bunkhouse. The young man who, with his touch, had somehow calmed her. The young man Paul had called 'witch'. Tia stood up drawn by the magnetism of him.

His eyes shone with barely supressed anger, which he managed to subdue before nodding to jailor George.

"Good breakfast?" George criticised, glancing theatrically at his wristwatch.

Tia took a deep breath and let her gaze wander the length of the witch's body. His chocolate brown hair was worn in corn braids, coloured stones glinted from their tips. His earthy green eyes locked onto her's for a fraction of a second before he swiped a large hand over his face. He wore a jewelled ring on one hand, which glittered as he continued his walk to the small table in the centre of the room. His white long-sleeved vest top stretched tightly over his well-defined abs, he wore faded jeans slung low on his hips. His trainers were tidy but old and looked sporty, but from this distance she couldn't really tell.

"Tia!" yelled George, making her jump out of her trance.

"What now?" she groaned.

"Where is your ghost?"

"Obviously not here," Tia replied obnoxiously while spreading her arms wide and giving a little head jolt to emphasise the point. Before she knew it, George was before her, his anger hissing through his teeth like steam.

"Then call her," he growled.

"Yule," she called lamely.

After throwing his hands in the air with exasperation, George grabbed Tia's wrist, hauled her to the desk in the centre of the room and shoved her into the wooden chair opposite the witch.

"Stay!" he roared.

I'm not a damned dog. Tia thought as he then turned to the witch who watched on casually. "You- house witch- watch the girl. I'll be back when I've talked some sense into my nephew." He turned to walk away but stopped. "You, ghost. If you want to move on, you had better bloody well help me! Now come on!" They exited the room with matching expressions of exasperation.

Tia slumped in the chair, the long skirt ruffling to her knees. Determined to keep her gaze from the witch sat opposite, Tia focused on the crystal ball and desperately tried to see into it.

What the hell? She thought, peering to take a closer look as the crystal's surface fogged over, and tiny images began to flicker rapidly within its depths.

She gasped, shock and awe mixing a lethal cocktail inside her mind. She felt drawn to the crystal, entranced.

A tap on the table's surface made her jolt to attention, accidentally catching the witch's gaze. He drummed his fingers along the edge of the desk, his eyes shining with more curiosities about her then an undiscovered galaxy.

"The art of divination is a soul art." His words were measured, soft and smooth in their tone.

"So?"

He wiped a hand over his face and locked his eyes- "Both you and I using the crystal makes the images flicker."

"You-you what?" She asked, eyebrow raised. Jinx leaned in close mouthing the words slowly- "You heard me." His lips twitches at the edges.

Tia's felt her mouth gape. "I...I didn't use your stupid crystal! I don't even know how!" she defended as a whisper on the wind tickled her ear.

The witch stared at her, clicked his fingers before her face and furrowed his brow in confusion after she showed no signs of acknowledgement.

Tia was entranced, too busy staring deep inside the crystal, where she saw an image of Reece manically scratching at his skin beneath a floaty woollen dress. She chuckled, which drew Jinx's attention.

Upon seeing the comical image, Jinx whistled and said, "Damn brave, wearing a dress like that."

"Damn stupid!" Tia corrected, peering deeper. "Where is he?" she asked.

Jinx let his awareness seep out through time. He located the pendant around Reece's neck which glowed like a beacon, summoning him. "Fishbourn 1797."

"And that is?" she drilled.

"Wales." He sniggered.

Tia spread her fingers out across the crystal ball attempting to touch the beautiful silken sky that stretched out over a calm winter sea. She could practically smell the salty waves lapping against the rocks.

"There's nothing like the rolling hills of Wales," Reece mumbled from inside the crystal ball, his eyes closed in contentment.

Tia leapt back, her chair scraping against the floor, her hand wrenched from beneath Jinx's.

"You can hear him? That's good." His eyes smiled at her knowingly.

"Good?" Tia questioned, scooting her chair back to the table and replacing her hand.

But Jinx did not elaborate. He just placed his hand on top of hers and the image slowly flickered back to life.

They watched Reece's long legs clamber over rocky Welsh ground. A large inn looming in the distance. A noise sounded, and they watched Reece spin himself around taking a defensive stance when three large men barrelled their way towards him. They were singing drunkenly at the top of their voices in something other than English. The men stood there looking at what appeared to be a young Welsh maiden.

"Bud, don't even think about it," Reece scolded as they came closer.

Tia watched them rounding on Reece saying what she could only imagine to be inappropriate remarks.

"Don't worry, Gwen. I got this," Reece said as they came closer, their bodies perspiring.

"I bet they stink of stale beer," sneered Tia. Her analysis was proven by the wrinkling of Reece's nose.

"Ferme la bouche!" Reece roared at the men. He then whispered, "Shh…its okay Gwen. "I only told him to shut his mouth."

Tia smirked. "Go Reece!"

Suddenly the man to the right of Reece reached out a roughened hand and stroked the length of his sleek black hair, which promptly fell off into his hand. The man reeled back, a scream strangling his throat as he attempted to combat his revulsion.

Reece spun, meeting an attack from the smallest man; his breath must have been rancid because Tia could see Reece's eyes water.

"Bud, you really think you can take me?" Reece sniggered while easily sidestepping the drunken man's loose punch. "Well, I do suppose I'm dressed like a girl." That comment earned him a bubble of laughter from Tia.

"I'm Welsh, bud, and whereas most youngsters play 'fifty out' as kids, us Welsh boys—" he pointed to himself for emphasis "—wrestle sheep for fun. There's no way you can take me!" he taunted, and then smirked when the man's punch shot wide, sidestepping another before a large knuckles scraped his chin, causing his head to snap around.

"Guess that's where over confidence gets you," commented Jinx.

Reece, feigning a knockdown from the next punch, crouched on his knees and swept the feet from under the two nearest men with brutal speed. They went down with roars of anger as the third man snarled. "You pretend be girl, so not fight Frenchman. Coward!" The Frenchman threw the wig at Reece who caught it and placed it back on his head with a wry smile.

The large man called his friends away and they all returned to the tavern, looks of disgust painting their faces as they ranted. "Well, that was fun." Reece rubbed the welt that was forming on his chin and added, "Kind of."

Jinx pulled his stare from the crystal ball, instead placing it on the girl before him; her lips pulled in a tight smile. He watched entranced as her tongue spread a trail of moisture over her plump, kissable lips. Her eyes shone with magic she could not see; unaware to her, he guided her in bidding the crystal. Her hand beneath his was smooth and melded perfectly in his palm. *My girl.* The thought ran through his head unbidden, and he tried to squash it. This girl was trouble. This girl was dangerous.

This girl is exciting, countered his heart.

"Why you staring?"

"I'm not. I was just… Hey, look." He rapidly shot his attention back to the crystal ball where Reece stood in an old barn packed to the brim with traditionally dressed women.

"Your pa's already left?" Reece whispered. "He's fighting with the soldiers at…?" he asked, nodding as Gwen gave him the answer in his mind. "Goodwick Sands. Okay."

Jinx tuned out of Reece's conversation to watch a strongly built woman take charge and direct the surrounding women as though they were soldiers. He knew her only from history, but Jemima Nicholas in person was amazing.

Her aura seeped into the village women who were afraid for their husbands, their fathers and brothers, their sons, nephews and cousins. She gave them spirit, strength and the opportunity to have a hand in their future. To support and protect their men. She gave them a vision of uniting under the Welsh flag to run the foreign, pillaging scum off their land – forever!

In admiring the legendary women, Jinx spotted a small group of girls where Reece now stood. The barely teenage girls hauled baskets of rocks on their hips and sat the younger girls, including a very much alive Gwen, in a circle around them while they gave instructions on how best to help their families.

From what Jinx could decipher from Reece's mumblings, the gist of their plot was to stay on the clifftops and hurl rocks at the unsuspecting French below. Jinx's eyes glanced up towards Tia; he watched contemplation subtly spread over her features.

"It could work," she offered.

A commotion outside drew Jinx's attention. Garth stood yelling at a man around Jinx's age, a man who looked incredibly like the young ascender Paul. *Does Paul have an older brother?* Jinx mused. The man had the same dark hair. He wore black shades, and was that an eyebrow piercing he could see glowing dark in the sunlight? The man certainly had the same temper, Jinx decided as their eyes met through a clear section of the stained glass window.

A shudder of magic ran down Jinx's spine. But before he could move, the man was gone. All he could see was Garth's profile in the window slowly walking away. *What were they fighting about?* he wondered.

Jinx's attention broke at Tia's comment.

"Ooh goodie, let the fun begin!" He swiftly turned back to the crystal ball where hordes of Welsh women were climbing the steep incline of cliffs overhanging Goodwick Sands. Behind them, unknown to the women, marched the young girls, including Gwen, all baring solemn expressions.

Jinx could understand how the French soldiers were fooled into thinking the rows of marching women were soldiers; their traditional dress was enough to subdue a man into the greatest of respects.

He watched in awe as Jemima Nicholas roared her famous battle cry with a pitchfork raised above her head. The women rallied around her on their ascent of the cliffs to fight for their land and men. Jinx was so caught up in the action that he almost missed Gwen caught off balance and tumble into a jutting rock.

"Shit!" screeched Tia. "Oh God, poor kid." Her hands trembled on the crystal's surface.

Applying a little pressure to console Tia, Jinx watched Reece trudge on- oblivious. He climbed to the top of the cliffs along with the girls, where they pelted rocks onto the unsuspecting victims below. When all the rocks had been thrown, the girls dispersed, affording Reece a glance of Gwen's final resting place.

Jinx watched sweat bead on Reece's forehead. He bent over trying not to gag when Gwen's ghostly essence sifted its way from her body in a shimmer of light.

"Diolch," she whispered as she turned to the air that was already rippling with the effect of Reece's transportation. Two seconds later, Reece rematerialized in front of them, his pallor a sickly green as he ran from the room, his skirt hitched up and one hand clutching his mouth and the other his stomach.

Poor Reece.

"Ti-a," a voice whispered.

Tia took a deep breath trying to calm herself and flew out of her seat, smacking into the witch's hand and knocking the wooden chair flying.

"Get out here, Yule! Get out where I can see you!" she stormed, her voice echoing around the large, almost empty, room.

"H-elp."

At that moment, the witch rose from his chair. He stepped around Tia taking a protective stance in front of her while a ghostly orb blinked in and out of view.

Pushing the meddling witch aside Tia screamed- "What kind of game are you playing now? Are you gonna throw something? Write on the walls? Or just moan eerily in the air?"

Chapter 15

Jinx

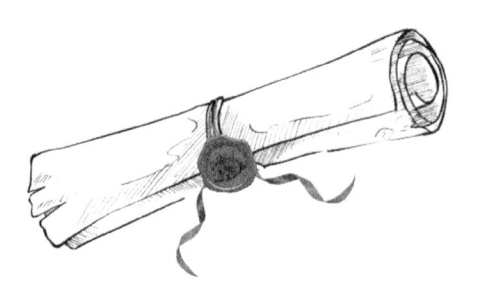

The bright orb blipped in and out of view like a beacon before the Ascender who had shoved him aside- not that he couldn't have stopped her if he had been aware she was so strong willed.

Jinx quirked an eyebrow at her 'don't mess with me' attitude and his lips parted in a slight smile. He liked powerful women who knew their own mind, and this girl was so tantalising. He just wanted to grab her and tie her to him forever. But he didn't, for she would probably bolt like a caged tiger. Or more likely attack him the first chance she got, and then he would never see her again. He sighed and refocused watching cautiously as the iridescent orb slowly bobbed closer. Its fading light flashed in and out of focus like a lighthouse alerting ships of rocky shores.

Jinx watched the girl who had stepped beside him, her modified puritan outfit clinging tightly to the contours of her tense body. Unwittingly he licked his lips. He could sense the fear beneath her rage. *Why is she afraid?* He wondered, studying her face in his perhibial vision as she glowered at the strange pulsing orb.

How could she possibly have a fear that runs so deep that I can see it within her soul? She is frightened, maybe even terrified, but what I've miscalculated before is the sadness flowing from her eyes. It was the kind of sorrow that shattered a person's soul, and damn him if he didn't want to pick up all the beautiful pieces and tenderly coax them back together. He'd never felt this way about anyone. None of the girls in his faction tugged at his heartstrings like a marionette; but this girl did.

Jinx shook his head and concentrated on her yelling at the blinking orb, the light from it fading further with its ever-begging plea. The possibility of this being the malicious spirit was high because the girl had said the spirit was 'playing games'.

He sent out his awareness in order to seek an insight on the potentially 'malicious' orb. He could see Tia's aura wrapped around her like a blood-red ribbon, pulsing in alarm, her strength and anger palpable beneath its radiance. He sent it further towards the blinking orb, letting its essence guide him until he had a true picture of the soul it bore.

Its aura, a calm indigo, barely glowed. Its matt appearance indicated a sad, sensitive person. There was no malice there. No anger.

When Tia died, with her being a ghost possessor and witch she could make one seriously powerful ghost. so he sent out a silent prayer: *Goddess help me if Tia died. She may just make the strongest Cacodaemon yet – if she decides to follow that path.*

Jinx could feel the orb had an unbearable sense of sorrow weighing on his psyche like a sponge in water. He could sense she masked it by a fear so intense he could practically smell it. Pulling his awareness back he gently reached out a hand and touched the orb.

It faded from sight, and the girl next to him glared angrily at his interference. *She's definitely a Gemini*, thought Jinx with a smile.

Slowly the orb re-manifested. Jinx felt his fingers touch it as its light rippled wearily around them. "Steady there," he cooed. "I won't hurt you." He coaxed the orb closer. "I'm here to help. What's your name?" Jinx listening intently as the orb vibrated on his fingertips, willing him to understand even though exhaustion had rendered it speechless.

A hand gently touched his arm and he gazed down into the beautiful cobalt blue depths of Tia's eyes.

Goddess. He sighed internally. *A man could drown in those endless pools; if not willingly, then she would definitely be capable of driving a man to it.*

"Her name's Yule. She is my ghost assignment. The reason I'm dressed like this," moaned the girl as she stared down at the plain cloth of the puritan costume.

Jinx smirked, a tiny dent forming to the side of his lips as he channelled his energy down through his hand. The power tingling through his fingertips and into the orb, pulsing with energy as it slowly sucked at it like a starving kitten.

Jinx jerked back, pulling his touch from the forming ghost.

He stared. The ghost woman's hair hung soiled and filth ridden down her back, her pale almost translucent neck bore the trademark branding of a hangman's noose. Nail marks raked the skin on her face. Her blackened eyes claimed brutality as she stared back through the blinding fog that clouded them.

Jinx found himself praying to the Goddess that this spirit, with help, could and would move on.

"See," the girl at his side gloated, "it's not like she's presentable." The girl smirked at him, a shadow of pain darkening her beautiful eyes as she turned her attention to the ghost and started ruthlessly scolding her.

Goddess, she's callous, thought Jinx. The girl's anger blazed when the ghost whispered her broken pleas, their effect like gasoline to the girl's sparking anger.

"Where the hell do you get off ghost peeping at me while I'm taking a bath?" she yelled.

Jinx captured Tia's flailing hands and pinned them in his own. "please- calm down. Tia, I apologise. I did not mean to intrude on your bathing. Alas, I beg you- help-"

"How dare you ghost write on my mirror, and with blood. Do you really think scaring me senseless will make me help you? Couse you can haunt me for eternity, scare me into madness, and I still won't help you! I. Hate. You. You'd have better luck scaring me if you'd just appeared out of nowhere. After all, your resemblance to the walking dead is profound!"

"Enough!" Jinx's voice bellowed. His power-filled tone radiated throughout the vast reception hall, steeling her breath.

Tia felt her mouth dry in response to the witch's command. Her ability to speak was made hard from the lack of moisture in her mouth, even though she was continuously gulping. Her eyes began to roll as her heart rate ratcheted. "Look at me!" Jinx ordered the panicked girl gasping at the dried air. "Please, look at me," he coaxed. He shifted one of his large hands to encompass one of hers and gently lifted a finger to tilt her beautiful, stubborn chin in his direction.

Looking into her striking eyes he could see the clouds of terror forming as his senses prickled with alarm at a presence forming behind him. Jinx shivered slightly at the cold spot that was the official calling card of a young spirit.

Without taking form, it reached up to touch his arm. Frozen daggers clawed the length of it as the spirit tugged at him, forcing him to crouch. A freezing wind blew into his right ear; "T-Bear is sad. hug her."

Strange, he thought. Then, just like that, the wind disappeared and the icy daggers melted away. The cold spot in which the small formless spirit resided had vanished.

Rising to his full height of six foot three, Jinx looked down at the girl who quivered in his arms. He didn't blame her for being scared; he was sure she would have felt the cold emanating from the formless spirit, too. But now, he had to calm her soul.

"Please, Tia." His words were no more than a whisper. A secret between the two of them, but there was no mistaking the heart breaking question in her eyes now glittering, their flood gates full to bursting.

Jinx placated her with the familiar words of the formless spirit, "T-Bear, calm down." But unable to meet the distressed eyes before him, swung the girl into a solid embrace; the stable warmth of his arms the only comfort he could offer her. He shivered. *When did it get so cold? Are you back?* He asked the little spirit.

Crash! A sudden darkness fell upon the hall when the destruction of a large Edwardian chandelier hanging from the centre of the hall exploded. Vibrant sparks of deadly glass rained like vengeful stars upon them. A warning scream shrilled through the spacious room and rattled the stained glass windows that were thick with ice.

Jinx felt his soul shrivel in an attempt to hide from the malicious energy seeping through the oak front doors like poisoned shadows. Its mastering form slammed the heavy doors back onto their now broken hinges with a resonating crunch.

A torrent of autumn leaves whipped around the malevolent spectre; all eyes widened with terror in his direction. It wore a long black coat with white ruffle collar, over the top of which hung a large wooden cross. His dark brooding features were shaded by a large black felt hat, which he wore on a head of dark curly hair. The malevolence he emanated was pure poison. The gardens haunters of shadow people, spirits and orbs had vanished. Even the ecto-plasmic clouds had run for cover.

Leaving the dark backdrop of the compound's graveyard standing eerily silent. Its blood moon hung low, lighting the manifestation like a macabre halo.

The bitter cold bit into Tia like the teeth of a cryogenic vampire. She shivered, teeth chattering, as her blood cells slowed their race around her veins. *Holy crap!* Thought was painful, but she forced her numb brain to think.

The screams echoing around the hall broke the eerie silence and sent shockwaves of icy stalactites crashing to the floor with deadly force. Tia watched the spectre drift forwards to the centre of the hall, horizontal penitentes sprouting from him.

He waved his hands around in an odd motion, as though pulling multiple things on an invisible chain.

Jinx's nose twitched and then scrunched up instinctively, his eyes watering. *Oh Goddess, what is that smell?!* It stank of putrid old meat, the festering kind left at the bottom of a café bin that someone forgot to clean. The kind with maggots worming their way through it. *But where in the Goddess's name was it coming from?*

That's when Jinx first noticed the ghostly shadows with sharp, hideous claws and razor teeth. Swarming around the malevolent witch hunter who was staring at Tia, a small smile of satisfaction playing on his lips. He cracked his hands apart, as if he was breaking something, and then suddenly the shadows whipped forwards to attack.

Icy tears fell from Jinx's eyes as the putrid stench of burning flesh filled his nostrils. Malevolence radiate from the spectre like a suffocating smog. Their poisonous essences were thickest above him and the girl he held protected in his arms.

Tia sensed Jinx's power vibrate within him. His diaphragm contracted tightly as he began to chant an unbreakable stream of foreign words. When his mantra came to a crescendo, one by one the old wall scones lit to brighten the black unseeing night with their rays. Tia felt more than heard the change in Jinx's chant; the tempo slightly altered and the language seemed slightly older and more commanding. The attacking shadows above him drew back a little. His concentration on their advances was so absolute that he didn't notice Tia gently prise herself from the protection of his arms. Sliding beneath their circling barrier, she slowly skidded her way over to Yule who was sobbing into her pale hands and trying unsuccessfully to shade the spectre from her view.

"You're what's been chasing her!" Tia raged, the pieces of the puzzle finally connecting in her mind.

The predatorily shadow that had been stalking Yule dissipated under the spectre's command to 'be gone'. His yellowed teeth snarled with anticipation as he turned his attention to Tia.

"Stand ye down, gal!" he sneered.

Tia winced and shrank back in a mix of bone shaking fear and stunned shock. *Why is he warning me?* A shift of motion caused her eyes to dart towards the open doors of the hall, where a figure moved stealthily through the maze of gravestones slowly gaining ground towards her, before pouncing onto the spectre's back and locking its head between his strong arms.

Garth was peering over the top of the spectre's shoulders "run!"

He's not a G-Poss. He's not a G-poss! How can he touch that thing?

As the two wrestled the spectres shadows began clawing their way back to him, sliding over his forms and ripping Garth away, dragging him from sight at an unnatural velocity.

The enraged spectre roared, and shards of ice fell, striking all around them. Screams of pain reverberated around the hall. Tia glanced quickly at Jinx who was still lost in his chant. His body shook with exertion while he seemed to keep the evil sharp-toothed shadows a distance away from inside.

Abruptly, the back entrance doors crashed open and a red faced George stomp in. "About time the boy transported, can't see what's taken him so long," he mumbled. "His ghost's only been deceased three years – it should be easy! Some bloody nephew he's turned out to be!" Oblivious to what was going on, he continued, "Boy's never been worth Yazmin's life. She should never have had him. Stupid…"

All of a sudden, George turned his attention to the situation in the room. "What the bloody hell is going on?!" he bellowed, his podgy form racing across the hall. His hand reached for the pouch of salt belted around his enlarged waist. But there was barely enough time to open it before the spectre stood behind him, knocking the salt in a steady stream until it cascaded over Yule like a waterfall of impending doom.

Yule screamed, her body withering and hissing as Tia watched the salt slowly burn her from existence. *No!* Tia couldn't believe it but her conscious- cared.

George turned to face down the spectre, but it was too late. With a sickening crunch, George hit the far wall at an unnatural angle.

Still chanting, Jinx somehow appeared beside him and gave a slight nod in Tia's direction. *Is this confirmation that he's okay? Or that I'm the only one who can…* Her thoughts trailed off as the spectre suddenly appeared before her.

Tia's terror forced her to step back from the green glow surrounding them, but she lost her footing, and then the revelation of six years ago dawned on her as she fell into Yules burning spirit, who unintentionally starting to possess her. She shrunk back as she felt Yule's presence invade her mind, just as the evil spectre had when she was a child. *Was it me who possessed the evil spirit?* She wondered. *Was it my fault? No. It couldn't be. It would mean that all this time it wasn't only Yule's fault but- but mine. No.* She shook her head. *I won't accept it. It was the spirit's fault, and Yule's. It ha nothing to do with me.*

Tia's mind spun from the muddle consuming it; she could feel the salt burning through Yule and bleeding slowly into her. Its scalding hot presence created enough pain to incapacitate her brain forever. But it was a sad relief to the bitter cold that had numbed her brain. *I'm definitely getting heat rash from this,* Tia moaned internally.

Suddenly, Yule's screams bled her brain to rawness as the salt travelled with speed throughout her internal system. Tia's screams joined her's as she scratched gouges out of her skin trying to rip the salt from her bloodstream- without success. Her stomach shrivelled under the attack, her heart beat erratically, all the while the salt spread like lightening through her veins- slowly burning away the essence of Yule's life force from within her.

Tia sucked deep, burning breaths into her lungs, their capacity to work failing her as she reached for the only place free of the salt's attack: her soul. She felt the protective strum of the chanting barricading her soul from the assault and knew in that moment that Jinx was not only protecting the academy, but also protecting the souls of those caught up in this horrific battle. And life be damned if she wouldn't fight back, too!

Tia let her rage boil. She was not some stupid maiden from a fairy tale waiting to be rescued. She looked up at the malicious spectre whose eyes were gleaming with evil satisfaction.

His large hand clasped the expanse of Tia's throat, firmly restricted her airways. "Aren't ye a clever little witch?" he sneered.

While the stench of burning flesh filled her nostrils, Tia concentrated on the peace in her soul, blocking out Yule's horrific screams. Her life force seemed to beat to a different rhythm and suddenly she felt her whole body thrum along to Jinx's undistinguishable words. It was as though her soul knew the language, but her brain had forgotten the words.

Pressure built inside her as she hummed to the rhythmical chant as the crescendo slowly peaked, a bone-deep scream of raw power shot the burning salt back through her pores. Then exploded in the air around her like a nova bomb.

Suddenly the world was silent. Her throat was no longer cinched, no longer being crushed. She watched with heavy eyes as the malevolent spectre flailed, scratching and hissing under the purifying salt.

Tia slipped to the floor- exhausted as she gasped in deep, stinging lungfuls of air. Sweat soaked her body, dripping like a lit candle she looked up to see the spectre had disappeared – and so had everyone else!

Chapter 16

Jinx

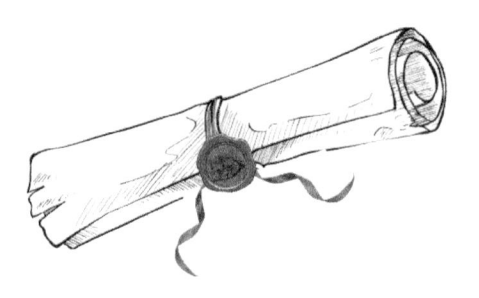

Hissing and steaming from burns inflicted by the salt, the spectre had turned to Jinx after Tia vanished. Its malevolence gleamed through sinister eyes that bored ice shards into his flesh.

Salt shrapnel snapped at the spectre as it screamed a vendetta of retribution that sent shivers playing his spinal column like a xylophone. 'Thou shalt not suffer a witch to live!'

Exodus 22:18. Jinx's bones froze. *Maybe Grandmother was right to fear the witch trials might return.*

The spectre before him vanished, its shrill cry echoing around the reception hall whilst a semiconscious George groaned and potentials murmured.

Panting, chest heaving, Jinx released his protection spell and fell wearily to his knees. Suddenly the back door to the hall flung open, and in raced scores of G-Poss warriors, a chanted prayer on their lips as they held fisted palms of salt, sifting through they're fingers as they ran.

What in Goddesses name happened? Jinx thought. Surveying the destruction around him. He had seen Tia In Jinx's peripheral vision he'd vaguely noticed Tia expelling the salt from her body. *Has she embraced her witch side, accessing her powers? Does she even know she has powers?* Jinx rubbed his head in thought. *Where have they gone? What will Tia's mission be before she can return home?* He rubbed a hand over his face. *Would she...change?* His eyes sparkled. *No, not his Tia. She would come back more impetuous than ever.* He smiled.

Jinx, weary to the bone, bowed his head to his knees. "Thank you, Goddess, for the magic I bear." *For a lesser witch wouldn't have stood a chance,* thought Jinx. His worst fears were recognised when he laid eyes on the evil spectre. He felt the death stains of innocence upon its wicked soul.

The stench of burning witch flesh upon its sinister soul was enough to contest to his assault of Fiona; her murderer.

. *Oh, Goddess*, Jinx rationalised, *the spectre is not only a Cacodaemon – a spirit most evil – but it is also a hunter. A witch hunter!*

Jinx ignored the G-Poss warriors taking protective stances around the academy's fractured oak doors and staring intently at him like a mutating disease under a microscope. His depleted magic attempted to make some of the more stubborn G-Poss stand aside.

"Move!" he roared. The G-Poss turned to stare at him belittlingly, turning their backs in a blatant show of their ignorance. They stood like bloodhounds, awaiting the scent of their prey, ready to pounce and destroy. Still they were ignorant of the fact that this was no ordinary spectre. *This ghost had evolved – he is truly an abomination- a spirit of horror*, Jinx thought. The G-Poss's rage had shrouded their minds.

Fearing that their precious ghost barriers were being breached had them protecting their home, instead of doing the job they were born to do: ridding the world of lingering spirits – no matter how dangerous.

If the G-Poss were anything, they were sticklers for rules. Years of traditions had been handed down to them, along with the G-Poss's most primal instincts to hate anyone witch born. Whether they had magic or not.

The G-Poss viewed witches as the enemy. The whole reason the G-Poss existed in the first place was because of witches. Or rather, their evil counterparts: warlocks. They were the number one cause for traumatic ghost producing deaths, due to their ill intent and ritualistic work. And to clear up their ghostly mess, Death himself had created the G-Poss, or so their story went. *Why Death suddenly intervened?* Jinx had no idea. *Maybe he was bored?* But the G-Poss's legendary prejudice was blinding; that's why Jinx found himself shunned from the room where he could do the most good.

"Bloody prejudiced G-Poss," Jinx mumbled as he reluctantly backed away from the warriors at the doors. He caught a glimpse of a young girl waving frantically at him from the corner of his eye. Slowly, he backed towards her, keeping a wary eye out in case the G-Poss noticed. "What?" He whispered when he was in range.

"Ya wanna get out of here, right?" she asked blowing her blue bubble gum, popping it with her teeth and then chewing it back up again. "I know a way," she coaxed. Jinx raised a tired brow.

"Come on," she said, taking his hand. "Ya don't remember me, do ya?"

Jinx, sighed, his body tremored with fatigue but shoving the exhaustion aside, he stared intently at the young girl. -as if he could forget her. She was practically a carbon copy of Tia, the half-G-Poss, half-witch he found himself taking too much of an interest in. The young girl before him had badly dyed hair tied up in tight pigtails, highlighting the strong features of her face.

"I remember you, Ella. I would be grateful for any assistance you can provide me." He sighed and pointed to the main doors. "Those ghouls dragged Garth away, and I have no way of knowing what state they've left him in." *Or if he's even alive*, he added silently.

The young potential instantly started sprinting, dodging and weaving as Jinx willed his weary bones to keep up with her through the corridors littered with notebooks and rucksacks from the evacuation. Jinx leapt over bags, skidded on some papers and kicked at water bottles in his way.

Ella ushered him through the corridors towards the canteen, which he remembered the potentials calling the 'pigpen'- *it certainly looks like a sty now.* He thought as they raced through amongst trays, food, drinks and Goddess knew what all scattered around the floor. They raced out the back door, which was propped open by a box of toppled groceries.

A gravel path swept around the building and into the graveyard surrounding it. *Sill no ghosts.* He thought, taking a deep lungful of air, but instead of fresh flowers and grass he was greeted by the stench of decomposed flesh. He sneezed, turned back towards Ella and said- "Thank you, now go back inside."

"But I can help ya." Ella huffed, her eyes gleaming with defiant irritation.

"Inside, Ella. Now! I;m not joking this is serious!" With a childish pout and defiant stomp of her foot, she turned and sulked back into the building. Jinx tried to suppress a grin of amusement on his way around the gravel pathway and towards the front of the ivy entrapped building. He had no time to be stealthy so he was thankful adrenalin had kicked in to speed up his loud crunching steps.

He could see the dark poisonous shadows of the ghouls the Cacodaemon's presence had summoned them from their prison graves. They swarmed Garth, his raucous wails of agony displacing the air around him as their insidious evil claws raked at his tender human skin.

Jinx snuck forwards and hid behind a large moss-covered gravestone. The ragged crack running down its centre had created tiny perforations where it had crumbled away. Through the crack, he spied a slight clearing where the ghouls viciously attacked Garth.

A sudden *crunch* rang out as a ghoul struck the round headstone before him. Its partially formed body now impaled; it lay there contently sucking on Garth's skin wedged within its claws. With every pull, the life energy flowing through him was extracted, rendering the ghoul drunkenly intoxicated by its essence.

Jinx thumbed the protection gemstones weaved into his braids. They reminded him of the day he received them from his sister. His hand trembled slightly when he touched a single crystal. They were all he had left of his sister since his grandmother sent her away. The last dribble of power sparking erratically from his fingertips as he watched the ghouls surrounding Garth. He watched as the closest one licked its blade-like teeth glistening with blood.

Jinx ran, sliding on the wet dirt, darting beneath the clutches of an angry ghoul. After he whispered a prayer on his lips, the ghoul that attempted to claw at him retreated. A shrieking hiss coming from it, steam smoking from its claws.

The ghouls ghosted closer, their shadowy forms bleeding over the grass like sick imitations of Rorschach patterns. Jinx tore his gaze away as they oozed closer towards him; the air around him turned bitterly cold by their malicious presence. He turned to run, but he stumbled over the bloody form of Garth. Jinx struck the cobbled earth alongside him with a thud as he let his Goddess guide his fingers to a braid of hair containing an energy-soaked gemstone. He prayed it would help him.

Ripping it from his head, his eyes watering from the pain, he caressed its greyish-blue surface. "Goddess, let it be," he begged before tossing it high into the air, letting his reserve magic spark free to join it.

Its surface glowed like magma as it exploded into dozens of tiny particles that ricocheted out at the ghouls. They shrivelled and shrieked while melting into sickening stench-ridden puddles of decay. Jinx watched with satisfaction as they slowly seeped into the pores of the earth where they once again became chained by the gravestones above them.

Breathing a sigh of relief, Jinx turned to Garth and only then noticed the squelch of the blood-soaked earth beneath him. He stared in horror at his friend's shredded body.

"Goddess, they've torn you apart," gritted Jinx through anger-clenched teeth. He cursed at the blood seeping through the shirt he'd pulled from his body and wadded it against his friend's wound. Garth's pallor was grey and dark circles sunk his eyes as his life slowly bled from his body.

"No, no. Hang on. Don't die now!" Jinx yelled rising from the ground, his eyes sparking like lightening rods, he began to cast:

"Goddess divine,

My soul to thine,

The earth she hath fed,

From blood of innocence,

I beg thee rewind,

And encase us in time,

Until help doth arrive!"

A deathly roar swelled from the pit of Jinx's stomach as he screamed his will into the wind. Collapsing on the earth beneath him, he devotedly awaited his Goddess's power to invoke the spell he had cast.

"That's some…bloody stone!" Garth gurgled, blood bubbling from his mouth. "Always said…I'd go out with a…bang!"

Jinx frantically raked his hand through his hair watching the blood slow from his friend's torn up body. Gradually it lessened to a pulsating drip until finally suspending its frantic escape.

With the blood of his friend soaking his shirtless body, he slowly slipped his mobile from his jeans pocket and punched in his grandmothers number. It rang for a few seconds before she picked up with a haughty, "What now?!"

"It's me, Grandmother – Jinx," he slurred.

"Jinx, you sound awful. And since when did you stop calling me High Elder? Why are you calling? I thought we had agreed that you'll stay at the—"

Jinx cut in and mustered all the authority his voice could manage as he ordered, "I need Hope's number. My friend is dying, and she can help."

He listened to the tapping of a pen hitting his grandmother's desk as she took her time to contemplate his request. "No."

"What!?" Jinx roared in indignation.

"She is powerless! Dead to us! I thought you'd accepted that a long time ago." His grandmother sighed pityingly, the drum of her fingers still audioable over the connexion. Jinx took a deep breath. It would not help to argue with his grandmother, when her mind was made up she stood like a rock in the water.

But his friend was dying, and his sister was the only one he knew capable of saving him.

"High Elder," he tried again, focusing on her love of power to gain an advantage, "evil spirits attacked my friend. The spirits of ghouls. But they were only partially formed. I thought only witches could be harmed by such spirits." Jinx left the question open, hanging it in the air like bait on a rod.

After a long pause, she answered, "It is true that the undead, unless fully formed, cannot touch mortals. How have they harmed him?" she asked.

Jinx quickly reeled in her in. "They've clawed pieces of flesh from his body. I saw one suck at the flesh. It appearing drunk afterwards." Fatigue laced his voice, his arm began sagging.

"Yes. Yes, on life essence. Interesting."

"High Elder, please," Jinx begged as the old woman crooned over the information he'd provided.

"Yes, yes of course, it would not do to have this...special being die before we can question him. "Jinx heaved a sigh of relief. He would figure out how Garth could escape being his grandmothers guinnypig later- if he survived. "I will talk with the G-Poss leaders and have them pick him up. You have done well, Jinx. I can see this situation helping with the petition we are proposing. Blessed be, Grandson"

Her words reverberated around his mind; time encased him in a frozen stasis. Although motionless, Jinx could see the traumatic impression left by the ghouls on the earth around the compound. Blood stained the grass a rusty red, dripping from gravestones where they had flung chunks of Garth's bloody flesh. The graves were cracked where their evil malevolence had been returned and chained beneath the earth.

Jinx's, his adrenalin burnt out, felt his mind whirling with an erratic tornado of thoughts. It drifted first to his friend. *Will*

Hope arrive to save him in time? Is he suffering from being a frozen moment in time, or has the Goddess mercifully suspended his pain while we're locked in this stasis? He sighed, his thoughts flitting to his sister. *What will she think of me?* It had been nine years since he'd seen her, and he had to admit he was a little nervous. *Will she recognise me? Will I recognise her? When I become High Witch Elder, the first thing I'll do is shut down the academy for defective—* he frowned internally; the word 'defective' repulsed him —*witches.* Angry thoughts switched to flickering peace as he thought of the girl with sumptuous raven hair. *Where has she gone?*

Chapter 17

Tia

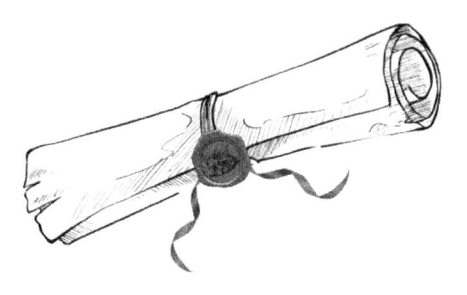

The swirls of noise penetrating Tia's subconscious drew her from a nightmare of ghostly faces screaming at her like a choir from hell. Her eyes fluttered open, pain lanced them as she realised she was staring up into the burning embers of the setting sun.

"What the…? Where am I?" Her voice hissed through cracked lips *how long have I been unconscious?*

Just minutes, a voice resonated inside her mind.

What the…? And then she remembered the academy, the witch hunter and Yule. *Oh God, I possessed Yule!* Tia's inner scream made her ears ring with white noise as she tried to deny her new reality.

Tia lay on her back in some kind of alley, squished between… *Are those buildings wooden?* She blinked twice. *Yes, yes they are. Where the hell am I?*

1645. There was the voice again. The voice from her past that haunted her every nightmare was now haunting her future.

Yule?

Aye. I be here, Tia.

Shit! Tia wrenched herself from the alley cobbles digging into her back and propelled herself forwards, desperate to escape. But all too soon, her eyes blurred beyond function and her head spun with indecipherable words from Yule. She hunched over with one hand on her churning stomach, fighting the urge to throw up.

Deep breath in. Deep breath out, she urged herself, her nose scrunching at the pungent smell. *Oh God, is that urine? Gross.* Her hand flew to her mouth as she tried to swallow the bile rising in her throat.

Ti-a.

Tia's head whipped around and promptly smacked into the wall with a thud. She fell backwards, unconscious.

Chapter 18

Jinx

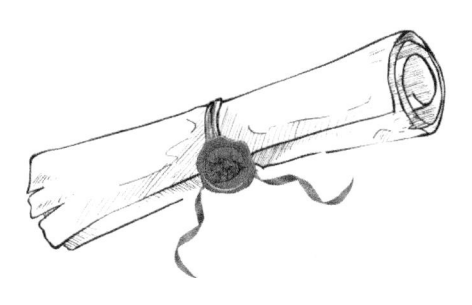

Frozen by his time spell, Jinx watched as a girl walked from the shadowy depths of the graveyard. She stood bathed in the light of the eerie blood moon. Her paisley nightgown swayed gently at her thighs, at least that's what he hoped it was, and she wore a putrid olive-green trench coat draped over top.

Looks like a bloody tent, Jinx grumbled to himself. *A male's coat for sure.* But he couldn't help the exhausted half-smile he gave her – it was his sister. *She's really here*. Something inside him uncurled from his memories and the exuberant feeling of having a sibling close rerooted itself in his soul, filling him with warmth.

Jinx watched Hope stuff her hand into an oversized pocket and pull out a small wooden box. His eyes narrowed at a flash of movement behind her. *What was it – a ghoul?* He thought they were all gone. He tried to rise, but his muscles were too tired and gave way. He called the magic from his soul, but nothing came. Exhaustion consumed him as he prepared to shout a warning for Hope to run. He opened his mouth...

"What's that?" a wistful voice asked.

Its familiarity sent shock waves of relief through Jinx's body. It was Ella. Her attention drawn to the box. Hope stared at her quizzically. "Healing crystals," she said, frowning.

"Really?!" Ella gasped excitedly and grabbed the box.

"El-la!" Jinx hissed. Huge blue eyes met his as the box was shoved back at a distressed Hope, who she glanced at Jinx and then the newly chastised Ella.

"Hello, Ella. I'm Hope, Jinx's sister. Would you like to help me?"

"Yeah sure!" Ella replied, bouncing on her toes. "What do ya want me to do?" Hope glanced at Jinx, but didn't meet his eyes.

"You can help Jinx. He needs to be taken h..." She gulped. "To wherever he lives."

"Okey-dokey." Ella marched up to Jinx, determination flaring her eyes to cerulean.

"Eww!" she complained as she helped Jinx to stand. "You're covered in...uh! God, that's gross."

Ignoring Ella's protest he leaned against her, his body covered in blood. He stared at his sister who was expertly placing her crystals along the length of Garth's shredded body.

Jinx focused trying to see if Garth's chest rose and fell, but he was too exhausted to see straight and stumbled when Ella started forwards.

"Is…is he?" Jinx struggled to rasp, but Hope couldn't hear him. She was too wrapped up in her task, and mumbling about the earth's energy being poisoned and how 'miracles just weren't her forte'.

It's okay, Jinx projected to his sister. *I'll cleanse the land after I recover my energy. Nothing bad will come. I will…stop it*, he promised, but Hope showed no sign that she'd heard him telepathically. *Why should she*, he thought with a shrug. *She has no power.*

Jinx, half propped up by a moaning Ella, stumbled his way to the bunkhouse. *Goddess, please let him live*, he beseeched.

"You didn't listen to me," he scolded. "I told you to go back inside."

Ella turned to face him. Her gaze, wise beyond her years, roamed his body; her eyebrows furrowing over sparking eyes as her delicate nose wrinkled in disgust. "As if," she huffed. "Just look at ya." She paused. "Ya needed me. And I knew it." She smiled and motioned towards the door with a nod of her head. "Ya gonna open it, or what?"

Jinx, pain shooting through his body like an electrical outlet, scavenged for the key in his pocket. *Now I know why they call themselves 'soul sisters'*. He harrumphed thinking of Tia. Ella snatched the key from him, rammed it in the lock and hurried them inside.

"Ooooh!" She scanned the room, her eyes wide and excited.

she swiped blood from her arm with a disgusted flick of her fingers before dumping him onto the bed and shutting the door.

"All good?"

"Yes thank you Ella." He heaved.

"Okay, so if we gotta stay here ya like got a T.V or sommat?" She nosed around the room poking and prodding in her investigation.

"Ella, wait I need your help. Go in that backpack and grab the silver candle."

"So I'm your servant now"- she quipped, a smile on her face as she unzipped the bag and dug out the shinny silver candle.

"Here." She handed it over and under his direction lit it, watching in awe as Jinx chanted over it, some of his energy slowly replenishing from its magical essence with little pops like burst bubble wrap.

"Disappointing really." Ella turned to face him. "I thought it would be more...ya know, scary." She shrugged her shoulders, pouting.

"Sorry, I left my sacrificial gear at home," he snapped.

"Really?" She bounced on her toes.

"No," Jinx replied drily. Disappointment shadowed her face, and guilt clenched at Jinx's heart. But before he could say anything, Ella changed her trail of thought and began her inquisition.

"So," Ella started, hoisting herself to perch on top of the cabinet, "ya gotta sista. Where's she from?"

Jinx sighed, slung a threadbare towel and tracksuit bottoms over his shoulder and stumbled into the shower room. Turning on the spray and slipping from his bloody clothes, he felt his muscles relaxed under the warm jet of water. He gargled some of the cleansing drops and spat them out before raising his voice so he could be heard over the noise of the shower.

"Her name's Hope. She's eighteen." He shouted through the locked door. *A year younger than me*, he thought to himself. "She lives at an academy for powerless witches- Goddess knows where." He sighed, tugging at a crystal in his braids. "And I haven't seen or spoken to her in over nine years." Jinx turned off the soothing stream of water, towelled off and sighed in relief –

he was no longer covered in Garth's blood. *Goddess, I hope he's okay. Jinx thought,* pulling on his sweatpants and tying the cord, he took a deep breath before exiting the shower room. Sure enough, Ella sat waiting to pounce with yet more questions.

"Why have ya not seen her in so long? Did she upset ya?"

Jinx walked to his bunk, slung on the shirt folded at the end of his bed and sat on the edge, his hands cupping his face. Memories flooded him and his heart gave a painful lurch. "Hope, me and my parents lived under my grandmother's rule in the Pren Ceri coven inside the Welsh mountain of Carnedd Llewelyn.. One day my parents were elected by the coven's council to dispose of a warlock." He rubbed his hands up and down his face, and then eyeballed a blank-faced Ella. "A warlock is a witch who has turned their magic dark with selfish thoughts or deeds that become dangerous and vengeful." He explained with a sighed. "My sister and I went along with my grandmother to the train station to see them off that day. Disposals didn't usually take witches very long, and there were two of them, so the mission was supposed to be easy. A cinch." He took a deep trembling breath. "We waved goodbye on the station platform. I never thought that would be the last time I'd see them."

"I'm uh- sorry. I lost my parents in battle too. I was very young. Tia was my only friend- my 'soul sista." Her eyes welled and Jinx nodded in remorse.

"Before they left, my father gave me the book you're sitting by." Jinx listened to Ella fidget, scoop up the book and then sigh in exasperation as she tried unsuccessfully to flick the pages.

"It won't open!" she explained.

"No, it doesn't. But on the last day I saw my father, he told me that a key possessed by the bloodline Calendula will unlock it and that contained inside are the secrets of the world."

"Cool! So where's the key?" She bobbed up and down.

"I haven't found it yet," he answered. *But for the first time ever, I have a place to start.*

"Huh," said Ella, pouting. "So you don't know what the secrets are, then?" she asked, dropping the subject with a disappointed pout.

"So, did they get the war-lop?"

"Warlock," Jinx corrected.

"Warlock. That's what I said," Ella protested. "Well, did they?"

"No. Neither of my parents were seen again. Hope and I were placed in the care of our grandmother- the High Witch Elder." He sniffed. "On Hope's ninth birthday, Grandmother declared her defective before the coven and cast her out," he barely whispered, his heart valves crushingly swollen. "Today was the first day I've seen her since." His voice broke on a swallowed sob, and the next thing he knew two warm arms were wrapped around him.

"It'll be okay, Jinx," Ella comforted. "She's here now."

"You don't understand." He sighed, pushing her away. "I sent her letters every month, I still do. Yaris, my grandmother's assistant, always spirited them away to her. But she only ever sent one a year – with nothing more than 'I'm alive. I hope you are, too' or something just as sarcastic. She hates me, Ella. She hates me!" He felt Ella's soft hand slip into his, giving it a little squeeze.

"She's angry. Hell knows I would be, too. Talk to her. Ya can fix it. I know ya can. Trust me. It's gonna be okay."

Jinx stared up from his palms, his eyes bloodshot as Ella squeezed his hand once more before reterning to the door to leave.

As the door clicked shut he remembered his promise to cleanse the earth, where the ghouls had attacked Garth and set about collecting the items he would need in a small square of black silk cloth.

Trudging out of the bunkhouse he made his way slowly back to where the ghouls had been, his steps slow and measured, his mind realing. Is Garth ok? Will Hope be happy to see me? What should I do?

Blood still soaked everything in the semi clearing and the energy of the earth he stood on felt wrong, not evil, just broken and destroyed. Almost sad.

Jinx made his way to the point where the energy felt like thousands of army ants stinging his skin. Walking until he could bear no more Jinx lay down his cloth. Five large candles rolled from its centre, like a rainbow of miniature pillars.

Picking up a dark green candle, Jinx set it to the north outside the graves beneath where the ghouls had returned. Then he picked up the yellow candle and placed it at a three o'clock from the green north candle. The amber candle was positioned at a six o'clock to represent fire and the blue candle at nine o'clock. Jinx returned to the centre and the last candle left waiting on the silk cloth. Picking up the silver candle, he set it in the centre of the cloth and lit it with the matches he'd packed. It burnt brightly, signifying the Goddess's presence. Jinx bowed his head and sat cross-legged on the rust-stained earth as he began to chant:

"Goddess divine, I welcome thee into my circle.

Spirit of the earth, I call to thee to attend.

> Air from the east, I ask thee to be near me.
>
> Fire of spirit, come, burn bright.
>
> And water of life, come aid my plight."

Jinx felt a tendril of magic bubbling inside himself, quashing the persistent sting of advancing negativity. Channelling the magic he forced it outwards through his skin and one by one the other candles lit, a dome forming between them. The energy inside was chaotic and malicious as the evil that had happened here was concentrated on one point, and Jinx continued his chant:

> "I ask thee, Goddess,
>
> And elements combined,
>
> To cleanse this horror,
>
> The earth alone cannot hide."

The hairs on Jinx's arms raised as his spell was adopted by the elements under the will of the Goddess. Jinx sighed in relief as the rust staining the ground was swallowed by the earth and the grass shone clean and fresh with glistening dew. The energy around him changed, too. It became calming without the bitter bite of evil upon it. Then, all at once, each candle extinguished and Jinx concluded his chant:

"Blessed be, Goddess divine,

And blessed be the elements,

For with none of these,

Our paths would surely lament."

Jinx, now full of relief and exhausted to the bone, collected his candles and placed them in the black silk cloth. Breathing in the newly cleansed air, he made his way back to the bunkhouse and fell fast asleep, dreaming of a sunny sky with large, puffy white clouds and a cool whispering breeze.

    The land in his dream was fruitful with trees and grassy hillsides as Jinx walked, his bare feet tickled by the fresh dewy grass. Suddenly, a darkness blotted the sky and the grass beneath his feet sharpened to teeth-like points. He stopped walking, his feet shredded and bloody, the air chilling to sub-zero. Jinx would have shivered, but his body was frozen and his breath barely escaped his lungs with the burning shock of grass blades. He woke with a start, his hand whipping to his throat as the lifelike dream faded from memory. Sweat poured down his forehead and into his eyes, stinging them as his mind slowly settled. *Thank the Goddess; thank the Goddess.*

With the midday sun shining through the windowpanes lit the crystals Jinx had strung there, their prisms creating miniature rainbows that danced like skittish fairies across the room. Jinx's body felt fully rested, but his mind was exhausted. He got up and checked his feet, just in case, before making his way to the tiny hospital on the edge of the compound. His strength was replenished and his magic had recovered. Now it was time to see if Garth was as lucky.

In the hospital, Jinx stared down at Garth grinning like an idiot and clapped a hand on his shoulder. "Man, you had me freaked." He ran a hand through his braids, sighing. Garth was whole and thanks to his sister, mostly healed.

"And here I was," he croaked, "thinking you witches would be celebrating to see one less G-Poss!"

"Okay," started Jinx in a tight authoritarian tone. "Let's get this straight, shall we? One, you're not exactly a G-Poss, as I heard you quit over some girl." He winked in secret approval. "Two, this situation helps the strained relationship between our factions. And three, Grandmother's hell-bent on getting that petition signed and agreed – that way the government will have no choice but to amalgamate our factions- making them work together for the benefit of duel-talented witches. She'd practically do anything to get some of our witches in here so they can learn some of your Ghost Possessing tricks." He laughed.

"Well, thank God for your grandmother and her petition, then – or I would've been dead, for sure." He grinned. "Now, how about you help me get cleaned up? I refused those nurses' help because they're damn right scary." Garth gave himself a once-over. His body was healed, but he was still covered in blood and gore. He gulped. "Come on, give me a hand. I'm making myself feel sick!" Jinx chuckled at the disgusted expression on Garth's green-tinged face.

"Well?" asked Garth, waiting.

"Yeah, all right," replied Jinx with a smirk, helping Garth rise and walk stiffly to the wash sink, Jinx waited for him to turn on the tap before calling a whisper of air magic forwards. He willed it to open the tiny room's window and then blew another at the running tap, which promptly turned it into a whirlwind as it hit Garth. The blood and dirt washed off his body and then flew out of the window, to rain on whomever was below.

"Gee, thanks mate," quipped Garth, his eyes shining with irritation beneath his drenched fringe. "I'm going to change, then you can introduce me to that angel who just saved my life."

Chapter 19

Tia

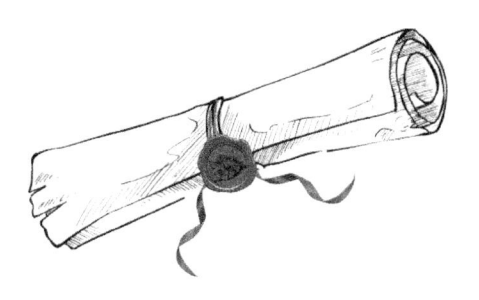

Whisperings of heartfelt joy seeped through Tia's mind and slowly stirred her into consciousness. "What the…? Where…?"

Tia I'm home, Yule rejoiced, from deep within Tia.

Images of the past few days filtered through Tia's awakening mind as she internally groaned. Slowly she pushed her bruised body up, off the cobbled street, which was outside some kind of ancient inn. She was not the only unconscious inhabitant of the alley. The stench of alcohol-intoxicated breath wafted from the bloated body of an unconscious man beside her.

"Filthy pig," she sneered, getting to her feet. Her head pounded and her back felt odd. She stretched releasing some of the tension as she strode around the big man, working the numbness from her muscles while her trainers ate up the path.

Great, so it wasn't all a bloody nightmare, then. Damn it! Now I've got no choice but to help the bloody bitch. Tia heard a woman clearing her throat, the noise resonating inside her head.

"Aww shit," she groaned. Yule was a consciousness inside her mind, as every ghost became when possessed. It was easy to transport them that way and even easier to help them fulfil their unfinished business where there wasn't two — one alive and one a ghost — walking around.

"So, let me guess," Tia snapped at Yule. "Your greatest regret is…not passing out from binge drinking?"

I do not doubt thee finds that comment amusing. But, Tia, if thee do not reach yonder house before noon, I fear thee will miss an important encounter.

Tia squinted open-mouthed at the pinprick of a wooden house perched on a hill so far away it barely rose in the distance.

"That house?" She pointed to the dot in the distance, her suspicions confirmed. "Shit!" She took off at a sprint, determined to reach the house taunting her from afar. Her mind revisited the events of yesterday: The way Yule had appeared. The judgement cast upon her by the new witch, Jinx. The way those dark shadows had clawed at her, and then attacked the gardener – his body disappearing into the gardens at an unnatural speed as they dragged him away.

She thought harder, remembering the salt that had coursed from Yule and into her when she had possessed her, remembered the burning as it spread through her veins. The intensity of pain had made her stomach clench, making her dizzy, the air around her swimming. Blurring her vision, the salt exploded from her body; the reverberating malice of the spectre's voice droning all the while.

"Thou shalt not suffer a witch to live!" As she slid- "Dong!" Transporting from present to past.

Dong? she thought, trying to place the oddity of the spectre's word. *Dong – why would he say...* "O.M.G!." She wheezed as her sweat-soaked body climbed the steep incline of the hill.

What burdens thee, Tia? asked Yule, sensing her mental disturbance.

"The bell, Yule. The bell struck the last chime of noon. I remember hearing it. That means... That means I transported you back after noon. Yule, I'm FREE!" The realisation was a revelation. Tia's body sparked to life, her blood zipped around her veins like a double shot of espresso.

Noon struck just as Tia reached the old house on top of the hill. She sat hunkered down behind an oversized holly bush. "So, you gonna tell me why I'm squatting behind this bush or are you gonna wait until I'm prickled to death? It's not like I stand a chance of transporting home with you stuck in my head." Tia could feel Yule sigh as she began to tell her story.

Once, long ago, I was eldest of the Calendula family and Derth as eldest of his; the house of Pren Ceri's, our bloodlines were destined to joined in holy matrimony.

"Jinx is a Pren Ceri," Tia interjected.

Aye, he be that. But I chose not to join with Derth, heir to one of the most powerful witch families of Wales, but instead chose a lowly farmer, Aaric.

At that moment, a young man came into view. "I'm guessing that's Aaric," said Tia. They watched for a few minutes before noticing a dark figure, obviously a woman by the shadowy flow of her skirt or dress. She exited the main house and followed the young man into a barn in the distance.

"Uh oh, trouble," taunted Tia.

Aye. Once again, Tia interjected before Yule could finish.

"Well, really? This is your greatest regret? Getting knocked by a farm boy? Tell me if I'm wrong, but isn't knocking supposed to be all sparks and fireworks?" she teased ruthlessly.

Tia, Yule reprimanded, *sadly, this be the last time we met. On the morrow, his blood kin named me his murderess.*

Screams and yells sounded out from the barn as the dark figure of the woman, a young Yule, Tia realised, was dragged out. Her corn-coloured braid being tugged violently by her father as Aaric stumbled out behind them, blood dripping in rivulets from his nose.

"Master Calendula, my love for thy daughter is true," Aaric said sincerely. "I would have her as my wife, with thy blessing."

"Wife! Thee hath defiled my insolent daughter, and now thee asks for her hand in marriage! Is thou dense of mind?!"

The yelling swept out like ripples on a pond, allowing Tia to listen in. "Wow," she remarked. "Your dad's a real blast." *Nothing like mine*, she added silently, remembering too late that Yule could hear her every thought.

He be not all bad, Tia, Yule whispered inside her mind.

Her father turned, pointed at Aaric and commanded, "Halt! I will deal first with my traitorous daughter, and then I'll return for you."

Tia watched the young man freeze as Yule was dragged away by her father.

Papa was merciless in his anger, Yule confided as Tia snuck her way into the barn where she would stay that night. She could hear Yule's quiet sniffles. If she wasn't possessing her at this very moment, Tia imagined her skin would be blotchy with tearstains, her eyes sunken. she felt her own heart soften in response.

Sitting on the most comfortable area of straw she could find in the barn's laddered hayloft, Tia listened to the sky roar with thunder. The effervescent dripping of raindrops seeped through the old wooden roof. She flicked her tongue in irritation, running it along the inside of her teeth. "Okay," she reasoned, "you owe me some answers."

Aye.

"Are you a poltergeist?"

No.

"But it was you who wrote on my mirror?"

It was no other.

"Why all the blood and pantomime? No, forget that." Tia wound a lose tendril of hair around her finger. "Are you even a ghost? A *real* ghost?"

Aye, that I am.

"But ghosts can't write." A steely edge of irritation laced Tia's voice. "They don't have the ability to manipulate an object long enough to form words. Especially not in blood," she added, reciting a lesson that had been droned into her since she was first brought to the academy. "So what are you? Some type of superghost?"

No, Tia. I be a witch, of the house of Calendula – a family more powerful than most. As such, I hold power over water.

"You have got to be shittin' me!"

I do not jest.

"So, you just expect me to believe you're a witch on top of the fact that you're a life wrecker and a supposed murderess? Are you bloody insane?"

Yule sighed. *Tia, I beseech thee, calm thyself.*

"Why? Why should I?" Her voice ascended into hysterical as she kicked the hay beneath her feet in frustration.

Because there is more I should confide in thee.

"More?!" Tia scoffed. "What more could there be?"

Thee have yet to connect thy apparel to my time, Tia.

Tia looked down at her costume, comprehension dawning as her face blanched. "Oh, holy crap!"

Aye, Tia, this be the seventeenth century, Yule replied sadly.

"How the hell am I supposed to save you from the witch trials if you really are a witch?" Tia asked, connecting the dots. "I don't even know if I believe in the witch trials. I mean, obviously, they're wrong to torture innocent people. But you're not innocent; you're a witch! Not that that means you deserve to be tortured and die, but the G-Poss have never liked witches and say we should never help them. Hey, maybe the G-Poss are behind the witch trials. *Nah, couldn't be. Doesn't matter, I already hate the G-Poss... Holy shit!* That spirit chasing you, he's a—"

Aye, Tia.

Tia fell silent. Thoughts raced through her mind as she slowly slipped into a fitful sleep, rising only to the sound of shuffling feet on the weathered cobbles outside. She groaned and wiped stray pieces of hay from her face, then flailing a hand attempted to silence an alarm clock that wasn't there. Striking the side of the barn, in her futile attempt, she winced and muttered obscenities under her breath as Yule greeted her from inside her mind.

Good morning, Tia.

"Is it?" she snapped, wiping the sleep from her eyes and stumbling to the window. "What the hell is that noise?" Tia watched Yule's younger self follow her parents out of the wooden house and into their horse-drawn carriage. It was suitable of nobility, with its fancy horseman and off-gold colour.

It raced off out of the small village of Meadow Vaile. Yule's younger self turned in Tia's direction, tears streaming down her face. She then picked up the midnight black kitten, weaving around her legs in a bid for attention, and rubbed her face into its silky fur.

Tia's eyes flickered back to the dusty road where a group of people came into sight. Cobbles crunched beneath eager feet, their raucous voices arguing viciously.

I fear they were laying in wait, whispered Yule.

Tia watched them surround the young and terrified Yule who ruffled the fur of her beloved kitten before placing a kiss on its little black head. *for luck!* Commented Yule, her tone resigned.

Tia watched the young Yule let the kitten leap from her arms onto the dusty cobbles.

"It be her familiar!" A blacksmith bellowed, face as red as the devil.

"Kill it!" screamed a woman, startling the confused kitten who had been approaching her in an effort to seek the woman's affections.

Suddenly, the crowd parted to reveal a man donning a black shirt with lace collar, black breeches and a tall ominous black velvet hat. In his weathered hand, he clutched an old book bound in polished leather with the words 'Holy Bible' inscribed in gold calligraphy.

Tia raised her eyes intent on meeting the malicious eyes of the monster whose murderous attempt at killing her and her ghost assignment had failed. She watched him open the book, allowing page after page to flutter open freely as if he were a preacher and had all the time in the world. The page he wanted finally fell into place.

His voice rumbled through the crowd with the promise of retribution. "Thou shalt not suffer a witch to live. Yule Winter, thy have been accused of murdering Aaric Smith and bespelling his mother, Charlotte. Hereby, I accuse thee, Yule Winter, of witchcraft and sentence thee to a trial, by ducking!"

Tia tore her gaze away from the malicious monster condemning the young Yule, focusing on the bundle of blood-soaked fur splayed beneath a tree. It was obvious the little thing had fled for its life, only to die by the tree. A splay of innards cascaded from its stomach where the rocks had repeatedly hacked into its skin. *You poor thing.* She cooed. *I wish I could have done something.* She thought, noticing the roots that cradled it.

"Yule, what type of tree is that?" asked Tia, mesmerised by the familiarity of the scene.

Oak, Yule replied, her voice tight with unshed tears.

Tia's eyes bulged with shock, her heart racing so fast it sounded like the beat of a rattlesnake about to attack. *It can't be. It just can't!* The blank gaze of the mutilated kitten. The deep bone splintering cold- the necklace of rope burns, the malicious spectre she had accidently possessed. *Oh God my nightmares!* "The kitten, it was—" Tia began.

Stoned, Yule interrupted.

"Killed, horrifically," she corrected, twirling a loose strand of her hair.

A punishment vicious in its execution, Yule agreed; her voice sombre in Tia's mind.

"For being your- familiar," Tia deduced, the ringing in her ears making her stumble over her words. "Killed. By the witch- hunter." *Oh God, It's all fitting together*, thought Tia. *The malevolent spirit – aka the witch hunter.*

I was drawn to the girl who laid my kitten's spirit to rest, Yule continued.

"It being the kitten who died horrifically, its death imprinting on time and deeming it a residual spirit, a spirit that was doomed to die again and again in a never ending loop, until..." Tia babbled, her stomach churning the curds of her last meal. "Until..."

Aye, Tia.

"But. But- I only touched it." Her voice quivered like a static loaded radio.

Thy buried her.

"Buried a residual spirit – impossible!" She laughed then realisation dawned, her smile turning sour. Unless... No," Tia denied, shaking her head.

'Twas thee who dispelled the salt from our bodies, Tia.

Tia gasped in shock. "I. Did. That?"

Aye, Tia, just like thy grandmother before thee. For she was a witch, too. Was she not?

"No, I mean, yes. I mean... Holy shit, Grandma Penny!" *But she's so-nice!*

Thy showed my kitten's residual spirit compassion.

"I showed it my cardigan," Tia sniped.

Aye, so she allowed thy to touch her, bury her, lay her spirit to rest. I manifested because for years I have felt the terror of her restless spirit. For her to suddenly feel peace, I was curious and grateful. I thought a being of such power would be able to aid me with moving on. But when I manifested, thy were but a child. Unfortunately, my presence drew the hunter.

"The witch hunter! The malevolent spirit! It was your fault?!" She gasped.

Believe me, Tia, for I speak true, Yule implored. *Had I known thy were but a child, I would never have appeared to thy. I beg thy forgiveness.*

"I lost my family! They took me away because of you. I never saw them again!" she screamed, the raucous scene outside veiling her anger as she stormed back and forth in the hayloft.

I know it was wrong. But since that day, thee hath not seen me, Yule admitted shamefully.

"Because you're a coward," croaked Tia.

Because never did I want him to come for thee, relented Yule.

Tia clutched her head, shaking it fearsly as she wished she could dispel Yule from inside so she could rant her anger at the ghost. "So that's why you were chosen for my assignment?" She huffed.

Not by magical means or any other can these assignments be changed, for Death himself is charged with their bestowing, reasoned Yule.

"Convenient," quipped Tia hands on her hips as she rolled her eyes.

We are of one blood, Tia Morgan, descendent of the house of Calandula. Even Death himself cannot separate a family for long.

Tia's mouth flopped open. *Shit! We're related!*

Chapter 20

Jinx

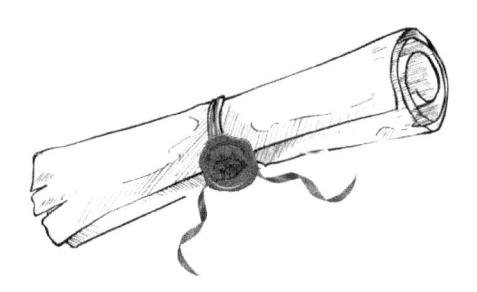

Back in the present, unknown to Tia, Jinx was also suffering difficulties with a long-lost relative. He had made sure Garth was settled in the tiny hospital on the outskirts of the compound before hunting down his sister, Hope.

He found her nestled in an old-fashioned armchair in the corner of the academy's in-house library. *I shouldn't be here* he thought. *I'm surprised that they let Hope in- but then again, she has no powers.* He stood, staring at her sleeping form. She had grown into a beautiful young woman since they last met. Her ebony skin glowed with a slight blush as a shallow sigh slipped through her delicately bowed lips. She looked so fragile. She always had.

They had missed so much of each other; solstices, naming day celebrations the equinox; things that didn't matter but played a big part in building sibling relationships. He sighed, rubbing a fist against his chest where like a separated puzzle, his heart began to fix.

He wondered what her school was like. Her friends. Whether or not she had a boyfriend. He was so full of questions that he didn't notice the sudden buzzing that shocked his sister from her silent slumber.

She jolted forwards, her eyes latching onto his and then immediately down casting them. Jinx frowned, an anger stirred making his magic restless like a disturbed hive.

What does she think? I'm gonna eat her? Berate her, maybe? Jinx felt his blood boil. It enraged him that someone had obviously instilled a deep sense off fear into her. Before he knew it, he was before her, his hand bearing the chrysoberyl ring resting on her soft knee whilst she frantically searched the pockets of a G-Poss coat.

"Hope... I..."

Her deep brown eyes flicked towards him. She replied, "Give me a minute," and tapped the small iPhone she had pulled from inside one of the interior pockets.

"You okay?" he asked.

She cringed at the message she had opened. "Yeah," was her whisper.

"But...?" He leaned in, his attention fixed on her.

"It's Olcan's," she said, sliding the phone back into her pocket. "He's gonna be angry when he finds out I've got it," she confided. "And all that blood last night, it ruined his coat." She harumphed.

Jinx, vibrating with anger silently questioned, *is that who's responsible for unnerving my sister so much that she jumps awake at the slightest noise?* He ran a hand through his thick braids, contemplated his retort.

"It's okay, you don't need to warn me off, I'm not gonna be here for much longer, anyway. Olcan's brothers are meeting me at the gates tomorrow." She pulled the phone back out, tapped its screen and corrected herself, "I mean today."

"But why?" he asked, tugging at his braids.

"So I can go home." He watched her tap the screen again, anger darkening her eyes as her eyebrows climbed. She read the highlighted twenty-four-hour clock. "Wow," she said. "What a day. *It's **one o'clock**.*"

"Yeah," snapped Jinx, retracting his hand sharply. "Goddess, in less than twelve hours my little sister, whom I've been **forbidden** to see since I was seven, is finally granted permission to come back into my life, and in those few hours she decides to disappear from it as though she'd never even seen me." He rubbed his chin in thought. *What can I do to make her* *stay?* Taking a deep breath, he muttered, "Why?" Knowing he wouldn't receive an answer by the way she had set her jaw, he stormed from the room. Wound up in the eye of an all consuming rage, torturing himself with events of the past, decisions he could not change and the life he had been forced to lead.

Jinx flew from the library, the oak door slamming in his wake. He stormed through the corridors, potentials scattering as he ploughed through them, caught up in his inner turmoil. He could feel the air around him thicken with his escaping magic. His soul was raw and the magic took advantage of his lapse in defences to vent its way from his body, along with his anger boiling like hot magma.

He had to calm down and focus his power before he did something he would regret.like when Yarik, had proclaimed his parents' disappearance was due to death. He had riled himself into such a temper that before he knew it, Yarik had fallen to his knees with his face blue from a lack of oxygen. Jinx had unintentionally sent his magic to suck it from his veins, leaving the air around him thick and full of carbon dioxide. He remembered his grandmother's scolding, his friend's screaming, but the only voice that managed to break through his heartbreak was his sister's.

By the time he could reverse the effect of his magic, Yarik was unconscious – but surprisingly since then, they had become good friends. Yarik was the only one he trusted to send his letters to Hope. Jinx found himself pondering on the irony of the situation. It was his sister who had helped him to calm down back then, yet now she was the cause of all his rage. *Goddess give me patients.*

He turned to survey his surroundings. Somehow, through his mind's conflict, his feet had lead him to the main hall. The doors stood open and the next thing he knew, he found himself ordering the potentials inside to vacate the room, determined to put his rage to sleep.

He took a deep breath. The rancid smell of death and decomposed flesh, which resonated from the ghouls and Cacodaemon invasion only a day ago, had now dispersed. The horrific memory was now left to fester in the back of the every potentials' minds.

He glanced around the large hall taking in its newly scrubbed surfaces, as the intense smell of bleach burnt his nostrils. *Goddess, why couldn't they have just used lavender– that would have worked.*

The thought of the delicate plant invoked an image of Tia. The smooth pale skin of her delicate hand as he held it and the deep burn of determination that shone from her cobalt eyes while she addressed the spirit.

The gentle caress of raven tendrils falling loose from her plait, glistening against his chest, where she nestled. Her being comforted by his strength while he drank in her heady scent of lavender and chalk.

He sighed, his magic suddenly calmer and his mind quiet. *I'm in way over my head*, he thought before slumping into a chair placed in front of a small table, upon which stood Fiona's crystal ball shrouded in the darkness of a small silk cloth.

Contemplating, he pushed his air magic into the lock of the drawer beneath it. The latch turned with little effort and the files of the five ascenders were brought forth.

He flipped open the first file, thumbed through the pages and looked into the crystal ball he had now uncovered. An image appeared, it was grainy and unfocused; it was only when he concentrated that the image became clearer.

Inside, Li was walking hand in hand with Anka. She waffled on about half the places she knew, their ghosts ever present in their minds as they wandered down the smartly clad streets of Victorian London. Slowly they walked down the dismal alleys, cobbles crunching under their feet in search of the dwelling in which Declan Barns once lived.

Jinx could see Victoria staring out of Li's eyes as they glistened with an unearthly iridescence. It was obvious to him that Victoria was, through Li, guiding them along the route she had travelled many times before. Jinx watched Anka cling to Li's arm while she surveyed the alleys clogged with buskers and homeless people who slept together in an attempt to emanate enough heat to see the light of another day.

Jinx saw Li cringe, Anka's grip depriving his much-needed arm of its necessary blood supply. It took them a while to locate Declan's dwelling, which was little more than a cellar beneath a large terraced house. Jinx could see the anticipation and fear etched onto the faces of both potentials as they took a deep, hopeful breath. Then Li raised a cold hand to knock on the wood-slatted door of the barely visible cellar dwellings.

The door creaked open to reveal the extraordinary beauty of a young Victoria, the bustle of her dress flowing in a blue fountain from her corset-pinched waist, her crystal blue eyes narrow as she regarded them, her body blocking the entrance.

Li held out a large tanned hand. "Lady Victoria, I have been looking for you," he said, watching her eyes darken with worry. "May we come inside?"

Abruptly, Victoria's younger self stepped back to allow their entry to Declan's dwellings.

Stepping inside, Anka looked around, a disgusted look playing across her dainty face. Declan's home was dark and musty. Jinx watched as Anka wrinkle her nose, before placing a delicate handkerchief against it.

Smiling Jinx watched everyone inside the crystal ball gather around a dingy little bed. The only light in the whole room flickered eerie shadows across the bedridden man.

"Oh, for heaven's sake, Li." Anka shouldered him aside and knelt on the grime-soaked floor next to where a very sick Declan lay. "I hope you know what you're putting me through," she chided the dying Declan. "This dress is practically an antique." Taking one of his hands in hers, she met his eyes. "You're dying."

"Anka!" despaired Li, running a large hand through his thick hair.

She pinned him with her eyes. "It's true."

A gurgled sob wrenched its way from the young Victoria who flew in a flurry of skirts to his side. She slipped a comforting hand beneath Declan's head, his body was bundled in the mottled blankets piled upon him. She raised her face and kissed his hand, her eyes full of heartbreak as she wept.

Can she feel her assignment's pain? Jinx wondered.

Anka held a hand to her heart, before being pulled to her feet and ushered away to give the lovers some privacy.

Declan's younger self clasped his hands over the sobbing Victoria's fragile ones. "Hush, hush now, I have words I need you to hear."

Huge teardrops fell from her eyes and down her lashes before she quieted.

"Mi'lady, not a flower alive can bare a bloom more perfect than you. You walk the road of travesty, and yet you remain by my side. I am honoured by the privilege of loving you." He blinked, startled by his pledge. "I love y—"

Victoria screamed. Anka spun around and shook as sweat beaded on her brow. The ghostly essence of Declan manifested. "You. I love you," he whispered, his hand outstretched in pleading. A terrified and heartbroken Victoria stepped forwards.

Jinx watched a blotchy-faced Victoria place a delicate hand in Declan's outstretched palm; the eyes of the two untimely lovers met.

Victoria's lips quivered. "I love you, too, my heart."

Jinx turned to the folder and made notes of the ascenders' assignments, ignoring the conversation in the crystal ball.

Two minutes later, Jinx felt the air beside him ripple and Anka appeared from the past. Tears streamed from her eyes as her body trembled. "Help, please help!"

Jinx stood, his chair scraping the floor-"Anka what's wrong?"

"Its Li. He-" she hiccupped- "he was upset. He said he thought that his assignment would be more taxing, more befitting of a leader." She rolled her delicate eyes. "He knows this assignment won't showcase his 'superior' leading skills. Please help him. I think he's going to do something stupid."

"He doesn't have much time before he transports back, Anka. Don't worry. He'll be fine."

"Please. Do. Something!" she begged, tears staining tracks down her face. "I'm scared. He'll do something stupid. I know he will. Please," Anka begged.

"All right, all right, I'll keep an eye on him," Jinx assured her, returning to his seat. "But I'm sure he'll be fine."

"You're sure?"

"I'm sure," he consoled.

"All right," she relented. Sniffing slightly and raising her chin, before sweeping from the room.

Jinx turned his attention back to the crystal ball, where Li trudge back along the canal walkway kicking stones into the deep, dark depths of the water. He slowly faded in and out of view. *It won't be long, Li's body is already trying to transport. It's was purely stubbornness keeping him there.*

Suddenly a ghost formed in the crystal ball, its hands held out in the universal 'stop' signal.

"Oh shit!" cursed Jinx. He could see Li shaking with adrenalin "Don't do it," he pleaded, gazing into the crystal ball.

Li made his way to the river where Anka's assigned ghost had worked. It was dark. The sky kissed the deadly ink waters that was the River Thames. He rubbed his roughened hands over his exhausted face.

Jinx watched Li walk with purpose, his gait quick as he approached his decided destination. *Goddess, is that…? Oh yes it is.* Isambard Kingdom Brunel's suspension footbridge stretching eagerly over the River Thames, right before the ghost baying for Li's attention.

With conviction, Jinx watched Li approach and mollify the ghost of a middle-aged man of gentry.

"They call me Jack," replied the ghost through a veil of misery.

"Did you kill yourself?" Li asked impertinently.

"No, I did not commit suicide, however much I wish I had. In the end, I just couldn't help it. I saw their faults and judged them guilty – and just like that my family were gone. Then I stood with their blood on my hands, all alone. I should never have killed them.

"People called it justice, but death snared me with its addiction and remorse alluded me until the day I died of old age. That was when justice found me, and Death reaped my soul for his punishment. But as you can see me, boy, I must impart on you the necessity of my destruction this day. I beg you, kill the young boy I once was and end my reign of terror before it begins again. Destroy my former self and free the souls that haunt me in my death."

Jinx found himself staring deeper into the crystal as Li tried to decipher the numerous orbs surrounding the older ghost's body. "Don't do it," Jinx hissed. He watched horrified as the orbs violently pierced the ghost man's illusive flesh before whipping in and out with brutal intensity. If he listened hard enough he could hear their screams, their pleas for justice.

Jinx tuned out of the conversation and ran a hand through his braids, his chrysoberyl ring snagging on his hair. *Goddess, what is Li thinking? Surely there's another way he can prove himself? How is it possible that he cannot see the evil emanating from this spectre?* Jinx refocused his attention on the crystal ball, but the inevitable had already happened. Li had possessed the ghost.

Jinx watched as Li stalked a young boy along the river's edge. He was no more than ten, but undoubtedly the boy the ghost had once been.

As if commenting on Jinx's thoughts, the ghost hissed through Li's lips, "In five years, he'll beat our mother to a bloody pulp for her transgressions that placed food on our table this night. Two years from now, we will hunt our first victim; and without remorse, eradicate her presence from this earth. From that day on, the draw of death will summon us – we will become snared in its addiction."

Li trembled as Jinx let out a heavy sigh, but the ghost continued to speak through him. "Please, I beg you. Kill the young man I was before he kills my chosen family. Please."

Jinx watched in horror as Li reached out a hand, his fingertips barely brushing the tattered sleeve of the boy's shirt.

At this point, Jinx didn't know what to do. He had no experience with ghosts. But he thought practically. *Would it really be so bad if Li killed a notorious killer – to be? Oh Goddess, what a mess!* Jinx watched the possessed ghost force its malicious essence into Li's mind, forcing his arm forwards. Jinx sighed in defeat. It seemed Cacodaemons were more common than he thought.

The young boy spun around, his arms frantically flailing. He caught Li in the shoulder, knocking him off balance. The boy fell over the edge screaming and plummeted into the icy water below.

Li, regaining his balance, watched him fall into the river, where he was swallowed from sight.

"Now, I'll never hurt anyone," ground out the ghost. The pain of its combustion knocked Li back; his foot came down in thin air searching unsuccessfully to find earth beneath it. His arms windmilled. Catching at his pendant in a futile attempt for help, Li clenched it too hard, ripping it from his neck, a thin blood trail spurting in its wake. He smacked the water with a bone-crushing descent.

"Oh shit!" screamed Jinx. Death had combusted the ghost's soul from within Li. He was sure of it. The ghost's last chance of redemption eternally destroyed as his evil essence was wiped from the history of the earth, along with Li's chance of ever coming home.

Jinx muttered a spell that opened the pendant just as it slipped from Li's fingers. The boy's broken body sinking, the air bubbles he expelled slowing. Jinx roared in anger and slammed the crystal from its stand of ancestral bones, smashing it into thousands of pieces that reflected the image of the dead ascender – Li.

Chapter 21

Tia

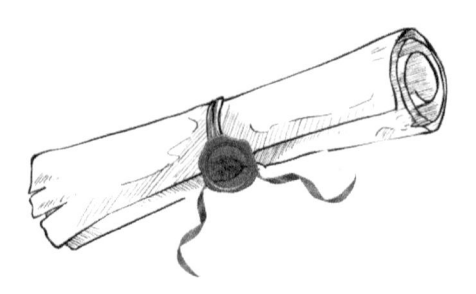

Meanwhile, back in the seventeenth century, Tia was attempting to cast a spell under the tutorage of Yule. She had followed behind the posse dragging the young Yule to a large wooden building in the centre of the small town, terrified she might be discovered. She now stood looking at rows after rows of ominous dark wooden doors lining what could only be called a seventeenth-century style prison. A shiver played the vertebra of her spine.

Peering through the small barred window of the witch hunter's headquarters she attempted to cast a distraction spell- she had no choice. after an all too quick 'how to' download from Yule. *If it's so easy, then why can't I do it?* moaned Tia internally. *It's not like she's got anything better to do.*

Obviously, the witch hunter had an assistant because inside sat an overweight guy manning a desk in front a large barred door leading to ominous rows of cells. Tia sighed. Once again, her attention to the spell was suffering from her lapse in concentration. Nothing happened.

"Okay, so tell me again how I'm supposed to save your ass from the past?" Tia sniped as Yule's collected calm resonated through her mind.

Breathe. Magic flows from the soul. Focus and say:

Magic entwined,

Through soul and past time,

I beseech you,

Open thy mind,

Show to me,

The power of blood kind.

"Yeah, yeah," groaned Tia. "I got it the first three times. Next you'll be tutoring me in fashion," she sneered, picturing Yule's tortured form, then sarcastically reconsidering- *maybe not.*

Amusing, Yule droned dryly as Tia smirked at her own snipe. *Thy have witch blood, Tia.*

Yeah, and apparently so do I. Not that I even like witches, Not that I've really known any exept Fiona–the bit-deceased house witch.

Tia took a deep breath. Feeling the air expand her lungs, she reached deep inside herself to a place she barely contemplated – her soul. A network of webs seemed to encase it, all sticky, attaching themselves to her mind, spreading throughout her body, crackling and sizzling like live wires as they reached her fingertips.

Aye now, Tia. NOW! Yule directed.

Tia chanted the stanza as fast as possible, before she could lose the threads of magic, and thrust her fingers through the bars of the tiny window.

Tia watched entranced and horrified as air molecules became visible, one shoving into another, the effect like a giant tsunami as the air wave rippled and pounded into her target – the overweight man.

His eyes shot to the back of his head, his chest crushed and his skin blue as he hit the wall behind him. His rigid form slumped with the receding magic to a deformed mass of man on the stone slab floor.

Tia gasped, her hands shaking, a single tear forming. *Oh God, no! Is he...? He's not... He's not dead, is he?*

Tia. Tia, calm thy mind. The man lives.

He does? Oh, thank God! thought Tia, not knowing how she would cope if she'd inadvertently committed murder. Wrestling back the numbness after the panic had retreated, Tia shot into action. She made her way to the door at the front of the wooden building. Inside the stench of rotten waste overwhelmed her. Sobs echoed throughout the building as she searched for a key.

Finally procuring the bronze key from the unconscious guard's pocket, Tia shoved it into the lock and wrenched the door wide open. She scooted through and then pulled it almost closed.

Hay stirred with her every footfall, plumes of dust choked her, her eyes stung as she pulled at the peephole on the first cell. Inside sat a woman clawing at her own skin and sobbing broken-heartedly.

"Don't tell me, I should rescue her, too?" Tia felt the subconscious shake of Yule's head inside her mind.

She clarified, *it saddens me to say that Ayla is guilty of the crime she is accused.*

"Oh, and what crime would that be? Making a bloody awful racket?"

Werewolfery.

"Ok-ay. You're kidding. Right?"

No, Tia. Ayla defies magic laws. She combined dark magic with a death curse to create the first of a new species: a werewolf.

"Shit!" Tia looked back in at the woman in the cell. "You sure? She doesn't look that deranged." Her heart beat sped up, doing laps on a treadmill.

Not deranged, Tia, enraged, Yule corrected.

"Looks devastated to me," mumbled Tia under her breath. She heard Yule's mental sigh as though concluding if she didn't explain herself, then Tia would persist in hounding her with her sarcastic interrogation.

Because the man the curse lay upon was her unfaithful lover – Lort.

"So, she cursed him to be the dog that he was." Tia chuckled quietly. "Fitting."

Werewolf. Yule's one-word answer echoed inside Tia's mind.

"Whatever." Tia shrugged it off, unbelieving. "Which cell's yours?"

I remember not, but listen and thy will hear—

"Sssh," Tia commanded. She concentrated to hear the eerie mumblings of the last cell on the right.

"Dead. Gone. Destroyed," were the murmurs of a deranged person – of a past Yule.

Tia crept along the cell block, careful not to scuff up too much of the hay and announce her presence. Her heart began its climb into her throat as she neared the wooden door where she suspected Yule was being held prisoner.

Tia stretched to slide open the peephole, the desolate hope of past Yule's unrequited love sliced straight through to her newly found soul.

This woman had lost more than just a man; she had lost her soulmate, her one chance of happiness dashed to pieces by his murder.

Peering through the hole, Tia watched as Yule scuttle away from the corner where she was rocking and into the small expanse of light from the opening. She shook from head to toe, her face scored by bloody nail marks, her body beaten and bruised as she stared into Tia's shocked eyes.

A deafening thud jolted Tia, her blood shot like a burst fountain though her veins, as she reeled back from the cell and scrambled to the safety of a darkened alcove. The monstrous footsteps of the dreaded witch hunter thundered throughout the prison. Screams bled from the inmates as waves of paramount fear spread throughout them.

"If thee be present, witch, I will find thee!" His foot steps beat a slow yet powerful presence as he stepped upon the earth. "Bran! Bring me the witch in number-" A long pause resounded, even the inmates were silent as Death. "Thirteen; today we shall have ourselves a pricking."

Cackling laughter stabbed Tia's spine like the needles from a rabid porcupine. She shuddered with the malicious tension radiating from the witch hunter's men.

Two minutes later, a young man strutted into Yule's cell, batons of splintered wood in their hands as they subdued her screams to whimpers and dragged her broken body out by her hair. "I did not do it. I did not kill him," she protested, rolling back and forth into the sides of the cell as clumps of her corn coloured hair dyed crimson with blood, fell to the hay sprinkled floor.

"Silence!" roared the man, slamming a booted foot into her spine, her skeletal form spun with the impact, knocking the air from her lungs.

"Timothy, let loose the dogs!" ordered the witch hunter, his voice resonating throughout the prison.

"But if the intruder is a witch, she will claim it as a familiar," answered Timothy, his voice quivering.

"She has not the time, or the power, I suspect. Or the condemned witch she came to rescue would be free." He chuckled, his voice thick like the blood of innocents he spilled.

Tia let out a breath, her lungs ached with the effort to hold when the witch hunter was close. Now, his footsteps receded from the building she felt a sense of deep relief relax her soul for the three seconds she forgot about Yule.

"Holy shit! Dogs?" *Beasts trained to kill.* "He's really gonna let loose dogs? In here?"

Of course. But—

"Holy crap!"

The clattering of claws against stone sounded. Hay sprayed in the wake of three giant Rottweiler as saliva dripped from their mouths in anticipation of feeding on their kill.

Tia clutched her arms over her head screaming, "Oh God, oh God, oh God!" She sprinted for the prison door, turning, her arms splayed wide as the dog catching her scent, attacked. Fear swirled like a whirlpool within her as huge jaws dripping saliva came thundering towards her face. Unsciously her soul screamed its horror, whipping her magic into a crescendo as she sent out a shockwave of air – molecules slamming into molecules. until suddenly the dogs were gone, smashed into pieces against the cell walls. A new morbid paint for the witch hunter to add to his fastidious collection.

Prisoners screamed in terror. Tia blasted the prison door open; Timothy was rendered unconscious as he hit the wall. She hid outside in a bushy border clutching her chest, her heart thrumming like a race car. Sweat dripped from her brow as she attempted to catch her breath and stave off the panic attack threatening to claim her.

You're. Afraid. Of. Dogs? Yule's voice asked, incredulous.

"Figured that, did you?" Tia panted, wiping the tears from her eyes.

Tia, please, you have to save me from my past.

"For God's sake, all I've been doing throughout this bloody ascension is saving your ass. I've faced malevolent spirits, ghouls, witch hunters, freaky werewolf-creating witches, and suddenly they find my Achilles heel – and you want me to what? Hurry up and get over it? Sorry for the inconvenience, Yule, but I have cynophobia."

I apologise, Tia, but you want me out of your life – forever – so you can go home. Forget we ever met. I beg thee- help me!

Reluctantly Tia straightened, surveyed her surroundings and harrumphed at Yule's chastising. She covertly watched a small crowd forming around a large barn-like structure.

Village hall, Yule corrected.

Smoothing down her hay-dusted clothes, Tia stalked forwards and mingled into the crowd of observers as they pushed their way into the hall.

The witch hunter stood centre stage preaching to a jury of men, the young man who had dragged out the young Yule was repeatedly stabbing a large needle into her now naked body.

"When did you get naked?"

When they searched for the devil mark, which they did not find.

"So they decided to give you one of their own?" Tia sneered.

They pricked me. If my blood was not spilt, justice would name me a witch.

"That's stupid." Tia snorted. "If anyone gets stabbed by something sharp, they bleed – common sense."

Aye, but if the pricking needle is blunted...?

"They're setting you up?"

Fearful people do desperate things, Tia.

"Like frightening an unsuspecting ten-year-old who is giving peace to their long-suffering cat."

In a rare fit of temper, Yule slammed about in Tia's mind; giving her a headache to challenge a saint.

"Bitch," Tia seethed, trying her best to ignore Yule's tantrum, tuning into the witch hunter's speech instead.

Past Yule's cries of pain echoed throughout the crowd of morbidly terrified onlookers. The whole village seemed to be watching, from the young to the old. Tia noticed a child holding her mothers skirt begging to cry. Picking her up, her mother hushed her, whispering in her ear before turning the blotchy faced child back to watch the scene.

"The accuser, mother to the deceased, has found no relief in scratching the accused witch. But I put it to you, jury, is this not just some mind trick – some spell? After all, the victim was last seen sneaking off to meet with the accused witch. My assistant is performing a pricking – but as of yet, you and I see no blood."

A chorus of agreement swept through the crowd.

"Blunt needle," gasped past Yule through a series of violent strikes across her abdomen.

The men restraining her showed no empathy as they stilled her quaking body.

"To the lake!" screamed an old, overweight woman.

"Duck her!" resounded another, the crowd taking up the call as the jury passed sentence.

"What's ducking?" whispered Tia, still clutching her head due to her nerve endings being crushed by Yule's temper tantrum.

Slowly the pounding stopped and she felt Yule centre herself, but she didn't answer Tia. Instead, Tia felt her recede to the back of her mind whispering soft prayers in a catatonic state, once again causing Tia's head to thrum painfully.

Tia decided her best option was to bustle along with the crowd, together with what looked like the entire village, she lost sight of young Yule as they made their way down to a water's edge.

Pushing her way forwards, she waited with everyone else for the witch hunter. He marched forth, followed by his assistants, one dragging Yule once again by her hair.

What is it with these Neanderthals- why can't they cuff you of something? But Tia never received an answer. She watched from the opposite side of the lake, where the men tied Yule's hands and feet to a long length of rope stretching the width of the river, before slowly lowered her into its freezing depths.

Gasps and jeers rang out from the crowd, but Yule didn't speak, cry or scream. She was as silent as the dead as they lowered her out of sight and waited---

God, she's gonna die. Tia surveyed the crowd, their anticipation sickening her to her soul. They were like Romans in an amphitheatre watching a blood sport deemed entertaining.

Tia crept forwards, unable to stand solitary a moment longer. *You might not be my friend Yule, but well, I'm kinda getting used to your back seat driving.* She knelt at the side of the lake, careful to conceal herself in the reeds, and crept out a hand to skim the frigid water's surface. "Should I?"

No response; Yule was still chanting prayers in the back of her mind.

Tia took a deep breath, feeling for the sparks that were her magic; but before she could attempt a rescue, Yule's lithe form came into view, bobbing in the water, her eyes wide open and glazed. "Shit! She's dead." Tia's hand broke the water's surface as shock took hold.

An audible gasp was heard from the crowd before a deathly silence as Yules body floated closer to the reeds where Tia hid, her glazed eyes staring straight up into Tia's. She was- breathing.

Screams split the air; people started mumbling prayers incoherently. Others shuffled backwards, some falling, others running for the safety of their homes.

"Witch!" screamed a young boy. "Witch! Witch! Witch!"

It was only when an elbow slammed into her face, her nose spurting blood as she rocked backwards on a wave of unconsciousness, that she realised the young boy had been pointing at her.

Tia awoke surrounded by darkness, her head pounding, dried blood crusting her smashed nose. Her stinging eyes watered when she closed them. The darkness eased her head a little. She shuffled her body and backed into the corner of a dark, oppressive room.

Safety? She wasn't sure. Slipping out a foot from beneath her huddled body, only now realising it was bare, she fondled the floor with her black painted toes. Her toes tensed, testing and releasing. *Is that – hay?*

"Holy shit!" Memories rushed back to her and she collapsed in agony remembering the river, the villagers and the boy, the boy who screamed witch – at her! "The witch hunter, he…"

Aye. Yule started to sob.

"So we're…"

Aye. A mental sniff this time.

"Crap!" Tia took out the pendant from beneath her dress. She turned it and studied it, pressed it, poked it, trying to switch it on. 'Like a beacon' Paul had said. 'They can see through it'. But why was it not moving, glowing, doing something?

"God, help me," she prayed, clutching the amulet close while rapidly surveying her surroundings, analysing them for her escape.

***

Days went by, maybe two, maybe twenty, but all Tia knew was the darkness of the cell, the sickening stench of human waste and the bone-deep, bitter cold. She rubbed her arms fiercely in an attempt to re-circulate her blood, failing miserably. Her stomach rumbled in petition against its state of neglect.

She scored her fingers down the cell wall, tearing her nails to their bed, attempting to claw her way free. "Crap!" she yelled as her nail tore off with a stab of pain. *Pain*, she thought. *Pain is good? Isn't it? Pain means its re—*

Real. I beg thee, Tia, forgive me.

Shit. Shit. "Shit! No!" she roared, slamming her fist into the roughened wooden wall. On impact splinters were left protruding from a river of blood from her fist. She slumped down against the wall, defeated. *There is no way out. No way except through that door.* She could hear moans reverberating from the sleeping hound left to guard her, its daily snuffles fuelled her terror, its nightly howls- her nightmares.

Her body shook in a constant state of shock, pain obscuring its normal control. She panted, fear consuming her every waking breath. She curled into a ball, closing her eyes fully for the first time in days. When you had to live in fear, you soon learn to live with it.

Sssh, steadied Yule in her mind. *All will be well, Tia. You and I, we shall think of our escape.*

"Es-ca-pe?" echoed Tia, her voice hollow. She lifted her head from her knees and stared at her cell. "The walls, they're...they're moving," she screeched hysterically. "They're moving!"

A growl echoed from the door as footsteps strode a path to her cell. The tiny peep hole was slammed down; creating a small rectangle of warmth before two bright blue eyes consumed it.

"Silence, witch! Or I will send the mutt in with you," it sneered, satisfied at the trembling through Tia's body- much to her shame. The window snapped shut and the footsteps receded leaving Tia alone once again, with only Yule to keep her sane.

Be at peace, Tia. Nothing moves. Hush. We want not that mutt in here.

Tia shook at the reminder of her jailer's threat.

"I have to get out, Yule." She sobbed into her hands, her body rocking to comfort itself. "Can't stay here, can't stay here, can't-."

Hush, Tia, hush. All will be well. I promise. There must be a way out, a way we have not yet found?

"I've tried. I've tried and tried and tried. It's useless." Sighing, she muttered a resigned, "I'm gonna die."

If only I was free of your possession, beseeched Yule. *Free us, I could, by sending rain to pelt a hole in this cell. I might have helped.*

"Why didn't you? I mean the past you?"

My heart was treacherous in its sorrow, much as yours is now. But magic seems untouchable when dark emotion clouds our minds. A deterrent, I think, for warlockism is the only path dark magic invokes.

"That's why none of those spells worked. Why didn't you tell me?" Tia demanded.

Because they were worth a try.

"I have tried kicking, scratching, spells, pounding, punching – everything."

Hush, Tia. Breathe, Yule coached. *No matter the outcome, I promise I will not leave you. I will be here. Being dead, is not so…bad.*

"What about dying?" Tia croaked.

Chapter 22
Jinx

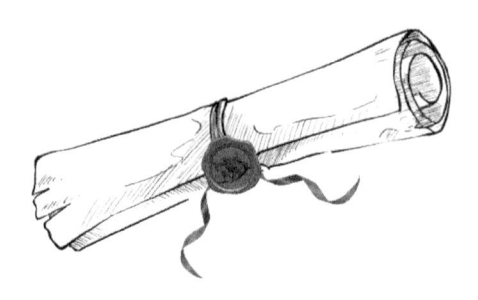

Jinx lay on his bed in the bunkhouse, the memories of that afternoon replaying in his tortured mind: Garth nearly dying, his long-lost sister appearing and rejecting him, then the crystal ball and Li, the ascender. The boy had died. Drowned. Jinx had been too late. He couldn't save him. He had watched Li as his lungs slowly inflated with water and he perished, in the past, alone. His soul ached. He should have been able to do something, anything.

A future for a future, resonated a voice inside his head. Jinx bolted upright, fully lucid from the torment the day had tolled upon him.

"Who's there?" His voice cracked. Jinx looked around confused. Had Garth snuck in while he'd been caught up in his own thoughts, too busy to hear him?

The boy altered the future, as you knew it. To stabilise the timelines and undo what he did, his future was forfeited.

"The Cacodaemon is alive?" That's just what he needed. Another ghost hell-bent on vengeance.

It is destroyed. Relief poured over Jinx as a wave of curiosity swamped him.

The witch hunter is a Cacodaemon, he thought. *And the being this voice belongs to can destroy them. How?* As if reading his mind, the bodyless voice spoke.

We will converse on this again, witch. But I warn you, next time it will cost you.

"Cost me what?" Jinx questioned, but the voice was already gone, leaving Jinx's mind to drift back into the dark torturous depths of guilt.

Minutes, maybe hours, later Garth appeared and slammed the door shut behind him. "You okay? I heard about the boy."

"Yeah," rasped Jinx, turning his back on Garth.

"I'm sorry. It must be hard. I know how it feels to lose someone." Clearing his throat, Garth continued, "Anyways, about earlier, you planning on telling anyone?"

"What?" huffed Jinx. "That you're something other than human, but I don't know what?" Jinx snapped, offended by Garth's lack of faith in his loyalty. "Or that you can touch and be touched by the dead?" Jinx spun around to face him with eyes glaring sharply like daggers.

"All right, take it easy." Garth sighed and rubbed a dirty hand over his face. "I'm sorry I didn't tell you, but I didn't lie to you either. You just never asked." Garth shrugged.

"Well, I'm asking now." Jinx glowered impatiently.

"And I'm not telling. Not yet," continued Garth with a deep sigh. "I can't." He blew out a frustrated breath and slumped against the cabinet.

Jinx leaned on his elbow, resting his head on his palms, his eyes hardening on Garth as a spark of magic misted his irises. "If you're a danger to this—" he circled his finger "—academy, I…"

"I'm no danger," Garth rushed out. "You can trust me on that." He gave Jinx a reassuring smile.

"How can I?" Jinx mumbled, the magic slowly seeping from his eyes.

"We're friends, aren't we?" Garth shrugged.

"Only if you can promise me you're no danger to this compound or the witches. And that one day very soon you will tell me—"

"What I am," Garth finished. "I swear it."

Fine. Jinx sulked and slumped his head back on the pillow, his magic receding completely as he wallowed in his own self-pity.

Garth's continual rustling prompted Jinx into asking, "What are you doing?" He stared down at Garth who was now shoving clothes into a rucksack.

"Head Mentor George told me your sister's stuck here for a few days, so I'm moving into Fiona's old place." He gulped painfully, his voice quaking. "I thought Hope could stay here. Maybe that way you guys can work through whatever issues you've got going on and get reacquainted?"

Jinx stared at him, his eyes softening. "Thanks," he mumbled, hearing the soft click of the door and Garth's footsteps gently receding from the bunkhouse. Jinx sighed. *Hope is coming here. Is that a good thing or a bad thing? What should I do? What-should-I-say?* Jinx lay on the top bunk, completely lost in thought, staring vacantly at the ceiling.

Jinx didn't acknowledge his sister's presence as she knocked delicately on the door and then proceeded to gently push it open. He didn't even take notice when she coughed.

She coughed again, but when she still received no attention she started, "The ascender…died?"

"Yes," he growled, finally noticing that she was there. *As if I don't feel bad enough, now Hope comes in here and the first thing she wants to talk about is that!* His heart seemed to fracture a little more.

"It's not your fault, you know – you weren't even there," said Hope trying to console him.

"How the bloody hell would you know if it's my fault or not?" His voice darkened. "You. Don't. Know. Me!" He turned to glare at her. Rage sparking air magic to cloud his eyes.

"Not through lack of trying," she muttered.

Pouncing on her words, he roared through gritted teeth, "What's that supposed to mean!?"

She turned on him, for the first time since she'd been made an outsider, uncaring of her powerless position. "Uh, let me think," she replied sarcastically. "Maybe if you'd responded to the letters I sent you, I might've actually had the chance to get to know you a little better." She blustered like a dragon about to roast its victim.

Jinx sat up, spinning his legs over the bunk as he dropped with a thud to the floor. He stalked forwards, eyes misting with anger, teeth gritted as he backed Hope into a corner. "You send one letter a year!" he roared. "I've sent you one a month since our grandmother separated us! You've never responded to any of my questions! Never given me a mobile number or address to visit you! Nothing!" he yelled in Hope's face.

"You've never sent me a letter," Hope spat back, shoving her hands into his chest, knocking him backwards, allowing her to escape the corner he'd backed her into. "Just think!" she screamed. "Why would I lie?!"

Jinx stood up, Hope's words finally sinking into his mind.

Her voice calmed. "You received the letters I sent," said Hope, "but I don't get yours. Why?"

"I don't... Goddess!" he roared, his voice taut. He turned to face Hope. "Yaris." He ran a hand through his braids, tugging at the loosened hair. "He's the only one who knew," Jinx admitted, finally comprehending the problem. "Shit!" He slammed his foot into the wall in frustration. *I'm gonna kill him. So help me Goddess I'm going to make him pay for keeping us apart.*

"I'm sorry," she consoled, stepping closer.

"You wanna stay here a few days. Right?" Jinx asked, running a hand through his braids, the crystals clattering noisily as they collided.

"Yeah, Olcan's had a nasty tumble, so his brothers can't pick me up." She sighed and slumped down on the end of the bottom bunk. "They're watching over him," Hope continued in a whisper, staring at the floor, her hands intertwining waiting for her brother's decision.

"I hope your friend's okay."

Hope's cheeks reddened.

"Give me your number, and you can stay," Jinx cajoled.

"But I don't know mine. I'll give you Olcan's, he and I are..." She blushed.

"You and he are...? What?" he asked irritably, motioning to his mobile that lay open on the fold-out bedside table.

"Nothing. I just mean you can trust him. He'll pass on your number to me. If he ever forgives me for ruining his coat, that is," she said, glaring down at the garment.

"Fine. And Hope, you need to know that when Grandmother finally steps down and names me her successor, as the Pren Ceri Coven's High Witch Elder, you so-called defectives will be welcome back home," he vowed, climbing stoically back into his bunk, whilst Hope speed-typed Olcan's number into his mobile.

Jinx woke from his silent slumber with an odd sensation, as though someone was watching him. He shivered, deciding to check on his sister. Peering down at her from the end of the bunk, he stuttered, "Is t-hat...?"

"Yes, it's Mum's crystal. I...took it when Grandmother sent me away, it's not like she noticed." Hope stroked the crystal. "It's normally cold, but it's acting weird tonight. It's hot. I think maybe someone's trying to make contact."

Jinx stared at the crystal in his sister's hand. His heart beat a little faster as tears formed in his eyes. He wiped them away and held out his other hand to his sister. "It's not...them trying to make contact," he told her as the crystal's warm weight touched his palm, "but we can find out who."

Jinx jumped from his bunk, snatched the crystal from his sister's delicate hands and placed it on the floor. He sat cross-legged before it and motioned for his sister to join him.

"Who do you think it is?" asked Hope, full of excitement and leaning in to stare at the crystal.

"Tia," he whispered hopefully as he focused his attention and thought of only her, her raven hair, her glistening lips. The pitiful state he had last seen her in.

Suddenly, the crystal began to fog, a shrill scream emanating from its depths.

"He-lp! Help me!" The plea resonated throughout the room, prickling Jinx's skin like an acupuncturist. *No. No*, Jinx thought. *That's not right. That's not Tia.*

"Someone's drawing the crystal's attention," Hope interrupted. "Jinx, they're begging for help." Hope drew closer, staring into the crystal's depths.

"But I want…" Jinx shook his head in frustration, his braids clattered together as his sister gently touched his hand.

"I know, but someone else is drawing the crystal's attention. They have power. The crystal won't ignore it…"

Suddenly, Paul appeared in the crystal's surface, he was on his knees desperately clutching his head. "I can't. I can't," he begged.

"What is he doing?" questioned Hope.

"Expelling," observed Jinx, his attention focused on the ascender.

"Expelling what?"

"Expelling his ghost assignment from his body," said Jinx.

"But I thought that was—"

"Impossible? Yes, unless…" Jinx started wearily. "Unless he is something more…than a G-Poss."

"You mean he could be a witch?" asked Hope, raising an eyebrow. "Two half-witch Ghost Possessors. Extraordinary!"

"Perhaps. Or maybe he's...something else," Jinx contemplated as a roar tore from Paul's throat.

The crystal shook with intensity as Cain's essence seeped from Paul's pores like oil, reforming him into his ghostly being, his eyes flaring amber as he bellowed. "You little shit!" he yelled, at Paul. The ascender was still on his knees, shaking, his face red and eyes shiny with unshed tears. "What am I supposed to do now? Haunt this bloody rundown warehouse for the rest of eternity?" Cain drew back a large fist and let it fly at Paul, who instinctively recoiled. But there was no impact. His meaty fist ghosted straight through Paul's cheek. Cain roared his frustration, the dust in the warehouse vibrated off the floor with his potential poltergeist activity.

"I'm sorry," said Paul, sniffing.

"You're a failure. A bloody waste of space. A worthless piece of shit! It's no wonder your uncle couldn't wait to get rid of you."

As Hope and Jinx watched on, the crystal once again started to vibrate. But this time, it hummed with power.

Paul knelt down and rocked slightly as he shouted, "I'm not worthless! Not useless I'm not!"

Cain got as close to Paul's face as possible, a wickedness gleaming in his eyes. "I bet that's why your mother died too. Couldn't stand the sight of you! Could she?!"

Magic hummed in the air. Jinx could see it through the crystal, and then he felt the fiery heat that signified the presence of a- *Oh Goddess no-* a warlock!

A blinding light burst out of nowhere, a figure silhouetted against its magnificence and Jinx watched as Cain exploded from a burst of salt flung from the warlock's hands.

"There now, isn't that better?" The voice- somehow familiar- chuckled. "I never did like him." Paul glared in open astonishment as the dark figure of the warlock stepped into the light.

"Wh-o?"

"Do not look at me, fool. You'll damn us both!" He bellowed.

"But why?" Paul sniffed.

The figure waved a hand dismissively. "Do not bother me with questions, I am a busy man." He held out his hand expectantly. "Now come."

"Why?" repeated a wide-eyed Paul.

"How did he put it?" the warlock mused, a hand at his temple in thought. "Ah, yes. I remember; To change the future Paul, you must first change yourself."

"Seriously?" Paul asked, rising to his feet, his eyes still on his trainers. "What kind of cryptic shit is that?"

"Our kind of cryptic shit!" roared the warlock. He grabbed Paul's arm, spinning him, and ripped the pendant from his neck, shoving him into the light.

"Shit! Ah, Goddess, shit!" roared Jinx in outrage, his magic sparking with his temper. He had already lost one ascender and been blamed for his death. He didn't need to lose another; the consequences would be too steep. But it was too late. Paul had already disappeared.

"What the?" Hope chimed in as the warlock lowered a boot-clad foot and smashed the pendant beneath its sole. The image of the warehouse where Paul had stood was faded until the crystal showed nothing.

"Great, that's all I need," Jinx snapped. "First, I'm blamed for Li's death. Now—" he motioned to the crystal "—they'll be accusing me of kidnapping their ascenders."

Hope watched him. "Should we continue looking in on the ascenders?" she probed.

"Yes," he commanded, his vigour renewed. "Let's find Tia."

Hope sighed in resignation. She picked up the quartz crystal and walked over to the small cabinet in the room, where a sage smudge stick lay. It was perfect to cleanse the crystal so it could be used again without interference from the previous vision of past-future events. The sage stick smoked, its herbal essence filling the room and Hope replaced the crystal on the floor between them.

Jinx let out his awareness, using the crystal as a conduit to search the past for the pendant that marked Tia and her location. He watched hunched over the smooth crystal as Tia's image appeared in its surface.

"Goddess, she's so thin," he growled, a wave of anger rolling over him. *Whoever's done this to her is going to pay. And pay dearly*, he vowed.

Through the crystal, Jinx could see Tia sat rocking in a corner, her hands clasping her knees as she mumbled. *To Yule*, he thought. Her head lay bowed on her knees. The sound of footsteps nearing the cell where she was being held had her raising a tear-stained face, defiled by blood and grime. As the footsteps became louder. She began to shake. Screams and pleas of 'innocent' filled the air and the crystal shook with their impact.

"What the...?" Hope gaped at the shaking crystal.

"What?" snapped Jinx. He tore his gaze from Tia to see his sister backing away with her finger pointing shakily at the crystal.

"Did you...see...that?" she stuttered.

"The crystal, yes. Why?" he questioned, his eyes fixated on Tia's shaking image in its surface.

"Is it supposed to do that?" she asked, waving her finger manically.

"How should I know? You're the crystal expert. I've never used them for divination before," Jinx replied with a huff.

"But you're the one powering it," Hope implored.

Jinx flicked his eyes to the crystal in irritation, a confused frown spreading over his features as he reached out to touch it. Sparks shot from the surface to dance upon skin. Every spark that touched him was full of power, projecting a distress call from witch- "...I beg thee...!" to witch-

"...Help us...!" to witch-

"...Innocent...!"

Their begging sobs punched holes in his heart. His ancestral brothers and sisters were in pain. *So much pain.* Sweat broke out on his brow; his hands shook as he tried to focus on his Tia. *My Tia?* All of a sudden, the booming voice of Tia's captor reverberated through the crystal.

"Against the wall, witch!" Tia stood, her face smashed into the wooden wall, a terrified expression claiming her features. A trance of fear glazed her eyes when she spotted the hound that stalked her captor's boots in her peripheral vision. Her body shook like the London underground on a night from hell.

Jinx watched as the man wrench her hands painfully behind her back and bound them tightly in rope.

He could barely hear her prayers with a horse voice spoken through cracked lips. Her captor dragged her from the cell, her weakened body tripping and stumbling in an attempt to keep up as he wrenched her hair like a choke chain on a lead.

Jinx kept his eyes fixed on Tia while the man hauled her out of the building and into the light of day. He watched a small smile reach her lips as the sun streamed down on her too-pale skin before she was hustled through a crowd of villagers. Then, the throng of onlookers parted revealing-

"Gallows! Goddess! No!" Jinx's power roared furiously through his veins, which followed the stream he had already been summoning to flow into the crystal. It exploded, becoming too gorged on his power, causing small chunks of sharp crystal to pierce his skin.

"Shit!" screamed Hope as she, too, had crystals angrily stab at her.

Jinx lurched to his feet, power exploding from him. He bombed out of the small bunkhouse door; his so-called guards flew face first into the cobbled path. Uncaring, Jinx raced on – determination spurring him.

"I'm coming, Tia," he vowed through clenched teeth. "I'll get you out. I'll save you. Just...don't die!"

Chapter 23

Tia

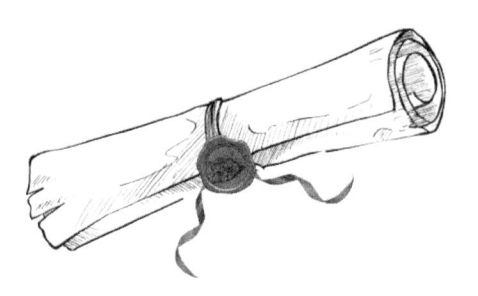

Cell after putrid cell swept by, hay and dust trailing in uproar at Tia's bare feet as she was dragged backwards by a hand twisted painfully in her dishevelled hair. She hissed, her eyes pricking with tears. Tia clenched the hand that pulled her in an attempt to lessen the pain and keep her hair rooted to her head. But it was useless. She could not free herself.

She watched through pain-teared eyes as a man with dark clothes and a velvet hat opened the door she knew led to Ayla: the witch – or warlock, as Yule had informed her – guilty of werewolfery.

Goddess, be with her, prayed Yule inside Tia's mind while crazed screams drew blood from her ears. Seconds later, the screams had died and the man, one of the witch hunter's assistants, dragged Ayla out like a dog on a lead. Except her lead was latched onto some sort of leather mask strapped over her face.

What the shitting hell is that? Tia asked Yule, trembling at the possibility that it might be her who wore it next.

A bridle, Yule whispered. *It be a witch's bridle.*

Be not afraid, sister. A voice, neither her own nor Yule's, echoed inside her head. *Thy vendetta shall be satisfied.* A half-crazy, half-psychotic laugh resonated around her mind as she looked at Ayla, the only one there who could possess the voice.

Ayla's wide eyes leaked bloody tears. She stumbled down the corridor of hay and into another cell where both Ayla and the assistant disappeared behind the deafening slam of the door.

Blessed be, sister, Yule prayed. *Thy path may have faltered, but may thy journey to Summerland be swift and merciful, and may the Goddess forgive thee, Ayla.*

Summerland? Questioned Tia.

Aye, Tia, Summerland. The place where our souls transcend after death.

Heaven – I don't even know if I believe in that anymore. Tia sighed within.

Aye, I understand, but the Goddess will watch over thy soul, Tia, no matter your beliefs.

[323]

Yeah, maybe. A hard wrench of her hair forced Tia's attention back to her ominous situation. That's when she realised they had reached the iron-barred door. She was dragged out, the light of day blinding her momentarily as she took in huge gulps of clean air.

Fresh air, thought Tia. *How long has it been since I could breathe without the stench of faeces making me gag? And look at that sky.* It was a beautiful blue, crossed with streaks of pink and amber, a scarlet streak lowlighting its beauty like a strategically placed ribbon.

Tia was dragged towards a mass of shouting villagers. Face upon face of old women, men and young children looked down on her. Tia twisted and turned in the hair lock. People spat in her face, others jeered and gawked – but no one helped her. The cobbled stones snared her feet and bit bloody chunks from their soles while she tried to regain her footing.

Suddenly, the air whooshed out of her lungs with a gruelling kick to her ribs. *Why?* Tia beseeched. *What have I ever done to you, you bloody bitch!*

Hush, Tia, calmed Yule. *Do not struggle; it will only incite them further.*

As if on cue, a young boy ran from the jeering clutches of his friends. A sardonic smile lit up his face before he threw his hand, palm open, in Tia's filthy face. A storm of white sand whirled and stabbed at her eyes. She recognised it as salt, as it attacked like a bee sting upon her bloodied face.

Tia swung and twisted in the man's grip, but to no avail. Finally, blissfully, he stopped. That's when Tia was jerked from the ground, her shoulders encompassed in a vice-like grip. Through her haunted bloodshot eyes she saw Yule. Yule from the past, atop a wooden structure, a rope circling her neck and a trapdoor at her feet. Her skin was tinted grey, her pallor ghostly as tears drew rivers down her blood-scored cheeks.

In that moment, past Yule knew she was going to die for a crime she never committed: the murder of her beloved Aaric. And Tia couldn't let that happen.

What can I do? she implored Yule inside her mind.

Nothing, Yule replied dejectedly.

There must be something, anything. Think! screamed Tia's mind.

All hope is lost, Tia.

There has to be a way. Oh! "God, I've got it."

TIA! Yule scolded as the witch hunter's assistant slammed his fist into her face, her already mashed nose splitting again on impact as her eyes watered. *Aaargh!*

"Filthy blasphemous witch!" he shouted. Tia stumbled backwards. "Silence!" He regained his hold and shook her so hard her teeth rattled. "Un-der-stand?"

Tia nodded with her lips sealed. She internally hypothesised, *y-your unfinished business is t-to what?*

Be found innocent of my lover's death, Yule answered.

So, if someone was to confess to his murder?

I would move on. But making his killer confess would prove impossible. I know not who it is. Yule sighed in Tia's mind.

But what if I was to?

To what? Yule asked, confused.

Confess?

Oh Goddess, I would be free to move on. To blessedly die and reach Summerland. Free. Tia…oh, Tia, no…no…you must not falsely confess to Aaric's murder. I would never again meet you. Unless…it is possible that my past self would demand vengeance. Tia, please. Do. Not. Do. This! Her voice became shrill with panic.

Tia's head screamed with pain, but she steeled herself against it and attempted to placate Yule. *But you are not a bad witch, Yule. I trust you*, she consoled.

Tia, I beseech you, do not take that risk, she begged.

Friends are formidable, Yule.

Friends. Yule broke on a mental sob. *I will have no knowledge of thee, Tia. I will die hating thee, cursing thee.*

But you'd never forget me, finished Tia resolutely.

Refocusing on past Yule, Tia listened as the witch hunter decreed, "Yule Winter has been condemned a witch guilty of the murder of Aaric, son of the widow Charlotte. When will they learn?" He clasped his dark Bible high, the golden calligraphy glinting in the sunlight.

"Thou shalt not suffer a witch to live," roared the crowd in anticipation.

The witch hunter motioned to the hangman. "As our Lord God demands, she shall be hung by the neck till dead!" he ordered.

Knowing this was her only chance, Tia pulled together the strands of her new, raw magical energy and lifted her voice so that it carried over the crowd like a megaphone. "I killed him!!!" she screamed as the hangman loosened the trapped door.

Past Yule turned, eyes full of loathing as she swung free beneath the trap door, the rope snapping taut around her neck.

The sound echoed ominously throughout the crowd as Tia watched past Yule swing from the noose – dead. A roar of cheers rose up. Tia's heart sank into depression. The loss of past Yule was traumatising, but the crushing emptiness left in her mind was heart breaking. The first connection to her family since the G-Poss took her was now gone – forever.

"Move!" Rough hands shoved Tia up the steeply constructed steps that led to the gallows.

Tia counted them in her mind as she tried to calm her racing heart.

One. Her foot slammed down like lead on the shabbily constructed surface. She could hear the sickening roar of the crowd still chiming in her ears, but the sound that chilled her blood was the taut squeak of the rope as Yule swung by her neck beneath the trapdoor.

Tia's stomach lurched, bile rose in her throat until her head was wrenched back from the hand fisted painfully in her knotted raven hair.

Dark brown eyes blazed hatred down upon her as the man above spat, "Move!" through gritted teeth. Tia's legs wobbled and her head hurt, but at least the pain had stopped her from throwing up. She stumbled up the high wooden steps.

Two, three, four. She heard the dull thwack as Yule was released from the noose, her body hitting the floor. Feeling the man's presence behind her, she stomped up three more steps.

Five, six, seven. When the gallows slowly came into view, Tia's breath hitched in her throat, her lungs burnt and her hands shook. Tia's feet rooted themselves as she stared around praying for an escape route. But there were none. She was all alone. Condemned to hang as a witch, hundreds of years before she was born.

Tia received a smack to the head as the man crowded the space behind her. She fell, her teeth retailing when her jaw hit the wood hard.

Eight, nine, ten. She stood up on shaky legs watching a man sling Yule's body into a waiting cart, before eagerly looking up at her. Tia, her throat like the Sahara Desert, gulped hard. She stepped automatically.

Eleven, twelve…thirteen.

Silence. Nobody spoke. Nobody moved, but all eyes were fixed on Tia. Over half of the crowd stared at her with hatred and fear burning in their eyes. The remaining few with a mixture of pity and what looked like pride. *Why the hell do they look so bloody proud?* thought Tia. *I'm gonna die. Oh God! I'm. Gonna. Die.*

She could already feel the rope around her neck, her breath coming in gasping pants as she trudged the final steps to her impending doom.

At first, her mind raced with flashes of her mother's face sick with worry as she leaned over her in the hospital where she was abducted by the G-Poss. Her mother's soothing scent of honey and almond milk soap had calmed her, along with a memory of her father playing a brand new Ratchet and Clank game he had bought them. The smile on his face as he showed Donnal how to make Ratchet jump into the spaceship.

Tia's lip quirked in a bloody smile; her eyes glazed with past memories of her brother, Donnal. *Is he...? Could it be that he is really...? What had happened to him?* Whatever it was, she knew it was her fault. It had to be because although they fought a lot, Tia had always been the one to look out for her brother. *Without me there for him-* A tear leaked from her eye, stinging her bloodied face. Her heart howled in loss.

Not only had she lost Yule's presence in her mind, which left a painful emptiness, but now she had to die in front of this twisted, evil witch hunter who had killed Yule – her friend and relative. Not only did she have to walk to her own execution, she had to do it alone. There was no comfort in this time for her. Yule was gone and any family she had would not know her, for the family she belonged to were not even born.

Then she remembered Ella and knew at once if she died, Ella – just as she figured Donnal had – would do something stupid. *Something permanent.* Something that placed them side by side, no matter what realm it was in.

Steeling a great, shuddering breath, a revelation hit her: *my family would not want me to feel guilty over my abduction.* So, she finally accepted that she no longer owed her family an apology for not fighting hard enough and not escaping. Deep down she knew they loved her, no matter what. *And if it wasn't for the bloody G-Poss being a government compound, they probably would have found me already* – the Morgans were not quitters. Tia sighed internally, a tear beading in her eye. *I love them. That's all that matters. I. Love. Them.*

Tia let her broken heart swell with love and slowly felt the fractured pieces click back together. *At least I will die whole and complete; no celestial hauntings for me*, she thought with a smirk, allowing her mind to go numb with the acceptance of her imminent death.

Resigned to her fate, she ceased stumbling and dragging her feet. She held her head high and her back ramrod straight as the hangman slipped a heavy length of rope around her neck.

Dignity, she projected into her own mind. *If I'm gonna die, I'll be damned if I die a coward!* Her battle cry roared through her mind as the witch hunter's malicious eyes promised a torment worse than death. Her eyes glued to his, his challenge met, she barely heard the trapdoor open on squeaky hinges. The world around her silenced. Everything moved into slow motion as her feet dropped out beneath her, her stomach rolling. The rope snapped taut around her neck, burning with friction it rubbed her skin raw, her breath slowly strangling from her.

Her body began to convulse, but her blurred vision never left the witch hunter's deep brown eyes pulsing with eager anticipation. She knew at that moment he wouldn't stop. His goal was too vast to fulfil. She knew deep down the witch hunter's malicious spirit that haunted the time she had come from would be out to destroy the people she had left behind. *Like Jinx*, her mind provided irritatingly. *Jinx. Ha! He could look after himself.*

Tia watched, her eyes obscured with bloody tears and black spots, the witch hunter raced from the hangman's platform and settle into the crowd below to watch her slowly strangle. The sky opened up and huge, heavy droplets hammered down onto the hastily departing horde. But the witch hunter stood still as a rock to see his justice carried out, a malevolent grin lighting his sadistic face.

The faces of Tia's loved ones swam in the river of her mind. The face of her mother, as real as if she was ten years old again, standing right next to her. The face of her father laughing, his pallor pale. Her crush, Li, smiling in an old-fashioned black and white photograph. Reece, Anka and the annoying freak Paul also washed into view, their faces monochrome as they faded into black blobs, her eyes no longer functioning. And then Donnal broke through her mind's darkness, a bright light shining around him, her brother smiled his forgiveness as she felt her body and mind slowly shut down.

Dear God, Goddess or whatever. Please, I beg you, look after the ones I'll leave behind. Please, I love th— Tia's body stopped convulsing, her head hung loosely on the rope, sweat poured down her body. She took one last shuddering breath, content to die alone in the past. A martyr to the G-Poss.

Chapter 24

Jinx

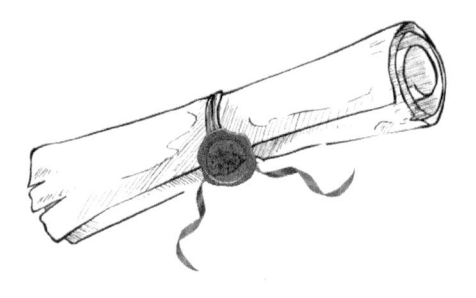

With the force of magic exploding through his body, Jinx ran along the cobbled path, jumped over a group of small sculpted Buxus and weaved his way through the cluttered maze of graves. *I have to do something. Anything. Oh Goddess.* He panted as he ran with the force of a tornado. *I can't let her die. Don't let her die. Please. Not like that. Witches, even half-witches, are supposed to have double the lifespan of a normal human – not less than a quarter of it. But there will be no recovery from a hanging.*

It was one of the three ways to kill a witch before their lifespan ended in old age, as was common since the end of the witch trials in the seventeenth century. The other two were by burning, not just at the stake, but anywhere. Or by drowning, which was most commonly called ducking in the seventeenth century, and so it had kept its name with the government's secret faction enforcers: the hunters. Not that Jinx needed to worry about those jacked up steroid freaks now. *I need to focus on Tia, on somehow reaching her. But how?*

Jinx sprinted, his footsteps light, as he smashed through the closest door into the academy. Unfortunately it was the kitchen delivery entrance. Jinx had to race through avoiding the chef waggling a wooden spoon coated with something red and runny at his co-worker. Knives and pots flew in his wake, but his natural magic buffered him from injury. He raced out through the door. Vaulting over the counters and out of the pigpen, gasping faces blurring from his vision, he sped down the corridors knocking potentials and G-Poss aside. *I cannot lose her!* His heart screamed as he crashed through the doors to the reception hall; his magic shoved the G-Poss from the room with barely contained force.

Jinx knelt on trembling knees, sweat dripping down his face. He raised his eyes to the ceiling beseeching his Goddess whilst drawing in great gulps of air. But before he had the chance to beg the Goddess, to plead for Tia's life, the air around him started to ripple. A cold whirl of air blasted him; the odour of waste and dirt filled his nostrils. Suddenly the air started to thicken, the molecules condensing to form...

"TIA!" he gasped, reaching to pull her into his lap before she collapsed to the floor. Sticky tendrils of raven hair clung to her pale face. Gently he wiped them away, a slick stream of grime and blood coating his fingers as they touched her chilled skin. Her nose lay smashed upon her cheek, imbedded in the swollen skin around it. Her bloodshot cobalt eyes fluttered open and locked on his of earthen green. She quivered.

In shock? Fear? Relief? Jinx had no idea, even though he secretly hoped it was relief and that she felt safe; he would protect her until his last breath.

Jinx stared down at the girl in his arms and assessed her injuries. *The nose can be fixed*, he decided, pushing himself to his feet, but the ugly rope burn that welted her neck would remain; a tribute scar to her warrior soul.

He picked her up, shifting her into the cradle of his arms. *She is so light*, he thought. Her feet hung over his arm, swaying with motion, bare, scraped raw and bloodied, as dirty as the rest of her. He began to walk gently. As her head lay nestled against his broad chest, he could see the missing patches of hair and bloody scalp. Jinx, fearful to his heart, listened to her short rattling breaths. *Thank the Goddess she is alive.*

Taking a deep breath, he steeled himself and took a quick glance at her neck. It ballooned beneath her raven hair, a necklace of rope burns scaring the tender skin as a welt formed. *Tia. My Tia. What have they done to you?* "Goddess," he pleaded, nearing the doors, "help her."

The doors burst open and in raced Hope. "Oh God!" she said, skidding to a halt. "Jinx, is she… Is she…?"

"No," he snapped. His voice was raw with stifled emotion as his heart thundered a warning in his ears and he pushed past her. Outside the hall a crowd of warriors had formed, led by George.

"Put her down, witch!" roared George. His podgy form wobbled as he stormed towards Jinx. "She is one of ours." He motioned with a wave of his chubby hand to the G-Poss warriors beside him. "Not one of you—" he looked Jinx up and down with an air of disgust "—dirty witches!"

"Get. Out. Of. My. Way," gritted Jinx back, careful not to jostle the unconscious Tia, who now lay like a dead weight in his arms. Worried when he could no longer hear her heart beat over the forming crowd, he sent a wave of magic out to her. Blood rushed to his ears; white noise filled them with pressure. He waited. And then...yes, there it was, faint but steady. She lived. But she might not if Jinx didn't get help soon.

"Our responsibility," bellowed George, now level with Jinx. He held out his arms in a cradle and glared at him. "Give her to me and leave." His words were snapped through gritted teeth.

Does he really care? thought Jinx. *Or maybe he just doesn't want to lose another one of his ascenders?* Jinx didn't know, and he didn't care. Tia was his responsibility. He had found her and he had made a promise – a promise he would keep.

Jinx gently lifted her higher, glaring at George. He felt the power of magic mist his eyes. He smirked sarcastically as George stepped back, afraid of him. Automatically he tapped into the forceful sensation crackling around him. His eyes glazed with magic as he sent it out to part the crowd. The air sent the G-Poss and potentials flying into the corridor walls. None of them hurt. But all, including George, satisfyingly stunned. Jinx harrumphed. None of them knew the extent of his powers, and now they'd had a taster.

Jinx licked his dry lips, his mind working overtime wondering where the hospital was located, when a cool hand touched his bicep. *Tia?*

Hope stood beside him, a look of horror on her face. "You shouldn't have done that, Jinx. I can see the fury in your eyes. You need to calm down before you do something you'll regret. And you are not a bad person – so think." She sighed. "Tia needs you. Focus on your magic," she scolded. "Now run!"

Jinx let his eyes fall once again to Tia. *My Tia.* His heart swelled with pride at the thought of her survival. *She has been through so much. My Tia is strong, a warrior. Much better than these G-Poss scum.* Awareness tugged at him. Finally, he remembered where he had seen the tiny hospital. Using his natural magic as an aid, he ran much faster than any human, much faster than any G-Poss. As fast as a witch with air magic could, he zoomed straight to the hospital doors. After kicking them open, he yelled for attention, then muscled the nurses out of the way to lie Tia's fragile form on a bed. "You're safe now," he whispered shortly before the nurses rolled her away and set to work.

Jinx's heart stuttered as he slumped into a chair waiting for news of Tia's situation. He raked a hand through his braids, the small gemstones whipping at his neck as he dishevelled them. "The people who did this to her…" His heart bled at the thought of being unable to help her. Tears of crushing guilt beaded in his eyes and anger boiled volcanically in his blood. Hope sat in the chair next to him and took his hand. "I want to kill them!" he confided, his teeth grinding with fury.

"Don't, Jinx. You can have revenge without cursing them, or yourself. You are *not* a warlock. Please don't go down that road. I don't think I could cope with losing someone else." Hope's voice warbled as Jinx stared up into her eyes, a single tear running down her cheek. "I've just got you back." Her lips wobbled and quirked into a sad smile.

"I…I love her," he confided, once again returning his eyes to the floor.

A tiny gasp seeped from Hope's lips. "You can't. She's a G-Poss. Grandmother will forbid it."

"I can do what I like. I love her. She is more than just a G-Poss, Hope. She has witch blood, too. Powers. She is exactly what Grandmother is looking for. A link between the G-Poss and the witch factions."

"God help her," prayed Hope.

At that moment, a panting George descended upon them, face red and eyes sparking furiously as he addressed Jinx.

"I have spoken to your High Witch Elder, boy. She will be sending a driver to collect you in the morning." He waggled a fat finger in Jinx's face, and Jinx had to fight the urge to snap his teeth at him. "Mark my words, boy, you will pay for this insult." He clicked his fingers and the twins appeared. "Stay with him," George instructed. "Take him back to the bunkhouse and make sure he stays there this time!" With that, George spun around, walked to the doors, pausing before exiting them. "You, girl, will be escorted off the property tonight. So I suggest you say your goodbyes," snapped George. He left the doors swinging in his wake.

Jinx turned to his sister. "Someone is coming for you?" he asked with concern.

"Yes, Olcan's brother, Kurt, texted me earlier. He says we need to talk, so he'll pick me up around ten."

Jinx looked up at the clock behind the reception desk. "That's in twenty minutes." He sighed, defeated.

She winked cheekily. "How about I make you a little time to say goodbye to your girl Tia, before I go?"

Jinx smiled his thanks as Hope intercepted the delinquent twins bearing down on them and directed them away, before stalking through the hospital in search of Tia.

After a few wrong turns later, Jinx stumbled on the right room. Tia lay peacefully on a bed covered in a duck egg, blue blanket, her skin clean and pale, her hair tied loosely off her face. He crouched next to her bony body and cursed. Her captors had not fed her. They had barely kept her alive. She looked so weak, so fragile. So *not* Tia. Gently, he manoeuvred one of her hands into his. It engulfed hers. He noticed the bloodied beds of her chipped black nails. *Evidence that she fought her captors with everything she had*, he thought.

My Tia, his heart proclaimed whilst planting a tender kiss on her palm. "I have to leave. I have no choice. If I don't go, my grandmother, the High Witch Elder, will come here and that will cause a whole lot more trouble than I'm in now." Jinx leaned closer to her ear, whispering, "It is said that when a witch pledges his heart, a gift he should then impart." He chuckled lightly. At the tender age of twelve, he swore to his mother that he would never use that phrase.

He stared back at Tia, his head hung, his braids clattering around his face as he choked the words, "I nearly lost you today, Tia." His throat constricted as he continued, "And if it is within my power, I shall never see you in this state again." He lifted his head and dashed away a stream of tears with the back of his hand. Sniffing, he resumed, "So, I hereby bestow on you a gift." He smiled indulgently as though hearing her ask 'what?' and the anxiety behind it. Ever cautious was his Tia. But smart, ever so smart. "I shall gift you my heart. If you can hear me, I hope you understand; the spell I'll now cast will bind my heart to yours. But yours will remain free, unless one day you feel the same way and bestow yours upon me." He bent his head to kiss the tender skin of her palm. She moaned. In acknowledgement? He could only hope. Sliding his chrysoberyl ring from his forefinger to her thumb, he cast:

"From my heart to yours,

I bind my love,

And seal my pact.

Through the chrysoberyl I impart,

Forever it will stay,

As my love will for thee.

Goddess divine,

So let it be!"

Gently he lifted her hand to rest it back on the bed, pulled up her blanket and tenderly tucked it under in.

Just then, Hope appeared. "Time to go," she whispered, trying not to disturb the unconscious Tia.

Jinx grabbed his sister's hand. "Do you think you could…? Fix her nose?"

Hope chuckled delicately. "I thought you'd never ask. Poor girl couldn't get a nose job to fix that. I'll do my best. As always. You'd better go, the twins are outside and they're getting really impatient."

"They can wait a minute," stated Jinx bluntly as he gazed from Tia to his sister. He took her small hand in his, stilling her. Hope's eyes quickly fluttered away when he looked directly at her. Jinx pulled his sister towards him and locked her in an embrace that showed the years they'd been apart didn't matter to him anymore. "Thank you. Don't be a stranger again. Okay?" Releasing a confused looking Hope, he smiled and stood, before leaning over Tia and tenderly kissing her forehead. "Tia, you complete me." He sighed as if a heavy burden was cursed on him for leaving. "Merry part, my love, and with the Goddess's blessing I shall see you soon."

Walking away from Tia lying helplessly in the hospital bed was one of the hardest things Jinx had ever had to do. *Goddess willing, she will not die.* The nurses had said she was stable and as he gently closed the door, he heard his sister rustling around with her crystals. He knew Tia was in good hands.

But in linking his heart to hers, he knew deep down on some level that she would never be the same again.

Chapter 25

Tia

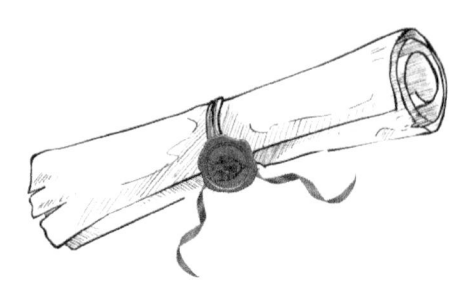

From within the haunting mist of her dreams, Tia watched a scarlet ribbon flutter its way towards her on a calm breeze. She smiled, playfully stalking its descent, before grabbing it. But at the last minute, as her fingers stroked its silky texture, everything changed. A deeply malicious voice cackled eerily in the air around her. Tia's pulse hammered erratically as an icy storm shot lightening through the dark clouds. The smell of singed earth rose around her. Then, suddenly, she fell through a wooden hatch, sharp splinters bit into her bare feet. Her hands flew to her neck, scratching as they strained manically against the scarlet ribbon now lashed around her throat like a whip, scoring, suffocating, and shredding into her skin.

The dream's storm raged above. Lightening clawed across the sky as thunder roared in anger. Tia struggled to fight, struggled to breathe, to survive. She fell to her knees, her eyes wide with horror at an image of the witch hunter taking form in her nightmare.

He stood there, a dark phantom of her imagination, clutching his old Bible inscribed with gold calligraphy. With one withered hand outstretched, his finger pointing damningly at Tia, he roared, "Thou shalt not suffer a witch to live!"

The words echoed around her like the scream of an owl about to strike its prey. Tia's eyes began to blur, black spots filled her vision until she could barely see, and then suddenly there was Jinx.

Jinx? What's he doing here? A bright orb of light surrounding him dissipated the darkness. His mere presence quashed the witch hunter's ghostly essence in her strange dreamscape.

She didn't know how she knew it was Jinx. In the mist of her dream, he was taller with a heavier build and held a power so strong his body crackled with static. His hair was no longer in corn braids with jangling crystals at their ends, it was now cut short. *Strange*, she thought, *somehow it makes him look more...human.*

The storm began to recede as she stared into his deep earthen green eyes. Her stomach swam with a nauseating reality; somehow, the Jinx in her dream was trying to help her. *But why?* Tia's throat clenched with nerves as she tried unsuccessfully to thank him, yet she didn't know why.

The screeching seemed to die slowly when a soft mumble of incoherent words drowned out its residue. That's when Tia noticed her 'dream Jinx' chanting, his thick lips moving quickly over the words. Then his eyelids sealed, severing their connection. Tia's soul instantly mourned the loss of those knowing eyes, as if on some level they were…connected. *As if!* Tia snorted in disbelief. Instantly, the lethal scarlet ribbon began to vibrate before exploding into tiny fragments that rained down like confetti around her.

Tia sucked in a deep lungful of air, her chest slowly and painfully expanding, as her hands reached for her neck. Her fingers played over the scar that was quickly forming where blood should have been. She stared at Jinx just as her little brother, Donnal, appeared.

He was vaguely transparent and only a year older than when she had last seen him. She sighed. *What had happened to him?* His hair hung in unruly locks over his blue-grey eyes and his body looked half-starved. With tears still staining his eyes, he slipped his hand into Jinx's, which made Jinx flutter open his eyes. His chant made the air around her hum – and then they were there, both holding a hand out to her attentively.

Tia felt her body wrenched up into their embraces; she clasped at their hands like the lifesavers they were in this messed up nightmare – or dream.

They walked for a long while, Tia at their centre, her long-lost brother to her right and Jinx, the incredibly powerful witch, to her left. No one said anything. They just walked as comrades, all content and complete with each other's presence. Together they were safe. She felt it. The knowledge seeped deep into Tia's aching bones, an earth-shattering comfort for the girl who had been taken from her family so long ago.

The dream mist parted to reveal a small cobbled road. They travelled along in silence until an illegible signpost split the path in two directions. Both Jinx and Donnal let go of her hands, each travelling a different road and then stopping, as if realising she wasn't there. They both stood on separate paths, waiting.

Tia felt her heart break in two. Jinx had saved her from the phantom witch hunter in this nightmare, dream, or whatever it was. And Donnal was her little brother; the brother she had been fighting so desperately to return home to.

Tia stared at the signpost, unsure what to do until she noticed forms flickering in and out of view beneath it. "Yule!"

she gasped, barely recognising the beautiful corn-haired woman. Her heart soared with joy as she turned, her sparkling blue eyes on Tia.

Tia smiled. No longer did she wear the stain of torture upon her body; no longer did the ominous dripping of her waterlogged dress announce her presence. Now, she was truly enchanting; like a fairy tale come to life. Her skin was pale and unblemished, her aroma no longer made Tia's eyes water with revulsion. Yule had truly moved on. But she still wore the neckless of rope burns. *Why?* Tia wondered as Yule swept her into an embrace only dreams would allow, a tear sliding from her eyes.

"Be at peace, Tia. The angels let me remember thee, for we will meet again."

Tia blinked her tear-blurred eyes, and then Yule was gone. Her heart clenched in joy at the thought that Yule was allowed to remember her and their time as…friends. She rubbed an arm across her eyes, clearing her vision so she could look for Jinx and Donnal.

Good. They're still there. Yet the disturbed mutterings of a familiar voice had her staring back at the old, weathered signpost again. A gorgeous boy with cropped black hair whispered from his slouched position against the post. His knees were tucked into his chest and his palms cupped his face as he sobbed.

"I can't believe it?" He dropped his hands and turned to face Tia. "Can you?"

Oh my God! Water-blind eyes stared out from where the most perfect brown ones used to reside. The boy's once tanned skin was now tinted a sickly blue. *Li.* Tia sighed with pity finally recognising him. *What the hell happened?*

He slowly stood and raised his hands in surrender as though worried that Tia would panic at the sight of him. *As if!* she thought, and then he just faded away.

Tia looked back at the paths. Her heart broke when she realised her brother was no longer waiting for her. She rubbed her aching heart harshly and turned towards where Jinx still stood, his hand outstretched, beckoning. Tia gulped in a sobbing breath. She'd wanted to go with her brother. She hadn't seen him in so long, and he looked so lost, *so* alone, *so* unloved.

Instead, her heavy footsteps faltered slightly as she cautiously made her way to the witch, Jinx, who smiled indulgently, reassuring her like one would a skittish child. Dream Jinx bent down and whispered into her ear as she reached him, he then pulled her down the dream path and back into the painful grip of reality.

"...Goodbye..." was the last whispering word Tia remembered while slowly regaining consciousness. Unsure of her surroundings, with her eyes still shut, she flexed her feet, but panic gripped her when they became tangled and restrained as she fought. She bolted upright and snapped open her eyes. She stilled, gaping at her surroundings. Many a time Tia had found herself in an uncompromising situation in the compound's small hospital after trying, unsuccessfully, to escape. But she had never been happy then, not like now. Now, she was ecstatic.

Yule! Yule, look. We're home. We're finally... Tia's excitement dampened. *I'm finally home.* Her soul ached as it sought her friend, yet finding nothing but a gaping hole of despair where she had once resided. Tia ran her fist across her chest to rub at her pained heart. *I've not only lost the presence of Yule inside my mind, but the presence of a friend and...relative.*

"Te!" cried a relieved voice. "Thank God yer awake. I was so shittin' scared. So much has happened while ya've been in here." Ella sat in an armchair beside Tia's bed, her boot-clad feet crossed and resting on the metal rung. She looked well; her cheeks were full and about to explode with exciting gossip. But something was different about the girl before her.

Her hair has changed, Tia noticed. It now had more of an ombre effect than a bad dye job feel to it. *She must have got someone to fix it*, thought Tia, fighting the urge to be offended that her opinion wasn't sought and Ella had trusted someone else. She didn't know what she would do if she lost Ella as well.

Ella gasped and her face blanched as her eyes flitted to the corner of the room, then back to Tia again. She smiled, her lip wobbling slightly as the restraint on her babble of gossip overtook her, speed talking its way from her mouth in Ella's usual light tone.

"Jinx, the stunafrekin'lishus—" Ella sighed holding a hand to her heart, drew a stifled pain-filled giggle from Tia "—was picked up by some stuffy witch chauffeur—" she scrunched her nose "—this morning after being escorted by the delinquent twins from this very building." She fluttered her eyelashes and sighed when Tia continued to stare at her blankly. "From this very room," Ella elaborated.

Weird, thought Tia, *I dreamt about him, didn't I?*

"Or so they say." Ella shrugged. "Anyways. His sista, Hope…" Ella's eyes darted back to the corner of the room; a vein throbbed erratically in the side of her neck as she licked her dry lips.

What the hell is she staring at? wondered Tia, slightly unnerved and letting her eyes flicker to the corner.

"Do ya know Hope?" Ella asked, but Tia was unsure if the question was meant for her or the empty corner. "Well, she's Jinx's sista, a powerless witch," she continued, looking back at Tia with a fixed determination. "Funny. Right? What? Are ya growlin' at me?"

"What? No!" Tia replied, shock palpable in her expression.

An unfazed Ella continued to chatter on, "Seriously! You mangy m-un." She smiled sheepishly at Tia, as though remembering she was still in the room.

What the bloody hell is going on with her? Is someone messing with her head? Or is someone really there? wondered Tia.

Ella quickly picked up, over enthusiastically, where she had left off. "Anyways, she's the one who fixed your nose."

Tia probed her once smashed nose with gentle fingers, confirming Ella's statement.

"She was escorted off the compound last night, so I'll guess ya'll have to send her a thank-ya note."

Tia took a deep breath watching Ella stare unseeing into the space before her, her pupils were dilating and turning slightly cerulean while trying not to look into the corner. Something was definitely wrong. Ella's veins were visible through her pale skin, her teeth were gnawing at her bottom lip and she had begun to twirl the end of one pigtail with frantic motions.

Tia narrowed her sore eyes speculatively. She had always known when Ella was lying to her. "M-un?" she asked, unsure whether or not Ella had mentioned the word 'mangy'. She shivered involuntarily, as the word sent shivers down her spine. Her head was still spinning with the realisation she had barely escaped her own execution and that some of her friends were now dead.

"Oh, uh? Nothing, it's nothing, just some stupid ghost that's been following me around for a few days." Ella smiled fleetingly. "Yes, I said *stupid*!" she snapped, glaring daggers at the corner.

Tia stared at the space, then back to Ella while raising an eyebrow. "Hate to tell you this, Ell, but there's nothing there."

"Yeah there is. Look, just there." She pointed, chewing her bottom lip.

Tia stared past her pink prickling eyes and saw- nothing. Now becoming concerned, she turned back to Ella who was shaking her head and wincing at the pain.

"No one," Tia replied solemnly.

"It's definitely there, Te. One minute it's a stunafrekin'lishus, makes your Jinx look ugly, man-boy, and the next—"

"He's not my Jinx," interjected Tia with a puff of frustration.

Ella's eyes sparkled mischievously. "Okay," she conceded, too quicky. Tia knew by her instant backdown that she hadn't won the argument.

"Anyway, Reece is back," said Ella, fluently changing the subject. "I still didn't get a shot of him in that dress, though. Never mind, maybe next time." Ella winked at Tia. "Oh, Anka, she's back, too – but she's not the same since Li's death."

Tia turned her attention to Ella, staring perplexed and trying to process the information. *Did she just say…death? Li? Li…is dead? Oh God!* Tia's face paled. She could feel the tears choking her as she fought the urge to cry. She succeeded. Only one escaped to trickle down her face, streaking a ribbon of heartfelt sorrow. *My dream. Li was a ghost in my dream. Oh God, was he trying to contact me? Does he need…help?* The deep consuming ache in her heart, which seemed to be a constant presence since waking back in her own time, felt as though it had been crushed to suffocation. And in that moment of broken-heartedness, Tia knew she would never be able to heal that fraction of her heart where she kept her lost friends: Li and Yule.

Life is a cruel bitch, thought Tia, *and for some unjust, crappy reason I seem to know her, intimately.*

"Oh shit! I'm so sorry, Te, I forgot to tell you. Li, he's dead. He died on assignment. Jinx is being blamed, of course – after all, he is a witch," said Ella, but Tia's heart had stopped.

First Yule, now Li. Why? Lost in a wave of gut-wrenching pain, Tia tuned out of Ella's prattling as a sharp screech hissed through her ears, nearly knocking her unconscious. *Breathe, Tia, just breathe.* She coaxed herself into complying and the world slowly righted itself, the screech of depression deafening her reversed until she could once again hear the unobservant Ella- still talking.

"...Oh yeah, and creepy Paul – he's missing. Just vanished! No one knows what's happened to him. Weird, if you ask me. The guy's seriously crazed. Guess this means he won't be harassing ya now though, so that's gotta be a bonus. Right?" She stuck two thumbs up and grinned.

But Tia was too busy drowning in the loss of her friends to acknowledge Ella. Life just seemed to go from bad to worse, to damn right shitty! And Tia had had enough. She vowed, *somehow, someway, the witch hunter who tried to frame Yule for her lover's murder will pay. Whoever is responsible for Li's death will seriously regret it by the time I've finished with them, and whoever – or whatever – is haunting Ella, my soul sister, WILL BE EXORCISED!*

"Wait-a-minute. Rewind and start over. Your freaky ghost guy does what, exactly?" asked Tia, trying to focus.

Chewing her bottom lip until it ballooned with pressure, Ella replied, "He kinda changes. Ya know, looks gorgeous one minute, long brown hair, silvery grey eyes and a…" Ella reddened. "Really…gorgeous…body," she managed, in between clearing her throat. "And then I turn around, and he's an 'it'!"

Tia sniggered. "What, he's got male PMT or something?"

But Ella's eyes didn't sparkle with amusement; they merely set their sights on Tia and hardened.

"It's not a joke, Te."

"Okay, Ell. What… is…an…it?" Tia leaned forwards, clasping the young girl's hand and holding her flitting gaze.

"It's a wolf. I think. Maybe it's a shapeshifter. Ya know, cos it changes shape."

A wolf? A shifter? A werewolf? Oh God, how could this be? No, Tia corrected herself, *it isn't a werewolf, it's a were-ghost! And only Ella can see it. Shit! Could it have transported back with me from the seventeenth century? Is it my fault Ella's being haunted? Did it somehow use me as a transportation device – a lift? If it has, how do I get it back there? What do I do? And how can I help her if I can't even see it?!* Tia nervously twiddled a strand of messy hair around one slender finger.

"Te. There's worse news." Ella stared at her waiting for acknowledgement.

"Worse than a were-ghost that only you can see?" Tia laughed sarcastically. Her head pounded, her nose tickled and her throat felt raw, as if someone had their hand permanently clasped around it. Reaching for the cup on the nightstand, she sipped the water to relieve her parched throat.

"Uh, yeah," Ella answered, shifting in her chair.

"Oh God – what now?" rasped Tia with Ella's eyes fixed on her.

"You passed." Ella winced waiting for Tia to explode in a rage of curses. Instead, her brow furrowed.

"Your assignment," said Ella to a perplexed Tia. "You're a Ghost Possessor, Te! Well, after the ascension ceremony yer will be."

Tia shot bolt upright. "SHIT!!!"

Chapter 26

Tia

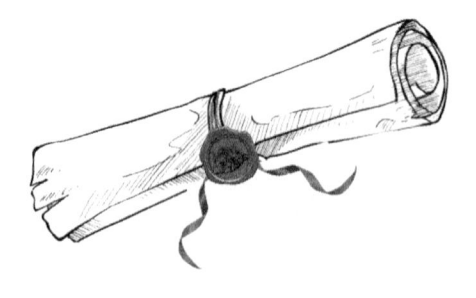

One week later...

Tia stood staring at the girl in her mirror; the girl who was so different from who she used to be. "G-Poss." She laughed, mockery lacing her voice. The girl looking back at her wore bell-bottomed jeans and a fitted black T-shirt. *Strange*, she thought, *suddenly I can wear normal clothes.* She stared at her flawless skin and couldn't get over the fact that she had nearly died a week ago, but there was nothing to show for it apart from the welted red scar encircling her neck, like a sick prank for Halloween. Even her busted nose had been re-formed thanks to Jinx's sister. *And isn't that weird*, she thought. *Jinx is a witch, yet he couldn't heal me – or maybe he just didn't want to. But his sister- a so say powerless witch I don't even know- took the time to fix me. Remarkable.* But now Tia owed her, and she didn't like owing anyone. Still, she had to wonder, why she hadn't healed her neck?

She lifted her fingers to skim its abrasion, the crystal ring on her thumb glinting in the light. "Bloody thing!" she cursed, once again trying to pull it off. She didn't even know how she'd acquired it – let alone why it wouldn't come off. But every time she looked at it, really looked at it, it seemed to remind her of the creepily powerful witch, Jinx. As though somehow he was watching her through it. She shook herself mentally trying to throw off the wave of intrigue.

Grabbing a brush, she ran it through her loose raven hair, and then walked over to Anka who sat perched on her bunk. Her usually tidy cabinet looked cluttered. Her perfect skin was blotchy and her eyes were puffy with unshed tears. *This is true love*, thought Tia as she sat alongside and brushed out Anka's hair, just like she used to do for her. Tia sighed. *I miss Li. We all miss Li. But Anka has taken it the hardest. She barely eats, confines herself to our room and doesn't even talk anymore. I miss her. I hope that one day I'll find a love that strong.*

It didn't take long for the two of them to be ready for the ascension ceremony, but Tia still wrestled with the idea of escaping. *Not that I'll get far with all these G-Poss warriors hanging around to celebrate a 'new year of ascenders'*, she thought. *Li wouldn't have been pleased, either; he would've wanted me to do the right thing. He always did. And with Anka all zoned out and 'nobody's home', like in a horror movie, there's no way she's going to get to the ceremony without me. So, here's to Li.* Tia saluted and stole a breath. She took Anka by the hand like a small insecure child and led her from their room just as a bell tolled the hour.

Tia unenthusiastically walked a stoic Anka down the old oak staircase to the main hall, where a huge buffet stretched along one wall. She sniffed the air, the delectable smell of chocolate and spices filled her nostrils. She would bet anything there was some sort of chilli and licked her lips in anticipation, her tongue watering with eagerness.

She watched potentials file into the tiered seating at the back of the hall. A stage stood in the centre with George's engorged form standing on top. A table covered in pouches and one scarlet-ribboned scroll were arranged behind him.

Tia strode forwards, admiring how quickly the central chandelier and gas lamps had been replaced. She made her way to Reece, who was nervously fidgeting at the bottom of the newly constructed stage staircase. The ascenders stood together. Only the three of them were left out of the five ascenders they had started with; the weight of their missing friends weighing heavily on their minds.

Suddenly the room fell silent, and George started his speech, babbling on as usual, until Tia no longer heard his words. Her attention lay elsewhere, on more interesting things.

Amongst the crowd of potentials sat the illusive G-Poss warriors she was about to join. Her worst nightmare finally coming true. *I'm about to become one of them*, she admitted to herself, resigned, as George called out her name. *At least I can help Ella. No sister of mine will be haunted by a were-ghost abomination, that's for sure. I'll get rid of it, even if I have to salt its ass and send it to limbo!*

"Tia Morgan." George's tone made the hairs on the nape of her neck stand on end. The last time he had called her to ascend the stage was to allocate her first assignment; now Tia's heart wrenched in her chest like a crowbar trying to yank it free. Yule was no longer with her, and the empty void in her mind wept with loneliness.

"Ti-a," growled George, his impatience showing with the rapid tapping of his fat little feet upon the stage. The noise echoed throughout the hall like her rapid heartbeat once she stepped forwards. The crowd clapped loudly as she walked to the foot of the stage. Staring at the wooden stairs, Tia began to count them in her mind.

One. Her foot slammed down like lead on the shabbily constructed surface. She could hear the sickening roar of the crowd chiming in her ears. Her blood turned to ice, sharp and lethal, shredding her heart from the inside. She knew what was coming next, but she couldn't stop the terror gripping her, the panic that had her fist rubbing her chest trying to calm her palpitating heart. She sucked in deep gulps of air, yet she felt unable to breath, and sweat soaked her clothes. Then she heard it, the sound of breaking bones and the rope snapping taut. The image of Yule charged into her mind, her head hanging loosely, her eyes glazed. Dead.

Tia's stomach lurched, bile rose in her throat, then her head was turned. A figure stood before her, but its image was a shadowy mess, Yule hung, swinging from her neck, *squ-eak, squ-eak, click!*

Fingers snapped before her face and the dark shadowy image pushed itself to the forefront of her vision.

Reece stood before her, one large hand grounding her. He bent down, his face close to hers, his dark doe eyes full of concern as he spoke in a soft lyrical lilt. "...That's it, deep breaths, deep breaths. That's it, Tia, you're okay. You're safe – I promise."

Her breath hitched and heart hammered wildly. With a pallid face, her hand fluttered nervously at the scar on her throat, sweat beading on her brow.

Then Reece took her hand in his and squeezed it reassuringly. "It's okay. You. Are. Safe. It'll be okay, Tia. It'll just take time. Now breathe, just breathe. We're with you." Reece tilted his head, his eyes showing empathy. With his hand holding hers, his strength comforting her, he walked her up the steps.

She stared down at their hands, hers atop, the crystal ring on her thumb drawing her gaze and somehow – magically – she didn't feel so alone. Reece retracted his hand before stepping back down the steps to embrace a distraught Anka.

Ascension was the only thing Li had wanted, Tia thought bitterly. *To become a G-Poss.* Her eyes rose from Anka to Reece who gave her an encouraging nod towards George. Reece was the rock now, the only one who stood *unchanged* amongst the ascenders.

"Tia!" George reprimanded. "When you are *quite* ready." He sighed in exasperation as Tia took centre stage and faced him. "For you, Tia Morgan, special exemptions have been made. One, because of the lack of ascenders to complete their assignment. And two, your empathetic decision to transport your assigned ghost during a potentially lethal situation. You have been accredited the minute and a half longer it took you to transport," he said sarcastically, as though the decision wasn't his. "And may I say on a personal level, I never thought I would see this day." He turned to the table behind him, scooping up a pouch.

"Congratulations, Ghost Possessor Tia!" He waited for applause before continuing- "In commemoration of your ascension into a fully fledged Ghost Possessor I present you with the right of exorcism." He handed over the small pouch. "With it may you be wise, safe and just in your decision to purify evil from our world.

God, I wish I could just salt the bloody git and end this torment forever. Tia thought, clutching the pouch tightly as her eyes searched for a familiar face in the crowd.

Ella whistled loudly through her fingers as Tia turned to disappear back down the steps, shivering when George's hand skimmed her arm.

"Before you go, Tia, I have a little something for you." He shoved the scroll into her hand and whispered, "I always deliver on my promises, Tia. Enjoy your punishment. You start your G-Poss duties straight away."

Don't forget to leave a review–

https://www.amazon.com/stores/Carrie-Weston/author/B08T8BBW1V

Or

https://www.goodreads.com/author/show/19206998.Carrie_West

on

Printed in Great Britain
by Amazon